AMERICAN COMMUNES TO 1860

SECTS AND CULTS IN AMERICA
BIBLIOGRAPHICAL GUIDES
(General Editor: J. Gordon Melton)
(VOL. 12)

GARLAND REFERENCE LIBRARY
OF SOCIAL SCIENCE
(VOL. 347)

BIBLIOGRAPHIES ON SECTS AND CULTS IN AMERICA
(General Editor: J. Gordon Melton)

AMERICAN COMMUNES TO 1860
A Bibliography

Philip N. Dare

GARLAND PUBLISHING, INC. • NEW YORK & LONDON
1990

Library of Congress Cataloging-in-Publication Data

Dare, Philip N.
American communes to 1860 : a bibliography / Philip N.
Dare.
p. cm. — (Sects and cults in America. Bibliographical
guides ; v. 12)
ISBN 0-8240-8572-8 (alk. paper)
1. Collective settlements—United States—History—Bibliography.
I. Title. II. Series.
Z7164.C69D37 1990
[HX654]
016.335'973—dc20   89-16930
                                                            CIP

Z
7164
.C69
D37
1990

Printed on acid-free, 250-year-life paper
Manufactured in the United States of America

CONTENTS

PREFACE

For ages people have sought to realize the ideal of the prophecy of Isaiah wherein the "wolf shall dwell with the lamb, and the leopard shall lie down with the kid...they shall not hurt or destroy in all my mountain; for the earth shall be full of the knowledge of the Lord..." (Isa. 11:8, 9, RSV). Whether they called it a "New Jerusalem," a "New Zion," "New Harmony," or referred to themselves as a society of believers in an inspired truth, they all sought and continue seeking to establish a kingdom on earth in which peace and justice and healing can occur. They welcome, then and now, anyone who is attracted to their ideals, beliefs, or system. Their effort at a reformation of society has manifested itself in several ways. For some, religion is the bond that cements them together. Others have held up economic or social principles as the focal point of their community. Still others have come together around literary and philosophical ideals. All of the communal groups have sought to create a new order which would provide the rest of society with a model for the restructuring of the nation or nations.

This bibliography reflects the phenomenal resurgence of interest, at all levels, in communitarian societies the past two decades. The objective in undertaking a reference source of this nature is to collate and update the contributions of earlier writings, such as the bibliographies in Socialism and American Life, edited by Donald D. Egbert and Stow Persons (1952) and Backwoods Utopias, by Arthur E. Bestor, Jr. (1950).

There has been a proliferation of research taking place related to communal societies. This research is not limited to the history of these groups. Sociologists, anthropologists, psychologists, musicologists, architects, and theologians are studying these groups. Several reprint series were developed to provide libraries and researchers with easier access to the writings of these communitarians. Historic communal villages have been restored and visitors by the tens of thousands journey to such places as Amana, Bishop Hill, Economy, Ephrata, Hancock, New Harmony, Pleasant Hill, Zoar, and scores of other sites that once were the locations of social and religious experiments.

But this fascination with collective settlements has not been limited to the historic groups alone. The so-called counterculture generated more such intentional communities than ever existed in the nineteenth century, and a new literature sprung up honoring and

encouraging an alternative lifestyle. Universities and colleges began
adding courses to their curricula on communal groups. The Center for
Communal Studies at the University of Southern Indiana, Evansville,
developed and serves as the headquarters for the National Historic
Communal Societies Association, formed in 1975. The Institute for the
Study of American Religion at Santa Barbara, California provides another
research center for communal studies.

This volume, therefore, will attempt to collate the historic
works and the results of the new research on communal groups that came
into existence in America in the pre-Civil War years. Two other volumes
will continue and complete this reference series. Timothy Miller's
volume will be a bibliography of American communes from 1860-1960.
Karol Borowski's bibliography will cover such groups that came into
existence after 1960.

While this volume is the result of an effort to locate the most
significant writings on communal groups it does not purport to be
comprehensive or exhaustive. The cut-off date for books and articles
was June 30, 1988. In addition to books and articles, it is a
bibliography that includes manuscript collections, dissertations,
theses, and other bibliographies. It is not limited to English language
works, but includes works in any Western language that contributed to
the development of communal groups that took root on American soil. It
is not annotated in order to save space to include more citations.
Doubtless, more works will surface that should have been included, and
there may be some questioning of the ones herein included, but
ultimately all any bibliographer can hope to accomplish is to provide a
guide to a subject which will take other students deeper into the field
or along one of the many paths that branch off.

Finally, a work of this nature cannot be completed without
painstaking attention to details and hours of typing. In this case, my
wife, Nancy, suffered a form of spouse abuse by agreeing to load these
citations into the word processor, and then manipulating all this
information to come out in camera ready format. I cannot express,
adequately, my appreciation for her efforts above and beyond the call of
our marriage vows.

American Communes to 1860

GENERAL AND COLLECTED WORKS

BIBLIOGRAPHIES

1. Bassett, T.E. Seymour. BIBLIOGRAPHY. DESCRIPTIVE AND CRITICAL.
   Volume 2 of SOCIALISM AND AMERICAN LIFE by Donald Drew
   Egbert and Stow Persons. Princeton: Princeton University
   Press, 1952.

2. Conover, Patrick. THE ALTERNATE CULTURE AND CONTEMPORARY
   COMMUNES, REVISED: A PARTLY ANNOTATED BIBLIOGRAPHY.
   Monticello, IL: Council of Planning Librarians, 1976,
   Exchange bibliography 952.

3. Fogarty, Robert S. "Communal History in America." CHOICE. 10
   (June 1973): 1-8.

4. Mariampolski, Hyman. "Communes and Utopias, Past
   and Present: A Bibliography of Post-1945 Studies."
   BULLETIN OF BIBLIOGRAPHY. 36 (July-September 1979):
   119-127, 143.

5. Melton, J. Gordon, and Rohen Martin. A BIBLIOGRAPHY OF AMERICAN
   COMMUNALISM. Evanston, IL: Institute for the Study of
   American Religion, 1984.

6. Negley, Glenn. UTOPIAN LITERATURE; A SUPPLEMENTARY LISTING OF
   WORKS INFLUENTIAL IN UTOPIAN THOUGHT. Lawrence: The
   Regents Press of Kansas, 1977.

7. Owings, Loren C. THE AMERICAN COMMUNITARIAN TRADITION, 1683-
   1940: A GUIDE TO THE SOURCES IN THE LIBRARY OF THE
   UNIVERSITY OF CALIFORNIA AT DAVIS. Davis: The Library,
   1971.

8. Pochmann, Henry A., comp. BIBLIOGRAPHY OF GERMAN CULTURE IN
   AMERICA TO 1940. Madison: University of Wisconsin, 1954.

9. Sweetland, James H. "Federal Sources for the Study of Collective Communities." GOVERNMENT PUBLICATIONS REVIEW PART
   A: RESEARCH ARTICLES. 7A (1980): 129-138.

10. U.S. Library of Congress. General Reference and Bibliography
    Division. COMMUNAL SETTLEMENTS IN THE UNITED STATES; A
    SELECTED LIST OF REFERENCES. Compiled by Helen
    Dudenbostel Jones. Washington, D.C.: Library of Congress,
    1909, 1947.

ARCHIVAL MATERIALS

11. Ashton, William Adolphus. Papers, 1818-1876.
     Indiana University. Lilly Library, Bloomington, IN.

12. Bestor, Arthur Eugene. Pictorial Materials on
     Collective Settlements. University of Illinois Library,
     Historical Survey Collections. Urbana, IL.

13. McGee, Anita (Newcomb). Papers. Library of Congress,
     Manuscript Division. Washington, D.C.

14. MacDonald, A.J. "Materials for a History of Com-
     munities." Beineke Library, Manuscripts and
     Collections. Yale University, New Haven.

15. Mitchell, Morris Randolph. Papers, 1898-1972. University of
     North Carolina Library, Southern Historical Collection,
     Chapel Hill.

ARTICLES AND BOOKS

16. Ahlstrom, Sydney E. A RELIGIOUS HISTORY OF THE AMERICAN PEOPLE.
     New Haven: Yale University Press, 1972.

17. Albertson, Frank, Annetta Hinzman, and Nancy Vonburg. "Seven
     Utopias of Mid-Nineteenth-Century New England." OLD-TIME
     NEW ENGLAND. 62 (October-December 1971): 47-52;
     (January-March 1972): 80-84.

18. Albertson, Ralph. "A Survey of Mutualistic Communities in
     America." IOWA JOURNAL OF HISTORY AND POLITICS. 34
     (October 1936): 375-444. Reprint. New York: AMS Press,
     1973.

19. Armytage, Walter H.G. HEAVENS BELOW: UTOPIAN EXPERIMENTS IN
     ENGLAND, 1560-1960. London: Routledge and Kegan Paul;
     Toronto: University of Toronto, 1961.

20. Bach, Marcus. STRANGE SECTS AND CURIOUS CULTS. New York: Dodd,
     Mead & Co., 1961.

21. Baldwin, Leland Dewitt. THE AMERICAN QUEST FOR THE CITY OF GOD.
     Macon, GA: Mercer University Press, 1981.

22. Barkun, David. DISASTER AND THE MILLENNIUM. New Haven: Yale
     University Press, 1974.

23. Barkun, Michael. CRUCIBLE OF THE MILLENNIUM: THE BURNED-OVER
     DISTRICT OF NEW YORK IN THE 1840'S. Syracuse: Syracuse
     University Press, 1986.

24. Baum, Patricia. ANOTHER WAY OF LIFE. New York: G.P. Putnam's Sons, 1973.

25. Bassett, T.D. Seymour. "The Quakers and Communitarianism." FRIENDS HISTORICAL ASSOCIATION BULLETIN. 43 (Autumn 1954): 84-99.

26. Beer, Max. SOCIAL STRUGGLES AND SOCIALIST FORERUNNERS. Transl. H.J. Stenning. Boston: Small, Maynard & Co., 1925.

27. Benedict, David. A HISTORY OF ALL RELIGIONS. Providence: J. Miller, printer, 1824.

28. Berneri, Mary Louise. A JOURNEY THROUGH UTOPIA. Boston: Beacon Press, 1950.

29. Bestor, Arthur Eugene. BACKWOODS UTOPIAS; THE SECTARIANISM AND OWENITE PHASES OF COMMUNITARIAN SOCIALISM IN AMERICA: 1663-1829. 2nd ed. Philadelphia: University of Pennsylvania Press, 1970.

30. ------. "The Evolution of the Socialist Vocabulary," JOURNAL OF THE HISTORY OF IDEAS. 9 (June 1948): 259-302.

31. ------. "Patent-Office Models of the Good Society: Some Relationships Between Social Reform and Westward Expansion." AMERICAN HISTORICAL REVIEW. 58 (April 1953): 505-526. Also found in BACKWOODS UTOPIAS, Supplemental Essay I.

32. ------. "The Transit of Communitarian Socialism to America." In BACKWOODS UTOPIAS, pp. 253-271. Paper presented to the Conference of the European Association of American Studies, Paris, Sept. 3, 1957. Reprinted from PROCEEDINGS OF THE EUROPEAN ASSOCIATION FOR AMERICAN STUDIES, HELD AT THE FONDATION DES ETATS-UNIS, Paris, Sept. 3-6, 1957, pp. 5-18.

33. Bliss, William D.P., ed. THE NEW ENCYCLOPEDIA OF SOCIAL REFORMS. 3rd ed. New York: Funk & Wagnalls, 1910.

34. Blunt, John Henry. DICTIONARY OF SECTS, HERESIES, ECCLESIASTICAL PARTIES AND SCHOOLS OF RELIGIOUS THOUGHT. Philadelphia: J.B. Lippincott; London: Rivingtons, 1874, 1886.

35. Bowden, Henry Warner. DICTIONARY OF AMERICAN RELIGIOUS BIOGRAPHY. Westport, CT: Greenwood Press, 1961.

36. Boyer, Paul. "'A Joyful Noyes': Reassessing America's Utopian Tradition." REVIEWS IN AMERICAN HISTORY. 3 (March 1975): 25-30.

37.   Branch, Edward Douglas. THE SENTIMENTAL YEARS,
      1826-1860. New York; London: D. Appleton-Century, 1934.

38.   THE BRETHREN ENCYCLOPEDIA. 2 vols. Philadelphia;
      Oak Brook, IL: The Brethren Encyclopedia, Inc., 1983.

39.   Brock, Peter. PACIFISM IN THE UNITED STATES, FROM
      THE COLONIAL ERA TO THE FIRST WORLD WAR. Princeton:
      Princeton University Press, 1968.

40.   Bryant, M. Darrol, and Donald W. Dayton. The Coming Kingdom:
      ESSAYS IN AMERICAN MILLENNIALISM AND ESCHATOLOGY.
      Barrytown, NY: International Religious Foundation, 1982.

41.   Buber, Martin. PATHS TO UTOPIA. Trans. R.F.C. Hull. New York:
      Macmillan; London: Routledge & Kegan Paul, 1949, 1950.

42.   Bushee, Frederick Alexander. "Communistic Societies in the
      United States." POLITICAL SCIENCE QUARTERLY. 20
      (December 1905): 625-664.

43.   Buss, D. "Meeting of Heaven and Earth: Literature of
      Millennialism, 1965-1985." FIDES ET HISTORIA. 20
      (January 1988): 5-28.

44.   Calverton, Victor Francis. WHERE ANGELS DARED TO TREAD.
      Freeport, NY: Books for Libraries; Indianapolis: Bobbs,
      Merrill, 1941.

45.   Cavan, Ruth Shonle. "Communes: Historical and Contemporary."
      INTERNATIONAL REVIEW OF MODERN SOCIOLOGY. 6 (Spring
      1976): 1-11.

46.   Carpenter, Delburn. THE RADICAL PIETISTS: CELIBATE COMMUNAL
      SOCIETIES ESTABLISHED IN THE UNITED STATES BEFORE 1820.
      PhD diss. University of Northern Iowa, 1972. Reprint.
      New York: AMS Press, 1975.

47.   Clark, Elmer Talmage. THE SMALL SECTS IN AMERICA. Nashville:
      Cokesbury Press, 1937; Abingdon-Cokesbury Press, 1949.

48.   Cohen, Daniel. NOT OF THE WORLD: A HISTORY OF THE COMMUNE IN
      AMERICA. Chicago: Follett Publishing Co., 1973.

49.   "Communal Lives and Utopian Hopes." SOCIETY. 25
      (January/February, 1988): 29-65.

50.   COMMUNITARIANISM IN AMERICA, 1799-1926. In University of
      Illinois, Illinois Historical Survey Collection. Urbana.
      Assembled by Arthur Bestor.

51.   COMMUNITIES; JOURNAL OF COOPERATION. Number 68 (Winter 1985).

52.   Conover, Patrick W. "An Analysis of Communes and

Intentional Communities with Particular Attention to
Sexual and Genderal Relations." FAMILY COORDINATOR. 24
(October 1975): 453-464.

53. COOPERATIVE COMMUNITIES: PLANS AND DESCRIPTIONS; ELEVEN
PAMPHLETS, 1825-1847. New York: Arno Press, 1972.

54. Cross, Whitney R. THE BURNED-OVER DISTRICT: THE
SOCIAL AND INTELLECTUAL HISTORY OF ENTHUSIASTIC RELIGION
IN WESTERN NEW YORK, 1800-1850. Ithaca: Cornell
University Press, 1950; New York: Harper & Row, 1965.

55. Desroche, Henri Charles. SOCIALISMES ET SOCIOLOGIE RELIGIEUSE.
Textes de Friedrich Engels traduits et presentes avec le
concours de G. Dunstheimer et M.L. Lefendre. Paris:
Editions Cujas, 1965.

56. DICTIONARY OF AMERICAN BIOGRAPHY. Ed. by Allen Johnson. New
York: Charles Scribner's Sons, 1928.

57. Dixon, William Hepworth. NEW AMERICA. 2 vols. London: Hurst &
Blackett; Philadelphia: J.B. Lippincott & Co., 1867.

58. Doig, Ivan. UTOPIAN AMERICA: DREAMS AND REALITIES. Rochelle
Park, NJ: Hayden Book Co., 1976.

59. Dombrowski, James. THE EARLY DAYS OF CHRISTIAN SOCIALISM IN
AMERICA. New York: Columbia University Press, 1936.
Reprint. Octagon Books, 1966. PhD diss., Columbia
University, 1937.

60. Douglas, Dorothy W., and Katharine Du Pre Lumpkin.
"Communistic Settlements." ENCYCLOPAEDIA OF THE SOCIAL
SCIENCES. Edwin R.A. Seligman, Editor-in-Chief. New
York: Macmillan, 1930; Reissued 1937, s.v.

61. Durnbaugh, Donald F. "Work and Hope: The Spirituality of
Radical Pietist Communitarians." CHURCH HISTORY. 39
(March 1970): 72-90.

62. Egbert, Donald Drew, and Stow Persons, eds. SOCIALISM AND
AMERICAN LIFE. 2 vols. Princeton: Princeton University
Press, 1952.

63. Egerton, John. VISIONS OF UTOPIA : NASHOBA, RUGBY, RUSKIN AND
THE "NEW COMMUNITIES" OF TENNESSEE'S PAST. Knoxville: The
University of Tennessee Press, in cooperation with the
Tennessee Historical Commission, 1977.

64. Ellis, John B. FREE LOVE AND ITS VOTARIES; OR AMERICAN
SOCIALISM UNMASKED. BEING AN HISTORICAL AND DESCRIPTIVE
ACCOUNT OF THE RISE AND PROGRESS OF THE VARIOUS FREE LOVE
ASSOCIATIONS IN THE UNITED STATES AND THE EFFECTS OF THEIR
VICIOUS TEACHINGS UPON AMERICAN SOCIETY. New York: United

States Publishing Co.; San Francisco: A.L. Bancroft, 1870.
Reprint. New York: AMS Press, 1977. Microfilm. Ann
Arbor: University Microfilms, 1969.

65. Ely, Richard Theodore. RECENT AMERICAN SOCIALISM. Johns
     Hopkins University Studies in Historical and Political
     Science. Baltimore: Johns Hopkins University Press, 1885.

66. THE ENCYCLOPEDIA OF RELIGION. Mircea Eliade, Editor-in-Chief.
     New York: Macmillan Publishing Co., 1986.

67. ENCYCLOPEDIA OF THE AMERICAN RELIGIOUS EXPERIENCE. Eds. Charles
     H. Lippy and Peter W. Williams. 3 vols. New York:
     Charles Scribner's Sons, 1987.

68. Erasmus, Charles J. IN SEARCH OF THE COMMON GOOD: UTOPIAN
     EXPERIMENTS PAST AND FUTURE. New York: Macmillan/Free
     Press, 1985.

69. Faux, William. MEMORABLE DAYS IN AMERICA: BEING A JOURNAL OF A
     TOUR TO THE UNITED STATES, NOVEMBER 27, 1818-JULY 21,
     1820. Vol. 11 of EARLY WESTERN TRAVELS, 1784-1846.
     Reuben Gold Thwaites, ed. London: W. Simpkin and R.
     Marshall, 1823. Reprint. Cleveland: Arthur H. Clark,
     1905.

70. Fellman, Michael. "Anachronism, Context and Progress in
     Nineteenth-Century American Communitarianism." CANADIAN
     REVIEW OF AMERICAN STUDIES. 15 (Spring 1984): 35-48.

71. ------. THE UNBOUNDED FRAME; FREEDOM AND COMMUNITY IN NINETEENTH
     CENTURY AMERICAN UTOPIANISM. Westport, CT: Greenwood
     Press, 1973.

72. Feuer, Lewis S. "The Influence of the American Communist
     Colonies on Engels and Marx." WESTERN POLITICAL
     QUARTERLY. 19 (September 1966): 456-474.

73. Fischer, Ernest G. MARXISTS AND UTOPIAS IN TEXAS. Burnet, TX:
     Eakin Press, 1980.

74. Fogarty, Robert S. "American Communes, 1865-1914." JOURNAL OF
     AMERICAN STUDIES. 9 (August 1975): 145-162.

75. ------, comp. AMERICAN UTOPIANISM. Itasca, IL: F.E. Peacock,
     1972, 1977.

76. ------. DICTIONARY OF AMERICAN COMMUNAL AND UTOPIAN HISTORY.
     Westport, CT: Greenwood Press, 1980.

77. Foster, Lawrence. RELIGION AND SEXUALITY: THREE AMERICAN
     COMMUNAL EXPERIMENTS OF THE NINETEENTH CENTURY. New York;
     Oxford: Oxford University Press, 1981.

78. Fryer, Judith. "American Eves in American Edens." AMERICAN
     SCHOLAR. 44 (Winter 1974-75): 78-99.

79. Gide, Charles. COMMUNIST AND CO-OPERATIVE COLONIES. New York:
     Thomas Crowell Company, [1928].

80. Goebel, Max. DIE GESCHICHTE DES CHRISTLICHEN LEBENS IN DER
     RHEINISCH-WESTPHALISCHEN EVANGELISCHEN KIRCHE. 2 vols.
     Coblenz: K. Badeker, 1862.

81. ------. "Geschichte der wahren Inspirations-Gemeinden von
     1688-1850." ZEITSCHRIFT FUR DIE HISTORISCHE THEOLOGIE.
     (1854): 267-322; 377-438; (1855): 94-160; 327-425;
     (1857): 131-151.

82. Gordon, Beverly. "Dress in American Communal Societies."
     COMMUNAL SOCIETIES. 5 (1985): 122-136.

83. Grant, H. Roger. "Missouri's Utopian Communities." MISSOURI
     HISTORICAL REVIEW. 66 (October 1971): 20-48.

84. ------. "Utopias That Failed: The Antebellum Years." WESTERN
     ILLINOIS REGIONAL STUDIES. 2 (Spring 1979): 38-51.

85. Harrison, John Fletcher Clewes. THE SECOND COMING, POPULAR
     MILLENARIANISM 1780-1850. New Brunswick: Rutgers
     University Press; London: Routledge & Kegan Paul, 1979.

86. Hayden, Dolores. SEVEN AMERICAN UTOPIAS. THE ARCHITECTURE OF
     COMMUNITARIAN SOCIALISM, 1790-1975. Cambridge, MA;
     London: MIT Press, 1976.

87. Hayward, John. THE BOOK OF RELIGIONS, COMPRISING THE VIEWS,
     CREEDS, SENTIMENTS, OR OPINIONS OF ALL THE PRINCIPAL
     RELIGIOUS SECTS IN THE WORLD, PARTICULARLY OF ALL
     CHRISTIAN DENOMINATIONS IN EUROPE AND AMERICA, TO WHICH
     ARE ADDED CHURCH AND MISSIONARY STATISTICS, TOGETHER WITH
     BIOGRAPHICAL SKETCHES. Boston: J. Hayward, 1842.

88. Hennell, Mary. OUTLINE OF THE VARIOUS SOCIAL SYSTEMS AND
     COMMUNITIES WHICH HAVE BEEN FOUNDED ON THE PRINCIPLE OF
     COOPERATION. London: Longman, Brown; Green and Longmans,
     1844.

89. Hertzler, Joyce O. THE HISTORY OF UTOPIAN THOUGHT. New York:
     Cooper Square, 1965, c1923.

90. Hess, Stephen H. "Criteria for Communitarianism." SOCIAL
     SCIENCE. 30 (June 1955): 157-166.

91. Hillquit, Morris. HISTORY OF SOCIALISM IN THE UNITED STATES.
     New York, London: Funk & Wagnalls, 1903.

92. Hinds, William Alfred. AMERICAN COMMUNITIES: BRIEF SKETCHES OF ECONOMY, ZOAR, BETHEL, AURORA, AMANA, ICARIA, THE SHAKERS, ONEIDA, WALLINGFORD, AND THE BROTHERHOOD OF THE NEW LIFE. Oneida, NY: Office of the American Socialist, 1878. Reprint. Secaucus, NJ: The Citadel Press, 1961, 1973.

93. Hine, Robert V. CALIFORNIA'S UTOPIAN COLONIES. San Marino, CA: Huntington Library, 1953; New Haven: Yale University Press, 1966; New York: W.W. Norton, 1973.

94. Holloway, Mark. HEAVENS ON EARTH: UTOPIAN COMMUNITIES IN AMERICA, 1680-1880. London: Turnstile Press, Ltd., 1951. Reprint. New York: Dover, 1966.

95. Holynski, A. "Le Communisme en Amerique." REVUE SOCIALISTE. 12 installments. (Sept. 1890-Sept. 1892): 12, 312-26, to 16, 196-307.

96. Hostetler, John Andrew. COMMUNITARIAN SOCIETIES. New York: Holt, Rinehart & Winston, 1974.

97. Hudson, Winthrop S. RELIGION IN AMERICA. 3rd edition. New York: Scribners, 1981.

98. Infield, Henrik F. UTOPIA AND EXPERIMENT; ESSAYS IN THE SOCIOLOGY OF COOPERATION. New York: Frederick A. Praeger, 1955.

99. James, Henry Ammon. COMMUNISM IN AMERICA. New York: H. Holt, 1879. Reprint. New York: Arno Press, 1977.

100. Kamman, William F. SOCIALISM IN GERMAN AMERICAN LITERATURE. Philadelphia: Americana Germanica Press, 1917.

101. Kanter, Rosabeth Moss. COMMITMENT AND COMMUNITY: COMMUNES AND UTOPIAS IN SOCIOLOGICAL PERSPECTIVE. Cambridge, MA: Harvard University Press, 1972.

102. ------, ed. COMMUNES: CREATING AND MANAGING THE COLLECTIVE LIFE. New York: Harper & Row, 1973.

103. ------. "Utopian Communities." SOCIOLOGICAL INQUIRY. 43 (1973): 263-290.

104. Kateb, George, ed. UTOPIA. New York: Atherton Press, 1971.

105. ------. UTOPIA AND ITS ENEMIES. New York: Schocken Books, 1963, 1972.

106. ------. "Utopias and Utopianism." INTERNATIONAL ENCYCLOPEDIA OF THE SOCIAL SCIENCES, David L. Sills, ed. New York: Macmillan & Free Press, 1968, s.v.

107. Kent, Alexander. "Cooperative Communities in the United
      States." U.S. Dept. of Labor. BULLETIN. 6 (July 1901):
      563-646.

108. Kent, Austin. FREE LOVE: OR A PHILOSOPHICAL DEMONSTRATION OF
      THE NON-EXCLUSIVE NATURE OF CONNUBIAL LOVE, ALSO A REVIEW
      OF THE EXCLUSIVE FEATURE OF THE FOWLERS, ADIN BALLOU,
      H.C. WRIGHT, AND ANDREW JACKSON DAVIS ON MARRIAGE.
      Hopkinton, NY: The Author, 1857.

109. Kephart, William M. EXTRAORDINARY GROUPS: THE SOCIOLOGY OF
      UNCONVENTIONAL LIFE-STYLES. New York: St. Martin's Press,
      1976.

110. ------. "Why They Fail: A Socio-Historical Analysis of Religious
      and Secular Communes." JOURNAL OF COMPARATIVE FAMILY
      STUDIES. 5 (August 1974): 130-140.

111. Kerby, William Joseph. LE SOCIALISME AUX ETATS-UNIS. Bruxelles:
      J. Goemaere, 1897.

112. Kern, Louis J. AN ORDERED LOVE: SEX ROLES AND SEXUALITY IN
      VICTORIAN UTOPIAS--THE SHAKERS, THE MORMONS, AND THE
      ONEIDA COMMUNITY. Chapel Hill: The University of North
      Carolina Press, 1981.

113. Laidler, Harry Willington. A HISTORY OF SOCIALIST THOUGHT. New
      York: Thomas Y. Crowell, 1927.

114. ------. HISTORY OF SOCIALISM; A COMPARATIVE SURVEY OF SOCIALISM,
      COMMUNISM, TRADE UNIONISM, COOPERATION, UTOPIANISM, AND
      OTHER SYSTEMS OF REFORM AND RECONSTRUCTION. New York:
      Thomas Y. Crowell, 1968.

115. Larrabee, W.H., et al. "Communism." THE NEW SCHAFF-HERZOG
      ENCYCLOPEDIA OF RELIGIOUS KNOWLEDGE. Samual Macauley
      Jackson, ed. New York; London: Funk and Wagnalls, 1909,
      s.v.

116. Lauer, Jeanette, C. and Robert H. "Sex Roles in
      Nineteenth-Century American Communal Societies." COMMUNAL
      SOCIETIES. 3 (Fall 1983): 16-28.

117. Lauer, Robert H. and Jeanette C. THE SPIRIT AND THE FLESH: SEX
      IN UTOPIAN COMMUNITIES. Metuchen, NJ: Scarecrow Press,
      1983.

118. Lawson, Donna. BROTHERS AND SISTERS ALL OVER THIS LAND:
      AMERICA'S FIRST COMMUNES. New York: Praeger, 1972.

119. Lindsey, David. NINETEENTH-CENTURY AMERICAN UTOPIAS. St.
      Charles, MO: Forum Press, 1976.

12   *General and Collected Works*

120. McIntosh, Montgomery E. "Cooperative Communities in Wisconsin."
      State Historical Society of Wisconsin. PROCEEDINGS. 51
      (1903): 99-117.

121. McKinley, Kenneth William. "A Guide to the Communistic
      Communities of Ohio." THE OHIO STATE ARCHAEOLOGICAL AND
      HISTORICAL QUARTERLY. 46 (January 1937): 1-15.

122. Madison, Charles A. CRITICS AND CRUSADERS: A CENTURY OF
      AMERICAN PROTEST. 2d ed. New York: Frederick Ungar,
      1959. pp. 83-134.

123. Mandelker, Ira L. RELIGION, SOCIETY, AND UTOPIA IN NINETEENTH
      CENTURY AMERICA. Amherst, MA: The University of
      Massachusetts Press, 1984.

124. Mannheim, Karl. IDEOLOGY AND UTOPIA: AN INTRODUCTION TO THE
      SOCIOLOGY OF KNOWLEDGE. New York: Harcourt, 1954.

125. ------. "Utopia." ENCYCLOPAEDIA OF THE SOCIAL SCIENCES. Edwin
      R.A. Seligman, Editor-in-chief. New York: Macmillan,
      1920, s.v.

126. Mansfield, John Brandt. HISTORY OF TUSCARAWAS COUNTY.
      CONTAINING A HISTORY OF THE COUNTY; ITS TOWNSHIPS, TOWNS,
      CHURCHES, SCHOOLS, ETC.: GENERAL AND LOCAL STATISTICS;
      MILITARY RECORDS; PORTRAITS OF EARLY SETTLERS, AND
      PROMINENT MEN: HISTORY OF THE NORTHWEST TERRITORY; HISTORY
      OF OHIO; MISCELLANEOUS MATTERS, ETC., ETC., ... Chicago:
      Warner, Beers & Co., 1884.

127. Manuel, Frank Edward, and Fritzie Prigohzy. UTOPIAN THOUGHT IN
      THE WESTERN WORLD. Cambridge, MA: The Belknap Press of
      Harvard University Press, 1979.

128. Marini, Stephen A. "Hymnody in the Religious Communal Societies
      of Early America." COMMUNAL SOCIETIES. 2 (Autumn 1982):
      1-25.

129. ------. RADICAL SECTS OF REVOLUTIONARY NEW ENGLAND. Cambridge,
      MA; London: Harvard University Press, 1982.

130. Masso, Gildo. EDUCATION IN UTOPIAS. New York: Teachers
      College, Columbia University, 1927. Reprint. New York:
      AMS Press, 1972.

131. Melton, J. Gordon. BIOGRAPHICAL DICTIONARY OF AMERICAN CULT AND
      SECT LEADERS. New York: Garland, 1986.

132. ------. ENCYCLOPEDIA OF AMERICAN RELIGIONS. Wilmington, NC:
      Consortium Books, 1973. 2d ed. Detroit, MI: Gale
      Research, 1986. 3d ed. Detroit, MI: Gale
      Research, 1988.

133. Mercer, John. COMMUNES: A SOCIAL HISTORY AND GUIDE. Dorcester, MA: Prism Press, 1984.

134. Miller, Ernest C. "Utopian Communities in Warren County, Pennsylvania." WESTERN PENNSYLVANIA HISTORICAL MAGAZINE. 49 (October 1966): 301-317.

135. Miller, Ernest L. "Some Tennessee Utopias." M.A. Thesis, University of Tennessee, 1941.

136. Moment, Gairdner B., and Otto F. Kraushaar. UTOPIAS: THE AMERICAN EXPERIENCE. Metuchen, NJ; London: The Scarecrow Press, 1980.

137. Morgan, Arthur E. NOWHERE WAS SOMEWHERE: HOW HISTORY MAKES UTOPIAS AND HOW UTOPIAS MAKE HISTORY. Chapel Hill: University of North Carolina Press, 1946.

138. Morse, Flo. YANKEE COMMUNES, ANOTHER AMERICAN WAY. New York: Harcourt Brace Jovanovich, 1971.

139. Mowery, Jeni. "Systemic Requisites of Communal Groups." ALTERNATIVE LIFESTYLES: CHANGING PATTERNS IN MARRIAGE, FAMILY AND INTIMACY. 1 (May 1978): 235-261.

140. Mumford, Lewis. THE STORY OF UTOPIAS. New York: Boni and Liveright, 1922. Reprint. Glouchester, MA: Peter Smith, 1959.

141. Muncy, Raymond Lee. SEX AND MARRIAGE IN UTOPIAN COMMUNITIES, NINETEENTH-CENTURY AMERICA. Baltimore: Penguin Books; Bloomington: Indiana University Press, 1973.

142. Negley, Glenn, and J. Max Patrick. THE QUEST FOR UTOPIA. New York: Schuman, 1952. Reprint. Washington, D.C.: Consortium Press, 1972.

143. Nordhoff, Charles. COMMUNISTIC SOCIETIES OF THE UNITED STATES, FROM PERSONAL VISIT AND OBSERVATION. New York: Harper & Brothers, 1874. Reprint. New York: Dover, 1966.

144. NOTABLE AMERICAN WOMEN, 1607-1950, A BIOGRAPHICAL DICTIONARY. Edward T. James, Editor. Cambridge, MA: The Belknap Press of Harvard University, 1971.

145. Noyes, John Humphrey. STRANGE CULTS AND UTOPIAS OF 19TH CENTURY AMERICA. New York: Dover, 1966. Reprint. Philadelphia: Lippincott & Co., 1870, under title: HISTORY OF AMERICAN SOCIALISMS.

146. Okugawa, Otohiko. "Appendix A: Annotated List of Communal and Utopian Societies, 1787-1919," In Robert S. Fogarty, ed., DICTIONARY OF AMERICAN COMMUNAL AND UTOPIAN HISTORY. Westport, CT: Greenwood Press, 1980. pp. 173-233.

147. ------. "Defining a Population of the Communal Societies in Nineteenth-Century America." RITSUMEIKAN REVIEW OF INDUSTRIAL SOCIETY. 34 (March 1983), 53-81.

148. ------. "Intercommunal Relationships Among Nineteenth-Century Communal Societies in America." COMMUNAL SOCIETIES. 3 (Fall 1983): 68-82.

149. Oved, Yaacov. "Communes & the Outside World: Seclusion and Involvement." COMMUNAL SOCIETIES. 3 (Fall 1983): 83-92.

150. ------. TWO HUNDRED YEARS OF AMERICAN COMMUNES. New Brunswick, NJ.: Transaction Books, 1986.

151. Parrington, Vernon Louis, Jr. AMERICAN DREAMS: A STUDY OF AMERICAN UTOPIAS. 2nd ed. enlarged. New York: Russell & Russell, 1947, 1964.

152. Pease, William H. and Jane H. BLACK UTOPIA: NEGRO COMMUNAL EXPERIMENTS IN AMERICA. Madison: The State Historical Society of Wisconsin, 1963.

153. Peters, Victor. "The German Pietists: Spiritual Mentors of the German Communal Settlements in America." COMMUNAL SOCIETIES. 1 (Autumn 1981): 55-66.

154. Pitzer, Donald E. AMERICA'S COMMUNAL UTOPIAS: THE DEVELOP-MENTAL PROCESS. (Forthcoming).

155. ------. "The Uses of the American Communal Past: Keynote Address for the Tenth Annual Historic Communal Societies Conference, New Harmony, Indiana, October 13, 1983." COMMUNAL SOCIETIES, 4 (Fall 1984): 215-242.

156. Prieur, Vincent. "De New Harmony a Twin Oaks: A Propos de Quelques Recurrences dans l'histoire des Mouvements Communautaires Americains." MOUVEMENT SOCIAL. 94 (Janvier-Mars 1976): 31-57.

157. Quint, Howard. THE FORGING OF AMERICAN SOCIALISM: ORIGINS OF THE MODERN MOVEMENT. Columbia: University of South Carolina Press, 1953.

158. Rexroth, Kenneth. COMMUNALISM: FROM ITS ORIGINS TO THE TWENTIETH CENTURY. New York: Seabury, 1974; London: Owen, 1975.

159. Richter, Peyton, ed. UTOPIAS: SOCIAL IDEALS AND COMMUNAL EXPERIMENTS. Boston: Holbrook Press, 1971.

160. Ruether, Rosemary Radford, and Rosemary Skinner Keller, eds. WOMEN AND RELIGION IN AMERICA. Vol. 1. THE NINETEENTH CENTURY. San Francisco: Harper & Row, 1981. pp. 46-100.

161. Sagot, Francois. LE COMMUNISME AU NOUVEAU MONDE: REDUCTIONS DU PARAGUAY, SOCIETES COMMUNISTES DES ETATS-UNIS. Dijon: L. Venot, 1900.

162. Schuster, Eunice Minette. NATIVE AMERICAN ANARCHISM; A STUDY OF LEFT WING AMERICAN INDIVIDUALISM. Northampton, MA: Department of History of Smith College, 1932.

163. Sears, Hal D. THE SEX RADICALS; FREE LOVE IN HIGH VICTORIAN AMERICA. Lawrence: The Regents Press of Kansas, 1977.

164. Seldes, Gilbert. THE STAMMERING CENTURY. New York: The John Day Co., 1927; Harper & Row, 1965. Reprint. Gloucester, MA: Peter Smith, 1972.

165. Skinner, B.F. "Utopianism: the Design of Experimental Communities." INTERNATIONAL ENCYCLOPEDIA OF THE SOCIAL SCIENCES. New York: Macmillan & The Free Press, 1968. s.v.

166. Skinner, Charles Montgomery. AMERICAN COMMUNES; PRACTICAL SOCIALISM IN THE UNITED STATES. Brooklyn: Brooklyn Daily Eagle, 1901.

167. Smith, David E. "Millenarian Scholarship in America." AMERICAN QUARTERLY. 17 (Fall 1965): 535-549.

168. Smith, Hannah Whitall, ed. RELIGIOUS FANATICISM; EXTRACTS FROM THE PAPERS OF HANNAH WHITALL SMITH, EDITED WITH AN INTRODUCTION BY RAY STRACHEY [RACHEL COUN STRACHEY], CONSISTING OF AN ACCOUNT OF THE AUTHOR OF THESE PAPERS, AND OF THE TIMES IN WHICH SHE LIVED; TOGETHER WITH A DESCRIPTION OF THE CURIOUS RELIGIOUS SECTS AND COMMUNITIES OF AMERICA DURING THE EARLY AND MIDDLE YEARS OF THE NINETEENTH CENTURY. London: Faber & Gwyer, Ltd., 1928.

169. Smith, Page. "Utopian Communities." In THE NATION COMES OF AGE, vol. 4 of A PEOPLE'S HISTORY OF THE ANTI-BELLUM YEARS. New York: McGraw-Hill, 1981.

170. Solis, Miguel J. AMERICAN UTOPIAS (1683-1900): EVOLUTION VERSUS REVOLUTION: A DESCRIPTIVE AND BIBLIOGRAPHICAL DICTIONARY. Material researched and annotated by the author from primary sources at the Lilly Library, Indiana University. Bloomington: Duplicated for the author by Indiana University, 1984.

171. Spurlock, John Calvin. "Anarchy & Community at Modern Times, 1851-1863." COMMUNAL SOCIETIES. 3 (Fall 1983): 29-47.

172. Stephan, Karen H. and G. Edward. "Religion and the Survival of Utopian Communities." JOURNAL FOR THE SCIENTIFIC STUDY OF RELIGION. 12 (March 1973): 89-100.

173. Stoeffler, F. Ernest, ed. CONTINENTAL PIETISM AND EARLY
      AMERICAN CHRISTIANITY. Grand Rapids: Wm. B. Eerdmans
      Publishing Co., 1976.

174. Stoehr, Taylor. FREE LOVE IN AMERICA. New York: AMS Press,
      1979.

175. Taylor, Barbara. EVE AND THE NEW JERUSALEM: SOCIALISM AND
      FEMINISM IN THE NINETEENTH CENTURY. New York: Pantheon
      Books, 1983.

176. Taylor, R. Bruce. "Communistic Societies of America."
      ENCYCLOPAEDIA OF RELIGION AND ETHICS. James Hastings,
      editor. New York: Charles Scribner's Sons; Edinburgh: T.&
      T. Clark, 1913. s.v.

177. Taylor, Keith. THE POLITICAL IDEAS OF THE UTOPIAN SOCIALISTS.
      London: Frank Cass, 1982.

178. Teselle, Sallie, ed. THE FAMILY, COMMUNES, AND UTOPIAN
      SOCIETIES. New York: Harper & Row, 1972.

179. Thomas, John L. "Romantic Reform in America, 1815-1865."
      AMERICAN QUARTERLY, 17 (Winter 1965): 656-681.

180. Tricoche, George N. "Le Communisme en action: Etude des
      Societes Communistes aux Etats-Unis." JOURNAL DES
      ECONOMISTES. 5e Serie, 25 (Mars 1896): 321-53

181. Tyler, Alice Felt. FREEDOM'S FERMENT: PHASES OF AMERICAN
      SOCIAL HISTORY FROM THE COLONIAL PERIOD TO THE OUTBREAK OF
      THE CIVIL WAR. Minneapolis: University of Minnesota
      Press, 1944. Reprint. New York: Harper & Row, 1962.

182. United States. Department of Commerce. Bureau of the Census.
      "Communistic Societies: Statistics, Denominational
      History, Doctrine, Organization." (From 1926 CENSUS OF
      RELIGIOUS BODIES). Washington, D.C., 1928.

183. "Utopia." DAEDALUS. 94 (Spring 1965).

184. Veysey, Laurence. THE COMMUNAL EXPERIENCE: ANARCHISTIC AND
      MYSTICAL COUNTER-CULTURES. New   York: Harper & Row,
      1973; Chicago: University of Chicago Press, 1978.

185. Wagner, Jon. "Sexuality and Gender Roles in Utopian
      Communities: A Critical Survey of Scholarly Work."
      COMMUNAL SOCIETIES. 6 (1986): 172-188.

186. Walters, Ronald G. AMERICAN REFORMERS. 1815-1860. New York:
      Hill and Wang, 1978.

187.   Waterhouse, E.S. "Pietism." ENCYCLOPAEDIA OF RELIGION AND
        ETHICS. James Hastings, editor. New York: Charles
        Scribners; Edinburgh: T.& T. Clark 1919, s.v.

188.   Webber, Everett. ESCAPE TO UTOPIA: THE COMMUNAL MOVEMENT IN
        AMERICA. In THE AMERICA PROCESSION series, Henry G.
        Alsbert, editor. New York: Hastings House, 1959.

189.   Weisbrod, Carol. THE BOUNDARIES OF UTOPIA. New York: Pantheon
        Books, 1980.

190.   Whalen, William Joseph. COMMUNES AND THE RELIGIOUS EXPERIENCE.
        Chicago: Claretian Publishers, 1972.

191.   Whitman, Alden, ed. AMERICAN REFORMERS: AN H.W. WILSON
        BIOGRAPHICAL DICTIONARY. New York: H.W. Wilson Co., 1985.

192.   Whitney, Norman Jehiel. EXPERIMENTS IN COMMUNITY: EPHARATA, THE
        AMISH, THE DOUKHOBORS, THE SHAKERS, THE BRUDERHOF [AND]
        MONTEVERDE. Wallingford, PA: Pendle Hill, 1966, Pamphlet
        149.

193.   Whitworth, John McKelvie. GOD'S BLUEPRINTS: A SOCIOLOGICAL
        STUDY OF THREE UTOPIAN SECTS. London; Boston: Routledge &
        Kegan Paul, 1975.

194.   Williams, Julia Elizabeth. "An Analytical Tabulation of the
        North American Utopian Communities by Type, Longevity, and
        Location." MA Thesis, University of South Dakota, 1939.

195.   Wittke, Carl Frederick. WE WHO BUILT AMERICA; THE SAGA OF THE
        IMMIGRANT. New York: Prentice-Hall, 1939.

196.   Wooster, Ernest S. COMMUNITIES OF THE PAST AND PRESENT. New
        Llano, LA: Llano Colonist, 1924. Reprint. New York: AMS
        Press, 1973.

197.   Zablocki, Benjamin. ALIENATION AND CHARISMA: A STUDY OF
        CONTEMPORARY AMERICAN COMMUNES. New York: MacMillan/Free
        Press, 1980.

AMANA COLONIES (1843-1932)

The Society of True Inspiration, or Amana Society, developed out
of an 18th century German pietist movement. They first settled
in Ebenezer, New York, and moved to Iowa in 1854, under the
leadership of Christian Metz. In 1932 it was reorganized into a
privately owned stock company.

ARCHIVAL MATERIALS

198.   Amana Society. Archives. Amana Heritage Society.
       Amana, Iowa.

199.   Pierce, Maris Bryant. Papers, 1793-1874. Buffalo and Erie
       County Historical Society Collections, Buffalo, NY.

ARTICLES AND BOOKS

200.   Amana Society. A BRIEF HISTORY OF THE AMANA SOCIETY OR
       COMMUNITY OF TRUE INSPIRATION, 1714-1900. Amana, IA: The
       Society, 1900, 1918.

201.   Amana Society. CONSTITUTION AND BY-LAWS OF THE COMMUNITY OF
       TRUE INSPIRATION, incorporated under the name of the Amana
       Society in county and state of Iowa. n.p., 1859?.

202.   Amana Society. DAVIDISCHES PSALTERSPEIL DER KINDER ZIONS; ODER
       SAMMLUNG VON ALTEN UND NEUEN AUSERLESENEN
       GEISTES-GESANGEN. Amana, IA: The Society, 1869.

203.   Amana Society. DAVIDISCHES PSALTER-SPIEL DER KINDER ZIONS;
       ODER, SAMMLUNG VON ALTEN UND NEUEN AUSERLESENEN
       GEISTES-GESANGEN. ALLEN WAHREN HEILSBEGIERIGEN SEELEN UND
       SAUGLINGEN DER WEISCHEIT, INSONDERHEIT ABER DENEN
       GEMEINDEN DES HERRN ZUM GESEGNETEN GEBRUCH MIT FLEISS
       ZUSAMMEN, GETRAGEN NEBST DEN DAZU NOTHIGEN UND NUTZLICHEN
       STEREO-TYPIRT.   Zweiter Abdruck. Amana, IA, 1869.

204.   Amana Society. J.J.J. AUFRICHTIGE UND WARHAFTIGE
       EXTRACTA AUS DEM ALLGEMEINEN DIARIO DER WAHREN
       INSPIRATIONS GEMEINEN. 1-   Sammlung; 1739-   .

205.   Amana Society. J.J.J. CATECHETISCHER UNTERRICHT VON DER LEHRE
       DES HEILS, DARGESTELLT NACH DEN AUSSPRUCHEN DER HEIL.
       SCHRIFT, AUF DEN EVANGELISCHE-APOSTOLISCHEN SINN DES
       GEISTES GOTTES GEGRUNDET. Neu aufgelegt. 2 vols. Amana,
       1863-1885.

206.   Amana Society. JAHRBUCHER DER WAHREN INSPIRATIONS

GEMEINDEN ODER BEZEUGEN VON DEM GEISTES DES HERRN. Vols.
1-2 published in Germany, n.p., 1842; vols. 3-21,
Ebenezer, NY, 1849-1863; vols. 22-58, Amana, Iowa,
1866-1884. Contains the EINSPRACHEN and AUSPRACHEN of
Christian Metz and Barbara Heinemann.

207.   Amana Society. LEHR-UND LESE-BUCH FUR DIE SCHUL-
           JUGEND IN DEN GEMEINDEN DER WAHREN INSPIRATION; ALS
           HILFSMITTEL ZUR AN LEITUNG UND FORTBILDUNG IN EINIGEN
           ZWEIGEN DER BURGERLICHEN WISSEN SCHAFTEN. Buffalo:
           Eben-Ezer, 1853.

208.   Amana Society. SEVEN VILLAGES PRACTICING MODIFIED CAPITALISM.
           Amana, IA: The Society, 1936.

209.   Andelson, Jonathan Gary. "Communalism and Change
           in the Amana Society, 1855-1932." Vols. I & II. PhD
           diss., University of Michigan, 1974.

210.   ------. "The Double Bind and Social Change in
           Communal Amana." HUMAN RELATIONS. 34 (February 1981):
           111-125.

211.   ------. "The Gift to be Single: Celibacy and
           Religious Enthusiasm in the Community of True
           Inspiration." COMMUNAL SOCIETIES. 5 (1985): 1-32.

212.   ------. "Routinization of Behavior in a Charismatic Leader."
           AMERICAN ETHNOLOGIST. 7 (November 1980): 716-733.

213.   ------. "Tradition, Innovation, and Assimilation in
           Iowa's Amana Colonies." PALIMPSEST. 69 (Spring 1988): 2-
           15.

214.   Bach, M.L. "Amana--The Glory Has Departed." CHRISTIAN CENTURY.
           52 (August 28, 1935): 1083-1086.

215.   Barlow, Arthur. RECOLLECTIONS...THE AMANA SOCIETY'S "GREAT
           CHANGE." n.p., 1971.

216.   Barthel, Diane L. AMANA: FROM PIETIST SECT TO AMERICAN
           COMMUNITY. Lincoln: University of Nebraska Press, 1984.

217.   Blakeman, Elisha. A BRIEF ACCOUNT OF THE SOCIETY OF GERMANS,
           CALLED THE TRUE INSPIRATIONISTS, RESIDING SEVEN MILES
           SOUTHEAST OF BUFFALO...FROM THE RECOLLECTIONS OF PETER H.
           LONG AND HIMSELF AFTER VISITING THEM IN THE MONTH OF
           AUGUST 1846. New Lebanon, NY: n.p., 1846.

218.   Caven, Ruth Shonle. "The Future of a Historic Commune: Amana."
           INTERNATIONAL REVIEW OF MODERN SOCIOLOGY. 8 (Jan-June
           1978): 89-101.

219.   ------. "Roles of the Old in Personal and Impersonal Societies."
       FAMILY COORDINATOR. 27 (October 1978): 315-319.

220.   Cavan, Ruth Shonle, and Man Singh Das. COMMUNES
       HISTORICAL AND CONTEMPORARY. New Delhi: Vikas Publishing
       House, 1979.

221.   Chafee, Grace. "Isolated Religious Sect as an Object for Social
       Research." AMERICAN JOURNAL OF SOCIOLOGY. 35 (January
       1930): 618-630.

222.   ------. "A Sociological Investigation of the Amana and
       Amish-Mennonite Communities." M.A. thesis. University of
       Chicago. 1927.

223.   Clark, Robert Edwin. "A Cultural and Historical Geography of
       the Amana Colonies." Ph.D. diss., University of Nebraska,
       1974.

224.   Davis, Darrell Haug. "Amana, A Study of Occupance." ECONOMIC
       GEOGRAPHY. 12 (July 1936): 217-230.

225.   Dickel, Martin. "Communal Life in Amana." IOWA JOURNAL OF
       HISTORY. 59 (January 1961): 83-89.

226.   Dow, James R., and Madeline Roemig. "Amana Folk Art and
       Craftsmanship." THE PALIMPSEST. 58 (March/April 1977):
       54-63.

227.   Durnbaugh, Donald F. "Eberhard Ludwig Gruber & Johann Adam
       Gruber: A Father & Son as Early Inspirationist Leaders."
       COMMUNAL SOCIETIES. 4 (Fall 1984): 150-160.

228.   ------. "Johann Adam Gruber: Pennsylvania-German Prophet and
       Poet." PENNSYLVANIA MAGAZINE OF HISTORY AND BIOGRAPHY.
       83 (October 1959): 382-408.

229.   Duval, Francis Alan. "Christian Metz, German American Religious
       Leader and Pioneer." PhD diss., State University of
       Iowa, 1948.

230.   Eiboeck, Joseph. DIE DEUTSCHEN VON IOWA UND DEREN
       ERRUNGENSCHAFTEN. EINE GESCHICHTE DES STAATES, DESSEN
       DEUTSCHER PIONIERE UND IHRER NACHKOMMEN. Des Moines:
       Druck und Verlag des "Iowa' statts-anzeiger," 1900.

231.   Ely, Richard Theodore. "Amana, a Study of Religious Communism."
       THE PALIMPSEST. 52 (April 1971): 177-197. First
       published in HARPERS. 105 (October 1902): 659-668.

232.   Farlee, Lloyd Winfield. "A History of the Church Music of the
       Amana Society, The Community of True Inspiration. PhD
       diss., University of Iowa, 1966.

233.   Godwin, Parke. "Letters from America: A New Community in
        America." PEOPLE'S JOURNAL (London). 4 (October 9, 1847):
        218-219.

234.   Grant, H. Roger, ed. "The Amana Society of Iowa:
        Two Views," ANNALS OF IOWA. 43 (Summer 1975): 1-23.

235.   Grossman, Walter. "The European Origins of the True Inspired of
        Amana." COMMUNAL SOCIETIES. 4 (Fall 1984): 133-149.

236.   Gruber, Eberhard Ludwig. CHRISTLICHES HAND-BUCHLEIN...ALLEN
        WAHRHEIT-LIEBENDEN ZUM HEILSAMEN NUTZ UND GEBRAUCH, SOWOHL
        ZU HAUSE ALS AUCH AUF REISEN UND IN GESELLSCHAFTEN SICH
        DESSEN NUTZLICH ZU BEDIENEN. VON JEREMIAS FELBINGER.
        RECHTEN UND ORDNUNGEN DES HAUSES GOTTES IN FRAG UND
        ANTWORT. GRUNDFORSCHENDE FRAGEN, WELCHE DENEN NEUEN
        TAUFERN IM WITGENSTEINISCHEN ZU BEANTWORTEN VORGELEGT
        WURDEN, NEBST BEYDEFUGTEN ANTWORTEN AUF DIESELBEN.
        Baltimore: Gedruckt bey Samuel Saur, 1799.

237.   ------. GRUNDFORSCHENDE FRAGEN, WELCHE DENEN NEUEN TAEUFERN IM
        WITGENSTEINISCHEN INSONDERHEIT ZU BEANTWORTEN, VORGELEGT
        WAREN. Germantown, PA: C. Saur, 1773; 1799.

238.   ------. KURZE UND EINFALTIGE VORSTELLUNG DER AUSAERN, ABER DOCH
        HEILIGEN RECHTEN UND ORDHUNGEN DES HAUSES GOTTES, WIE ES
        DER WAHRE HAUS-VATER JESUS CHRISTUS BEFOHLEN, UND IN
        SEINEM TESTAMENT SCHRIFTLICH HINTERLASSEN. VORGESTELLT IN
        EINEM GESPRACH UNTER VATER UND SOHN, DURCH FRAG UND
        ANTWORT, VON ALEXANDER MACK, EINEM MITBERUFFENEN, ZU DEM
        GROSSEN ABENDMAHL. 2. aufl. Germantown: Gedrukt u. zu
        finden bey Christoph Saur, 1774.

239.   ------. A SHORT AND PLAIN VIEW OF THE OUTWARD, YET SACRED RIGHTS
        AND ORDINANCES OF THE HOUSE OF GOD, AS COMMANDED TO BE
        OBSERVED BY THE TRUE STEWARD, JESUS CHRIST, AND DEPOSITED
        IN HIS LAST WILL AND TESTAMENT, ARRANGED IN A CONVERSATION
        BETWEEN A FATHER AND SON. By Alexander Mack; translated
        into English by a friend to religion. Philadelphia:
        Printed by John Binns. 1810.

240.   ------. ...UNSCHULDIGES, FREIES UND GEBUNDENES ZEITVERTREIB. AUS
        GNADEN GEFUNDEN, BEI MUSSIGEN STUNDEN: UND DENEN
        NACHKOMMENDEN ZUM VORWURF UND AUFMERKEN, ZEUGNISS UND
        ANDENKEN. AUFGESCHRIEBEN UND HINTERLASSEN VON EBERHARD
        LUDWIG GRUBER...UND NUN NACH SEINEM TODE ZU NUTZ UND
        ERBAUUNG REDLICHER SEELEN DEM DRUCK UBERGEBEN VON SEINEN
        BRUDERN UND MITVERBUNDENEN. Theil-Budingen: Gedruckt in
        der A. Heller'schen Hofbuchdr., n.d.

241.   Hadorn, Wilhelm. "Die Inspirierten des 18. Jahrhunderts,"
        SCHWEIZERISCHE THEOLOGISCHE ZEITSCHRIFT. 17 (1900):
        187-224.

242.   Hegler, A., and K. Holl. "The Inspired." THE NEW
           SCHAFF-HERZOG ENCYCLOPEDIA OF RELIGIOUS KNOWLEDGE.   Samuel
           Macauley Jackson, ed. New York; London: Funk and
           Wagnalls, 1910. s.v.

243.   Heinze, Ted W., HISTORICAL STORIES OF THE AMANA COLONIES.
           N.p.: The Author, N.d.

244.   HOW IT WAS IN THE ... COMMUNITY KITCHEN. Fairfax, IA: R.
           Trampold, N.d.

245.   Johnson, Irving Rydell. "A Study of the Amana Dialect." PhD
           diss., University of Iowa, 1935.

246.   Knortz, Karl. DIE WAHRE INSPIRATIONS-GEMEINDE IN
           IOWA; EIN BEITRAG ZUR GESCHICHTE DES CHRISTLICHEN
           PIETISMUS UND COMMUNISMUS. Leipzig: Wigand, 1896.

247.   Lankes, Frank James. THE EBENEZER COMMUNITY OF TRUE
           INSPIRATION. Gardenville, NY: n.p.

248.   ------. THE EBENEZER SOCIETY. West Seneca, NY: West Seneca
           Historical Society, 1963.

249.   Liffring-Zug, Joan. THE AMANAS YESTERDAY. Collected by Joan
           Liffring-Zug; John Zug, ed. Iowa City: Penfield Press,
           1975.

250.   Linder, Irene C. "A Study of the Birthrate of Amana." Master's
           thesis, University of Iowa, 1941.

251.   MacClure, Lulu. "Life in Amana." THE PALIMPSEST. 52 (April
           1971): 214-222.

252.   Metz, Christian. HISTORISCHE BESCHREIBUNGEN DER
           WAHREN-INSPIRATIONS-GEMEINSCHAFT, WIE SIE BESTANDEN UND
           SICH FORTGEPFLANZT HAT, UND WAS VON DEN WICHTIGSTEN
           EREIGNISSEN NOCH AUS GEFUNDEN WERDEN KANN, BESONDERS WIE
           SIE IN DEN JAHREN 1817 UND 1818 DURCH DEN GEIST GOTTES IN
           NEUEN WERKZEUGEN AUFGEWECKT WORDEN UND WAS SEIT DER ZEIT
           IN UND MIT DIESER GEMEINDE UND DEREN HERZUGEKOMMENEN
           GLIEDERN WICHTIGES VORGEFALLEN. Buffalo, NY: 1863.

253.   ------. INSPIRATIONS-HISTORIE; ODER, AUGZUGE AUS DEN TAGEBUCHERN
           VON BR. CHRISTIAN METZ, ENTHALTEND DAS WICHTIGSTE, WAS
           SOWOHL IN UND MIT DEM WERKZEUG SELBST, ALS AUCH IN UND MIT
           DER GEMEINE SICH ZUGETRAGEN. ALS FORTSETZUNG DER IN DER
           ZWANZIGSTEN SAMMLUNG ENTHALTENEN INSPIRATIONS-HISTORIE
           GEORDNET UND ZUSAMMENBETRAGEN. Amana, IA: 1875.

254.   Moerschel, Henry George. THE AMANAS. Amana, IA: Amana Society,
           1969.

255.   ------. "Historical Background of Amana." IOWA JOURNAL OF
       HISTORY. 59 (January 1961): 78-82.

256.   Nagel, Paul Giesbert. "Kurze Historie der so-genannten
       Inspirirten und Inspirations-Gemeinden; Auf Teutsch: Der
       Propheten-Kinder und Propheten-Schule." J.J.J. xvii.
       Sammlung n.p.; 1776. pp. 233-268.

257.   Noe, Charles Fred. "A Brief History of the Amana Society,
       1714-1900." IOWA JOURNAL OF HISTORY AND POLITICS. 2
       (April 1904): 162-187.

258.   Ohrn, Steven. "Conserving Amana's Folk Arts: A Community
       Remaining Faithful." PALIMPSEST. 69 (Spring 1988): 16-33.

259.   Perkins, William Rufus and Barthinius L. Wick. HISTORY OF THE
       AMANA SOCIETY, OR COMMUNITY OF THE TRUE INSPIRATION. Iowa
       City: State University of Iowa, 1891. Reprint. Westport,
       CT: Hyperion Press, 1976.

260.   Petersen, William. "Life in the Amana Colony." THE PALIMPSEST.
       52 (April 1971): 163-176.

261.   Phillips, Tom and Mary. AMANA, METAMORPHOSIS OF A CULTURE.
       Cedar Rapids: Kirkwood Community College, 1973.

262.   Purcell, L. Edward, et al. "An Amana Album." THE
       PALIMPSEST. 58 (March/April 1977): 48-53.

263.   Rettig, Lawrence. AMANA TODAY. Amana Society, 1975.

264.   ------. "Grammatical Structures in Amana German," Ph.D. diss.,
       University of Iowa, 1970.

265.   Rice, Richard Millburn. "Eighty-Nine Years of Collective
       Living." HARPER'S MAGAZINE. 177 (October 1938): 522-524.
       Reprinted in THE PALIMPSEST. 52 (April 1971): 198-213.

266.   Richling, Barnett. "The Amana Society: A History of Change."
       THE PALIMPSEST. 58 (March/April 1977): 34-47.

267.   ------. "Sectarian Ideology and Change in Amana." M.A. Thesis,
       McGill University, 1973.

268.   Ricker, Alan W. THE AMANA SOCIETY: A STUDY IN COOPERATION FROM
       THE VIEWPOINT OF A SOCIALIST. Girard, KS.: A.W. Ricker,
       1911.

269.   Ritschl, Albrecht Benjamin. GESCHICHTE DES PIETISMUS. 3 vols.
       Bonn: A. Marcus, 1880-86.

270.   Scheuner, Gottlieb. INSPIRATIONS-HISTORIE; ODER,
       BESCHREIBUNG DES GNADENWERKS DES HERRN IN DEN GEMEINDEN
       DER WAHREN INSPIRATION WIE DER HERR DASSELBE NACH DEM TODE

DES 1.BR. CHR. METZ DURCH SEINE MITBRUDER UND SCHW.
BARBARA LANDMANN FORTGEFUHRT HAT. 7 vols. Amana, IA:
1900-1925.

271. ------. INSPIRATIONS-HISTORIE; ODER HISTORISCHER BERICHT VON DER
NEUEN ERWECKUNG, SAMMLUNG UND GRUNDUNG DER WAHREN
INSPIRATIONS-GEMEINDE IN DEUTSCHLAND, SO WIE DEREN AUS
WANDERUNG NACH AMERIKA UND SPATERE UEBERSIEDLUNG VON
EBENEZER NACH AMANA, UND WAS WEITER IN UND MIT DIESER
GEMEINE [SIC] IN DEM ZEITRAUM VON 1817-1867 SICH BEGEBEN
HAT. Amana, IA: 1891.

272. ------. INSPIRATIONS-HISTORIE, ODER HISTORISCHER BERICHT VON DER
GRUNDUNG DER GEBETS-VERSAMMLUNGEN UND GEMEINDEN, WIE
SOLCHE VOM GEIST DES HERRN DURCH DIE INSPIRATIONS-
WERKZEUGE ANBEFOHLEN UND VON EBERHARD LUDWIG GRUBER
ANGEFANGEN UND EINGEORDNET WORDEN; SOWIE, WAS SICH MIT DEN
HIERIN GENANNTEN INSPIRITEN ALS AUCH IN UND MIT DER WAHREN
INSPIRATIONS-GEMEINDE WAHREND J.F. ROCKS LEBZEITEN UND
AUCH NACH IHM BIS ZUR ZEIT DER NEUEN ERWECKUNG IN DEN
JAHREN 1817 UND 1818 ZUGETRAGEN. AUS VERSCHIEDENEN,
THEILS GEDRUCKTEN, THEILS BESCHRIEBENEN BERICHTEN
ZUSAMMENBESTELLT VON GOTTLIEB SCHEUNER. Amana, IA: 1884.

273. ------. INSPIRATIONS-HISTORY; THE HISTORY OF THE INSPIRATION; OR,
HISTORICAL ACCOUNT OF THE FOUNDING OF THE CONGREGATION OR
COMMUNITY OF PRAYER AS SUCH WAS COMMANDED BY THE SPIRIT OF
THE LORD THROUGH THE INSTRUMENTS OF INSPIRATION AND BEGUN
AND ORGANIZED BY EBERHARD LUDWIG GRUBER. Assembled by
Gottlieb Scheuner; Janet W. Zuber, transl. Amana, IA: The
Society, 1884, 1978.

274. Schiff, Henry. "Before & After 1932: A Memoir." COMMUNAL
SOCIETIES. 4 (Fall 1984): 161-164.

275. Schiffer, Robert L. "Capitalist Revolution in Iowa."
REPORTER. 24 (January 5, 1961): 24-27.

276. Schulz-Beherend, George. "The Amana Colony."
AMERICAN-GERMAN REVIEW. 7 (December 1940): 7-9, 38.

277. Selzer, Barbara Jacoline. "A Description of the Amana Dialect
of Homestead, Iowa." PhD diss., University of Illinois
(Urbana), 1941.

278. Shambaugh, Bertha Maud Horack. "Amana." THE PALIMPSEST. 2
(July 1921): 193-228.

279. ------. "Amana-In Transition." THE PALIMPSEST. 17 (May 1936):
149-184.

280. ------. "Amana Society." ENCYCLOPAEDIA OF RELIGION AND ETHICS.
James Hastings, editor. New York: Charles Scribner's
Sons, Edinburgh: T.& T. Clark, 1913. s.v.

281.   ------. AMANA THAT WAS AND AMANA THAT IS. Iowa City: The State
       Historical Society of Iowa, 1932. Reprint. New York:
       Arno Press, 1976.

282.   ------. "Amana That Was and Amana That Is." THE PALIMPSEST. 44
       (March 1963): 91-124.

283.   ------. "Amana That Was and Is." THE PALIMPSEST. 31 (June
       1950): 215-248.

284.   ------. "Amana the Church and Christian Metz the Prophet." THE
       MIDLAND, A MAGAZINE OF THE MIDDLE WEST. 1 (August 1915):
       249-257.

285.   ------. AMANA, THE COMMUNITY OF TRUE INSPIRATION. Iowa City: The
       State Historical Society of Iowa, 1908.

286.   Shaw, Albert. "Life in the Amana Colony." CHAUTAUGUAN.
       (February 1888). Reprinted in THE PALIMPSEST. 52 (April
       1971): 163-176.

287.   Smith, Anna M. "The Amana Community." COMMONWEAL. 27
       (November 5, 1937): 42-43.

288.   Snyder, Ruth Geraldine. "The Arts and Crafts of the Amana
       Society." M.A. thesis, State University of Iowa. 1949.

289.   Strieb, Ruth B. and Gordon F. "Communes and the Aging: Utopian
       Dreams and Gerontological Reality." AMERICAN BEHAVIORAL
       SCIENTIST. 19 (November/December 1975): 176-189.

290.   Stuck, Peter. "Amana Protests." CHRISTIAN CENTURY. 52
       (September 25, 1935): 1212.

291.   THE TWENTY-FOUR RULES FORMING THE BASIS OF THE FAITH
       OF THE AMANA CHURCH SOCIETY. [Amana, IA]: Amana Church
       Society, n.d.

292.   Ungers, Oswald Matthias and Liselotte. "Utopische Kommunen in
       Amerika, 1800-1900, Die Amana-Community." WERK. (August
       1970): 543-546.

293.   West Seneca (N.Y.) Centennial Society, 1851-1951. WEST SENECA
       CENTENNIAL CELEBRATION. West Seneca, 1951.

294.   ------. WEST SENECA, ERIE COUNTY, NEW YORK, 1851-1951. Buffalo:
       Rauch & Stoeckl, 1951.

295.   Yambura, Barbara Schneider, with Eunice W. Bodine. A CHANGE AND
       A PARTING: MY STORY OF AMANA. Ames: Iowa State University
       Press, 1960.

296.   Zimmerman, Paul A. THE HISTORY OF BEER BREWING AS CONTINUED BY
        THE COMMUNITY OF TRUE INSPIRATION IN THE "NEW WORLD".
        Amana, IA: The Author, 1982.

297.   Zuber, Janet, transl. BARBARA HEINEMAN LINDMANN BIOGRAPHY {AND}
        E.L. GRUBER'S TEACHINGS ON DIVINE INSPIRATION, AND OTHER
        ESSAYS. Lake Mills, IA: n.p., 1981.

298.   Zug, Joan Liffring and John. THE AMANAS YESTERDAY: A STORY OF
        SEVEN VILLAGES IN IOWA, HISTORIC PHOTOGRAPHS 1900-1932.
        Iowa City: Penfield Press for The Amana Society, c1975.
        New edition as: SEVEN AMANA VILLAGES. Iowa City, IA:
        Penfield Press, 1981.

299.   ------. THE AMANA COLONIES: SEVEN VILLAGES IN IOWA, NEW WORLD
        HOME OF THE TRUE INSPIRATIONISTS. Amana, IA: The Amana
        Society, 1969.

BERLIN HEIGHTS, OHIO (1854-1858)

A group of "Free-Lovers" in Berlin Heights, Erie County, Ohio
led by Francis Barry.

300.   Fogarty, Robert S. "Nineteenth Century Utopian."
          THE PACIFIC HISTORIAN. 16 (Fall 1972): 70-76.

301.   Peeke, Hewson Lindsley. THE CENTENNIAL HISTORY OF ERIE COUNTY,
          OHIO. Cleveland: The Penten Press, 1925. II, pp.
          647-654.

302.   SOCIAL REVOLUTIONIST. Greenville, Ohio. Vol. 1-4. January
          1856-December 1857.

304.   Towner, James William. A GENEALOGY OF THE TOWNER FAMILY. Los
          Angeles: Times-Mirror Printing and Binding House, 1910.

305.   Vartorella, William F., ed. BERLIN HEIGHTS: FREE LOVE AND THE
          NEW FAITH IN OHIO, 1857-1871. New York: AMS Press, 1987.

306.   ------. "Free Love War Waged in Ohio." ECHOES.
          (June 1974).

307.   ------. "The Other `Peculiar Institution': The Free Thought and
          Free Love Reform Press in Ohio During Rebellion and
          Reconstruction, 1861-1877." PhD diss., Ohio University,
          1977.

BETHEL-AURORA COLONIES (1844-1880)

Founded by William Keil, a German Methodist, with a small group
of Harmonists from Economy, Pennsylvania. Bethel, Shelby
County, Missouri was the site for the first settlement. In
1856, Keil led a group to Oregon to establish the Aurora colony
in Marion County.

ARCHIVAL MATERIAL

308. Aurora Colony. Papers, 1855-1885. Oregon Historical Society
     Library. Portland. Microfilm from originals at Oregon
     State Archives.

309. Hendricks, Robert J. "Miscellaneous Papers Relating to the
     Aurora Community." Oregon State Archives Microfilm.

ARTICLES AND BOOKS

310. Bek, William Godfrey, transl. "From Bethel, Missouri to Aurora,
     Oregon: Letters of William Keil, 1855-1870." MISSOURI
     HISTORICAL REVIEW. 48 (October 1953): 23-41; (January
     1954): 141-153.

311. ------. "The Community at Bethel, Missouri, and Its Offspring at
     Aurora, Oregon." GERMAN-AMERICAN ANNALS. 7 (September
     1909): 257-276, 306-328; 8 (April 1910): 15-44, 76-81.

312. ------. "A German Communistic Society in Missouri." MISSOURI
     HISTORICAL REVIEW. 3 (October 1908): 52-74; (January
     1909): 99-125.

313. THE BETHEL COLONY, 1844-1877. Bethel, MO: Bethel Colony Foun-
     dation, n.d.

314. Burckhardt, J. Frederick. "A Historical Narrative of the Old
     Bethel Colony," Oregon Historical Society microfilm.

315. Darley, Harold. "The Old Communistic Colony Bethel."
     PENNSYLVANIA MAGAZINE OF HISTORY AND BIOGRAPHY. 52
     (1928): 162-167.

316. Grant, H. Roger. "The Society of Bethel: A Visitor's Account."
     MISSOURI HISTORICAL REVIEW. 68 (January 1974): 223-231.

317. Harkness, Ione Juanita Beale. "Certain Community Settlements of
     Oregon." M.A. thesis, University of Southern California,
     1925.

318. Hendricks, Robert J. BETHEL AND AURORA: AN EXPERIMENT IN
     COMMUNISM AS PRACTICAL CHRISTIANITY WITH SOME ACCOUNT OF
     PAST AND PRESENT VENTURES IN COLLECTIVE LIVING. New York:

The Press of the Pioneers, 1922. Reprint. New York: AMS
Press, 1971.

319.   Holbrook, Stewart H. "Aurora Communists." AMERICAN MERCURY.
       67 (July 1948): 54-59.

320.   Lyman, H.S. "The Aurora Community." OREGON HISTORICAL SOCIETY
       QUARTERLY. 2 (March 1901): 78-93.

321.   Olsen, Deborah M., and Clark M. Will. "Musical Heritage of the
       Aurora Colony." OREGON HISTORICAL QUARTERLY. 79 (Fall
       1978): 232-268.

322.   Simon, John E. "William Kiel and Communistic Colonies." THE
       OREGON HISTORICAL QUARTERLY. 36 (June 1935): 119-153.

323.   Will, Clark Moor. "Aurora Colony Church Bells." OREGON
       HISTORICAL QUARTERLY. 67 (September 1966): 273-276.

324.   ------. THE STORY OF OLD AURORA IN PICTURE AND PROSE, 1856-1882:
       AN INFORMATION HANDBOOK TO FILL THE NEED FOR A BRIEF
       RECORD OF AN HISTORIC OREGON EXPERIMENT IN COMMUNAL
       LIVING. Salem, OR: Panther Print Co., 1972.

325.   White, John G. "Bethel, A Town Awakened." MISSOURI LIFE
       (September-October, 1978): 11-20.

BETTINA KOLONIE (1847-1848)

Also known as Darmstadter Kolonie because of the origin of the
radical German students who settled the community on the Llano
River in Texas. The settlement was named for the German woman
author Bettina von Arnim.

ARTICLES AND BOOKS

326. Biesele, Rudolph Leopold. THE HISTORY OF GERMAN
         SETTLEMENTS IN TEXAS, 1831-1861. Austin, TX: von
         Boeckmann-Jones Co., 1930.

327. Reinhardt, Louis. "The Communistic Colony of Bettina,
         1846-1848." TEXAS HISTORICAL QUARTERLY. 3 (July 1899):
         33-39.

328. Wilmer, John. "The German Colony in Texas." TAIT'S EDINBURGH
         MAGAZINE. 15 (April 1848): 219-224. Microfilm. Ann
         Arbor: UMI, 1961.

BISHOP HILL COLONY (1846-1862)

A group of Swedish dissidents led by Erik Jansson, who settled in Henry County, Illinois.

ARCHIVAL MATERIALS

329. Bishop Hill. Papers, 1846-1914. Bishop Hill Heritage Association. Bishop Hill, IL.

330. "Proceedings of the Meetings of the Bishop Hill Colony in Henry County and the State of Illinois, May 6, 1854-May 27, 1861." In the possession of Mrs. Emmelyne A. Hedstrom, Galva, Illinois.

331. Stoneberg, Philip J. Papers. Knox College Library. Galesburg, IL.

BIBLIOGRAPHIES

332. Johnson, E. Gustav. "A Selected Bibliography of Bishop Hill Literature." THE SWEDISH PIONEER HISTORICAL QUARTERLY. 15 (July 1964): 109-122.

333. Vance, Mary A. HISTORIC BISHOP HILL, ILLINOIS; RESTORATION OF A SWEDISH UTOPIAN COMMUNITY. Monticello, IL.: Vance Bibliographies, 1980. Architecture Series, A-380.

ARTICLES AND BOOKS

334. Adams, Gale. "Bishop Hill: Colony on the Prairie." SAVER. (Fall 1975): 3-7.

335. Andersson, S. "Nagot om Erik Jansismen, sarskilt dess verksam het i Alfta." JULHALSNING TILL FORSAMLINGARNA I ARKESTIFTET. Uppsala: Almqvist & Wiksells, 1923. pp. 86-100.

336. Andersson, Theodore J.,compiler. 100 YEARS: A HISTORY OF BISHOP HILL, ILLINOIS. ALSO BIOGRAPHICAL SKETCHES OF MANY EARLY SWEDISH PIONEERS IN ILLINOIS. Chicago, 1947.

337. Ankarberg, Karin. "Nagra avsnitt ur Bishop-Hill koloniens historia." HISTORISKA STUDIER TILLAGNADE FOLKE LINDBERG, 27 AUGUSTI, 1963. Edited by Gunnar Torward Westin, Stockholm, 1963. pp. 123-133.

338. Benson, Adolph Burnett, ed. SWEDES IN AMERICA,

1638-1938. Published for the Swedish American
Tercentenary Association. New Haven: Yale University
Press; London: H. Milford; Oxford University Press, 1938.

339.   ------, and Naboth Hedin. "The Bishop Hill Colony." AMERICANS
        FROM SWEDEN. Philadelphia: Lippincott, 1950. pp.
        106-118.

340.   Bigelow, Hiram. "The Bishop Hill Colony." TRANSACTIONS OF THE
        ILLINOIS STATE HISTORICAL SOCIETY FOR THE YEAR 1902.
        Springfield, IL.: 1902. pp. 101-108.

341.   Bishop Hill Colony. THE BISHOP HILL COLONY CASE. ANSWER OF THE
        DEFENDANTS TO THE BILL OF COMPLAINT, FILED IN THE HENRY
        CIRCUIT COURT, TO THE OCTOBER TERM, A.D. 1868. MOTION TO
        DISSOLVE THE INJUNCTION, AND BRIEF AND POINTS, ON MOTION
        OF BENNET & VEEDER, SOLICITORS [SIC], AND OF COUNSEL FOR
        THE DEFENDENTS. Galena, IL.: N.W. Fuller, 1868.

342.   "Bishop Hill Settlement, Henry Co. The First Swedish Settlement
        in Illinois." In Helge Nelson, THE SWEDES IN NORTH
        AMERICA. Lund, Sweden: C.W.K. Gleerup, 1943. Reprint.
        New York: Arno Press, 1979. pp. 160-165.

343.   Booten, Joseph F., and George M. Nedved. CENTENNIAL CELEBRATION
        OF THE BISHOP HILL COLONY. Bishop Hill, IL., Monday,
        Sept. 23, 1946, State of Illinois, Department of Public
        Works and Buildings. Springfield, 1946.

344.   "Celebration of the Seventieth Anniversary of the
        Founding of Bishop Hill Colony." JOURNAL OF THE ILLINOIS
        STATE HISTORICAL SOCIETY. 9 (July 1916): 344-356.

345.   Cornelius, Carl Alfred. SVENSKE KYRKAUS HISTORIA
        EFTER REFORMATIONEN. 2 vols. Uppsala, Sweden: R.
        Almqvist & J. Wiksell, 1886-87.

346.   Dearinger, Lowell A. "Bishop Hill Colony. Rise and Fall of
        Swedish Dissenters Communal Society on the Illinois
        Prairie." OUTDOOR ILLINOIS. 4 (July 1965): 4-13.

347.   Elmen, Paul. "Bishop Hill: Utopia on the Prairie." CHICAGO
        HISTORY. 5 (Spring 1976): 45-52.

348.   ------. WHEAT FLOUR MESSIAH: ERIC JANSSON OF BISHOP HILL.
        Carbondale; Edwardsville, IL.: Southern Illinois
        University Press, 1976.

349.   Engstrand, Stuart David. THEY SOUGHT FOR PARADISE. New York:
        Harper & Brothers, 1939. (Fiction)

350.   Erdahl, Sivert. "Eric Janson and the Bishop Hill Colony."
        JOURNAL OF THE ILLINOIS STATE HISTORICAL SOCIETY. 18
        (October 1925-January 1926): xiv-xx, 503-574.

351. ERIK-JANSONISTERNAS HISTORIA. Galva, IL.; 1902.

352. Farman, Emma Shogren. "A Plymouth of Swedish America: The Town of Bishop Hill and Its Founder, Eric Janson." THE AMERICAN SCANDINAVIAN REVIEW. 2 (September 1914): 30-36.

353. Gladhi, Henrik. "Till halsingelaseriets och erikjansis mens karakteristik." KYRKOHISTORISK ARSSKRIFT. 47 (1947): 186-212.

354. Hatten, Minnie Maxwell. "Bishop Hill: A Sectarian Community." Masters thesis, State University of Iowa, n.d.

355. Havighurst, Walter Edwin. "From Helsingland to Bishop Hill." UPPER MISSISSIPPI: A WILDERNESS SAGA. New York; Toronto: Farrar & Rinehart, 1944. pp. 117-127.

356. Hedstrom, Emmelyne Arnquist. HISTORIC BISHOP HILL: 1846-1946. BISHOP HILL CENTENNIAL SOUVENIR. Observance September 22, 23, and 24, 1946. Aledo, IL: Times Record Co., Catalog Printers, 1946.

357. Hellstrom, Olle. "Erik Jansson." SVENSK BIOGRAFISKT LEXIKON. Erik Grill, ed. Stockholm: Norstedts Tryckeri, 1975. s.v.

358. Herlenius. Emil. ERIK-JANSISMEN I SVERIGE; BIDRAG TILL SVENSKA SEKT VASENDETS HISTORIA. Uppsala: Almqvist & Wiksells boktr, 1897.

359. ------. ERIK-JANSISMENS HISTORIA. ETT BIDRAG TILL KANNEDOMEN OM DET SVENSKA SEKT VASENDET. Jonkoping Svenge: Lundgrenskaboktr, 1900.

360. Illinois. Department of Public Works and Buildings. Division of Parks and Memorials. OFFICIAL GUIDE TO THE OLD COLONY CHURCH AND CATALOGUE OF THE COLLECTION OF PIONEER RELICS OF BISHOP HILL. Centennial Issue. Springfield, 1946.

361. Isaksson, Olov. BISHOP HILL, ILL.: A UTOPIA ON THE PRAIRIE. Albert Read, transl. Stockholm, Sweden: LT Publishing House, 1969.

362. ------. "Discover Bishop Hill." THE SWEDISH PIONEER HISTORICAL QUARTERLY. 19 (October 1968): 220-233.

363. Jacobson, Margaret E. BISHOP HILL, 1846. Photos by Russell Trall Neville. Bishop Hill, IL.: Bishop Hill Old Settlers Association, 1941.

364. ------. "The Painted Record of a Community Experiment: Olof Krans and His Pictures of the Bishop Hill Colony." JOURNAL OF

THE ILLINOIS STATE HISTORICAL SOCIETY.   34 (June 1941):
164-176.

365.   Jansson, Erik. EN HARLIG BESKRIFNING PA MENNISKANS TILL VAXT,
       DA HON HELT AR, ENLIGT JOHANNES 15 CAP., INYMPADE UTI DET
       SANNA WINTRADET CHRISTO, ELLER EN SANN FORKLARING O FRER 2
       KONUNGS BOKEN 2: HURU DEN SOM LIKA MED ELISA HAFNER
       OFRERGIFWIT ALLT, KAN TILLWARA UNDER DROENDA BON, TILL ATT
       TALE DUBBELT SA MYCKET, SOM SIN. MASTARE. ETT ORD I
       SINOM TID TILL LASAREN. Soderhamn. Printed by C.G.
       Blombergsson, 1846.

366.   ------. ETT AFSKEDSTAL, TILL ALLA SVERIGES INNEVANARE, SOM HAR
       FORAKTADT MIG, DEN JESUS HAFNER SANDT; ELLER FORKASTAT DET
       NAMNET ERIK JANSSON, SASOM ORENT, FOR DET JAG HAR BEKANT
       `JESU NAMN' INFOR MENNISKAR. Soderhamn. Printed by C.G.
       Blombergsson, 1846. 2d ed. Galva, IL., 1902.

367.   ------. ETT ORD I SINOM EID, ELLER EN KORT WEDERLAGGNING AF "ERIK
       JANSISMEN I HELSINGLAND." Soderhamn: Printed by C.G.
       Blombergsson, 1846.

368.   ------. FORKLARING OFVER DEN HELIGE SKRIFT, ELLER CATECHES
       FORFATTAD I FRAGOR OCH SVAR. Soderhamn: Printed by C.G.
       Blombergsson, 1826; Galva, IL., 1903.

369.   ------. NAGRA ORD TILL GUDS FORSAMLING. Soderhamn: Printed by
       C.G. Blombergsson, 1836.

370.   ------. NAGRA SANGER SAMT BONER. Soderhamn: Printed by C.G.
       Blombergsson, 1846. 2d ed. (with additional hymns)
       Galva, IL.: S. Cronsioe, 1857.

371.   Johnson, Eric, and Carl Fredrik Peterson. "Bishop
       Hill--Koloniens historia." SVENSKARNE I ILLINOIS.
       Chicago: W. Williamson, 1880, pp. 21-54.

372.   Johnson, E. Gustav. "A Prophet Died in Illinois a Century Ago."
       THE SWEDISH PIONEER HISTORICAL QUARTERLY. 1 (July 1950):
       8-12.

373.   Krohe, James, Jr. "Sweden on the Prairies." AMERICANA. 9
       (March-April, 1981): 64-70.

374.   Lagerberg, Matt. "The Bishop Hill Colonists in the Gold Rush."
       JOURNAL OF THE ILLINOIS STATE HISTORICAL SOCIETY. 48
       (Winter 1955): 466-469.

375.   Lilljeholm, John E. PIONEERING ADVENTURES OF JOHN EDWARD
       LILLJEHOLM IN AMERICA, 1846-1850. Translated by Arthur
       Wald. Volume 19. Rock Island, IL.: Augustana Historical
       Society Publications, 1962.

376. Lowe, David G. "Prairie Dream Recaptured." AMERICAN HERITAGE.
      20 (October 1969): 14-23.

377. McDonald, Julie. THE BALLARD OF BISHOP HILL. Montezuma, IA:
      Sutherland Publishing, 1985.

378. Mikkelsen, Michael A. THE BISHOP HILL COLONY: A RELIGIOUS
      COMMUNISTIC SETTLEMENT IN HENRY COUNTY, ILLINOIS.
      Baltimore: The Johns Hopkins Press, 1892. Vol. 10, no. 1.
      JOHNS HOPKINS UNIVERSITY STUDIES IN HISTORICAL AND
      POLITICAL SCIENCE. Reprint. New York; London: Johnson
      Reprint, 1973.

379. Morton, Stratford Lee. "Bishop Hill: An Experiment in Communal
      Living." ANTIQUES. 43 (February 1943): 74-77.

380. Murray, Anna Wadsworth. "Olof Krans." CHICAGO HISTORY. 10
      (Winter 1981-82): 244-247.

381. Nelson, Charles H. "A Socio-Cultural Interpretation of a
      Protestant Religious Movement: The Case of the Erik
      Janssonists of 19th Century Sweden." PhD diss., New
      School of Social Research, 1974.

382. ------. "The Erik Janssonist Movement of Pre-Industrial Sweden."
      SOCIOLOGICAL ANALYSIS. 38 (Fall 1977): 207-225.

383. ------. "Toward a More Accurate Approximation of the Class
      Composition of the Erik Janssonists." THE SWEDISH PIONEER
      HISTORICAL QUARTERLY. 26 (January 1975): 3-15.

384. Nelson, Ronald E. "Bishop Hill: a Colony of Swedish Pietists in
      Illinois." ANTIQUES. 99 (January 1971): 140-147.

385. ------. "The Bishop Hill Colony and Its Pioneer Economy."
      SWEDISH PIONEER HISTORICAL QUARTERLY. 18 (January 1967):
      32-48.

386. ------. "Bishop Hill: Swedish Development of the Western
      Illinois Frontier." WESTERN ILLINOIS REGIONAL STUDIES. 1
      (Summer 1978): 109-120.

387. Nelson, O.N. HISTORY OF THE SCANDINAVIANS AND SUCCESSFUL
      SCANDINAVIANS IN THE UNITED STATES. Minneapolis: O.N.
      Nelson & Co., 1893.

388. Nordquist, Del. "Olof Krans : Folk Painter from Bishop Hill,
      Illinois." AMERICAN SWEDISH HISTORICAL FOUNDATION
      YEARBOOK, 1961. Philadelphia, 1961. pp. 45-58.

389. Norelius, Erik. "The Swedish Background of the Settlement of
      Bishop Hill, Illinois." THE COVENANT QUARTERLY. 11
      (August 1951): 83-90.

390.   ------. DE SVENSKA LUTHERSKA FORSAMLINGARNES OCH SVENSKARNES
       HISTORIA I AMERIKA. Rock Island, IL.: Lutheran Augustana
       Book Concern, 1890.

391.   Norton, John E. "And Utopia Became Bishop Hill." Thesis,
       Augustana College, 1971.

392.   ------. "And Utopia Became Bishop Hill..." HISTORIC PRESERVATION
       25 (October-December 1972): 4-7.

393.   ------, "`For It Flows With Milk & Honey': Two Immigrant Letters
       about Bishop Hill." SWEDISH PIONEER HISTORICAL QUARTERLY.
       24 (July 1973): 163-179.

394.   ------. "Robert Baird, Presbyterian Missionary to Sweden of the
       1840's." SWEDISH PIONEER HISTORICAL QUARTERLY. 23 (July
       1972): 151-167.

395.   ------. "`...We Have Such Great Need of a Teacher': Olof Back,
       Bishop Hill, and the Andover Settlement of Lars Paul
       Esbjorn." THE SWEDISH PIONEER HISTORICAL QUARTERLY. 26
       (October 1975): 215-220.

396.   Ohlsson, Johan. "Om Erik Jansismen och kolonien Bishop Hill."
       HALSINGERUNOR (1964-1965): pp. 81-95.

397.   Olson, Ernst Wilhelm, and Martin J. Engberg. "The Bishop Hill
       Colony." HISTORY OF THE SWEDES OF ILLINOIS. 2 vols.
       Chicago: The Engberg-Holmberg Publishing Co., 1908. pp.
       197-270.

398.   Olson, Ernst Wilhelm. "The Bishop Hill Colony." In Gosta
       Nyblom, AMERICANS OF SWEDISH DESCENT: HOW THEY LIVE AND
       WORK. Rock Island, IL.: G. Nyblom Publishing House, 1948,
       pp. 124-131.

399.   Olsson, Olof. "Letter." Wesley Westerberg, transl. THE
       SWEDISH PIONEER HISTORICAL QUARTERLY. 23 (April 1971):
       60-70.

400.   "Paintings Tell Story of Prairie Communal Town, Bishop Hill."
       LIFE. 16 (January 31, 1944): 10-12.

401.   Pinzke, Nancy Lindberg. FACES OF UTOPIA: A BISHOP HILL FAMILY
       ALBUM. Chicago: n.p., 1982.

402.   Pratt, Harry E. "The Murder of Erik Janson, Leader of Bishop
       Hill Colony." JOURNAL OF THE ILLINOIS STATE HISTORICAL
       SOCIETY. 44 (Spring 1952): 55-69.

403.   Root, John. SEMI-CENTENNIAL CELEBRATION OF THE SETTLEMENT OF
       BISHOP HILL COLONY HELD AT BISHOP HILL, ILLINOIS,
       WEDNESDAY AND THURSDAY SEPT. 23 AND 24, 1896. Galva, IL.,
       1909.

404. Setterdahl, Lilly. "Emigrant Letters by Bishop Hill Colonists
      from Nora Parish." WESTERN ILLINOIS REGIONAL STUDIES. 1
      (Summer 1978): 121-175.

405. Setterdahl, Lilly, and J. Hiram Wilson. "Hotel Accommodations
      in the Bishop Hill Colony." THE SWEDISH PIONEER
      HISTORICAL QUARTERLY. 29 (July 1978): 180-197.

406. Skarstedt, Ernst Teofil. "Bishop Hill kolonien i Illinois."
      SVENSKA-AMERICANSKA FOLKET I HELG OCH SOCKEN. Stockholm:
      Bjorck & Borjesson, 1917.

407. Soderblom, Anna (Forsell). "Ett besok i Bishop Hill." EN
      AMERIKABOK. Stockholm: Svenska kyrkaus diskonistyrelses
      bokforlag, 1925.

408. ------. "Lasare och Amerika farare pa 1840 talet; brev, protokoll
      m.m. om Erik Jansismen." JULBELG FOR SVENSKA BEM.
      Stockholm, 1925, pp. 80-93.

409. Sparks, Esther. "Olof Krans, Prairie Painter." HISTORIC
      PRESERVATION. 25 (October-December 1972): 8-12.

410. Spooner, Harry L. "Bishop Hill: An Early Cradle of Liberty."
      THE AMERICAN-SCANDINAVIAN REVIEW. 47 (March 1959): 31-38.

411. Stephenson, George Malcolm. "Astrology and Theology."
      SWEDISH-AMERICAN HISTORICAL BULLETIN. 2 (August 1929):
      53-69.

412. ------. "Eric-Jansonism and the Bishop Hill Colony." THE
      RELIGIOUS ASPECT OF SWEDISH IMMIGRATION: A STUDY OF
      IMMIGRANT CHURCHES. Minneapolis: The University of
      Minnesota Press, 1932.

413. Stoneberg, Philip J. "The Bishop Hill Colony." In Henry L.
      Kiner, THE HISTORY OF HENRY COUNTY, ILLINOIS. 2 vols.
      Chicago: The Pioneer Publishing Co., 1910.

414. ------. "The Bishop Hill Colony." In THE SWEDISH ELEMENT IN
      ILLINOIS: SURVEY OF THE PAST SEVEN DECADES. Edited by
      Ernest W. Olson. Chicago: Swedish-American Biographical
      Association, 1917.

415. ------. "The Bishop Hill Colony and the Notes of the Western
      Exchange Fire and Marine Insurance Co." NUMISMATIST. 30
      (November 1917): 462-464.

416. ------. "Bishop Hill koloniens industriella lif." VINTER-ROSOR
      1908. Chicago, 1908.

417. Swainson, John. "The Swedish Colony at Bishop Hill, Illinois."
      In O.N. Nelson, HISTORY OF THE SCANDINAVIANS AND
      SUCCESSFUL SCANDINAVIANS IN THE UNITED STATES.
      Minneapolis: O.N. Nelson & Co., 1893, pp. 135-152.

418. Swank, George. PAINTER KRANS OF BISHOP HILL COLONY. Galva,
      IL.: Galvaland Press, 1976.

419. ------. BISHOP HILL, SHOWCASE OF SWEDISH HISTORY; A PICTORIAL
      HISTORY AND GUIDE. Prepared for the Bishop Hill Heritage
      Association, Galva, IL., 1965.

420. Swanson, Alan. "The Music to the Jansonist Song Book: a
      Preliminary Report." SCANDINAVIAN STUDIES. 53 (Spring
      1981): 165-170.

421. ------. "The Texts of the Janssonist Song Book: a Preliminary
      Report." SCANDINAVIAN STUDIES. 54 (Summer 1982): 205-19.

422. Westerberg, Wesley M. "Bethel Ship to Bishop Hill." SWEDISH
      PIONEER HISTORICAL QUARTERLY. 23 (April 1972): 55-59.

423. Widen, Albin. "Bishop Hill: A Coming Centennial." THE
      AMERICAN-SCANDINAVIAN REVIEW. 30 (Autumn 1942): 216-227.

424. Wiken, Erik. "New Light on the Erik Janssonists'
      Emigration, 1845-1854." SWEDISH-AMERICAN HISTORICAL
      QUARTERLY. 35 (Summer 1984): 221-238.

425. Wilson, Carolyn Anderson. "Revitalization, Emigration, and
      Social Organization: An Ethno-historical Study of the
      Bishop Hill Colony, 1846-1861." Honors thesis, Knox
      College, 1973.

426. Wilson, J. Hiram. "Visions of Heaven: Religious Community in a
      Swedish Commune." ANTHROPOLOGICAL LINGUISTICS. 23
      (September 1981): 245-261.

427. Wright, Rochelle. "Stuart Engstrand and Bishop Hill." THE
      SWEDISH PIONEER HISTORICAL QUARTERLY. 28 (July 1977):
      192-204.

BROOK FARM (1841-1847)

Founded by George Ripley at West Roxbury, Massachusetts with a nucleus of transcendentalist literary figures, it became associated with Fourierism two years later.

ARCHIVAL MATERIALS

428. Brook Farm. Records, Massachusetts Historical Society. Boston.

429. Dwight, John Sullivan. Papers, 1832-1892. Boston Public Library. Boston.

430. Orvis, Marianne (Dwight). Letters. Massachusetts Historical Society. Boston.

BIBLIOGRAPHY

431. Myerson, Joel. BROOK FARM, AN ANNOTATED BIBLIOGRAPHY AND RESOURCE GUIDE. New York: Garland Publishing, 1978.

ARTICLES AND BOOKS

432. Baym, Nina. "The Blithedale Romance: A Radical Reading." JOURNAL OF ENGLISH AND GERMANIC PHILOLOGY. 67 (October 1968): 545-569.

433. Bestor, Arthur Eugene. BROOK FARM, 1841-1847: AN EXHIBITION TO COMMEMORATE THE CENTENARY OF ITS FOUNDING. Compiled from the exhibition notes written by Arthur Eugene Bestor, Jr. New York: n.p., 1941. (Columbia University. Libraries. Exhibition notes, no. 1).

434. Blanchard, Paula. MARGARET FULLER. New York: Delacorte Press, 1978.

435. Bradford, George P. "Reminiscences of Brook Farm, by a Member of the Community." CENTURY MAGAZINE. 45 (1892): 141-148.

436. Brooks, Van Wyck. "Retreat From Utopia, What Happened to the Brook Farm Colonists After Their Communistic Experiment Collapsed." THE SATURDAY REVIEW OF LITERATURE. 17 (February 22, 1936): 3-4, 14, 16, 18.

437. Brownson, Henry Francis. ORESTES A. BROWNSON'S EARLY LIFE FROM 1803-1844. Detroit: H.F. Brownson, 1898.

438. Brownson, Orestes Aronson. "Brook Farm." UNITED STATES MAGA-ZINE AND DEMOCRATIC REVIEW. 11 (November 1842): 481-496.

439.   Burton, Katherine (Kurz). PARADISE PLANTERS, THE STORY OF BROOK
        FARM. London; New York: Longmans, Green & Co., 1939.
        Reprint. New York: AMS Press, 1972.

440.   Burton, Warren. THE DISTRICT SCHOOL AS IT WAS, BY ONE WHO WENT
        TO IT. Boston: Phillips, Sampson & Co., 1850.

441.   ------. HELPS TO EDUCATION IN THE HOMES OF OUR COUNTRY. Boston:
        Crosby and Nichols, 1863.

442.   ------. MY RELIGIOUS EXPERIENCE AT MY NATIVE HOME. Boston: Gray
        & Bowen, 1832.

443.   Carter, Robert. "The Newness." CENTURY MAGAZINE. 39 (November
        1889): 124-131.

444.   Cary, Edward. GEORGE WILLIAM CURTIS. Boston: Houghton Mifflin,
        1896.

445.   Channing, William Henry. "Ernest the Seeker." DIAL. 1 (July,
        October 1840): 48-58, 233-242.

446.   ------. A STATEMENT OF THE PRINCIPLES OF THE CHRISTIAN UNION.
        New York: Hunt's Merchants' Magazine, 1843.

447.   Codman, John Thomas. "The Brook Farm Association." COMING AGE.
        2 (1899): 33-38.

448.   ------. BROOK FARM, HISTORIC AND PERSONAL MEMOIRS. Boston: Arena
        Publishing Co., 1894. Reprint. New York: AMS Press,1971.

449.   Commager, Henry Steele, editor. "The Constitution of the Brook
        Farm Association." In DOCUMENTS OF AMERICAN HISTORY.
        8th ed. New York: Appleton, 1968. Doc. no. 162.

450.   Conway, Moncure D. "Concerning Hawthorne and Brook Farm."
        EVERY SATURDAY. 7 (January 2, 1869): 13-18.

451.   Cooke, George Willis. "Brook Farm." NEW ENGLAND MAGAZINE. New
        series. 17 (December 1897): 391-407.

452.   ------. "`The Dial': an Historical and Biographical Introduction,
        with a List of the Contributers." THE JOURNAL OF
        SPECULATIVE PHILOSOPHY. 19 (July 1885): 225-265; 322-323.

453.   ------. EARLY LETTERS OF GEORGE WILLIAM CURTIS TO JOHN S. DWIGHT,
        BROOK FARM AND CONCORD. New York; London: Harper & Bros.,
        1898.

454.   ------. JOHN SULLIVAN DWIGHT, BROOK-FARMER EDITOR, AND CRITIC OF
        MUSIC: A BIOGRAPHY. Boston: Small Maynard & Co., 1898.
        Reprint. Hartford, CT.: Transcendental Books, 1973.

455.   Crowe, Charles Robert. "Fourierism and the Founding of Brook
        Farm." BOSTON PUBLIC LIBRARY QUARTERLY. 12 (April 1960):
        79-88.

456.   ------. GEORGE RIPLEY; TRANSCENDENTALIST AND UTOPIAN SOCIALIST.
        Athens, GA.: University of Georgia Press, 1967.

457.   ------. "This Unnatural Union of Phalansteries and
        Transcendentalists." JOURNAL OF THE HISTORY OF IDEAS.   20
        (October-December 1959): 495-502.

458.   ------. "Transcendentalist Support of Brook Farm, A Paradox?"
        THE HISTORIAN. 21 (May 1959): 281-295.

459.   Curtis, Edith Roelker. "A Season in Utopia." AMERICAN
        HERITAGE. 10 (April 1958): 58-63, 98-100.

460.   ------. A SEASON IN UTOPIA; THE STORY OF BROOK FARM. New York:
        Nelson, 1961. Reprint. New York: Russell & Russell, 1971.

461.   Curtis, George William, ed. EARLY LETTERS TO JOHN S. DWIGHT,
        BROOK FARM AND CONCORD. New York; London: Harper, 1898.
        Reprint. New York: AMS Press, 1975.

462.   ------. "Hawthorne and Brook Farm." FROM THE EASY CHAIR. vol.
        3. New York: Harper & Brothers, 1891-1894.

463.   Dana, Charles. A LECTURE ON ASSOCIATION IN ITS CONNECTION WITH
        RELIGION, MARCH 7, 1844. Boston: B.H. Greene, 1844.

464.   Delano, Sterling F. THE HARBINGER AND NEW ENGLAND
        TRANSCENDENTALISM; A PORTRAIT OF ASSOCIATIONISM IN
        AMERICA. Rutherford, NJ: Fairleigh Dickinson University
        Press, 1983.

465.   THE DIAL; A MAGAZINE FOR LITERATURE, PHILOSOPHY, AND RELIGION.
        Vol. 1-4. Boston, July 1840-April 1844.

466.   Dowden, Edward. "The Transcendentalist Movement and
        Literature." CONTEMPORARY REVIEW. 30 (July 1877):
        297-318.

467.   Duffy, John J. "Transcendental Letters from George Ripley to
        James March." EMERSON SOCIETY QUARTERLY. 50 (1st
        quarter, 1968): Supplement 20-24.

468.   Dwight, John S. A LECTURE ON ASSOCIATION IN ITS
        CONNECTION WITH EDUCATION. Boston: B.H. Greene, 1844.

469.   Elliott, Walter. THE LIFE OF FATHER HECKER. New York: Columbia
        University Press, 1891. 2nd ed. New York: Columbia
        University Press, 1894, 1898, pp. 61-193.

470.   Emerson, Ralph Waldo. "Fourierism and the Socialists." DIAL. 3
        (1842): 86-89.

471. Flanagan, John T. "Emerson and Communism." NEW ENGLAND
      QUARTERLY. 10 (June 1937): 243-261.

472. Francis, Richard. "The Ideology of Brook Farm." STUDIES IN THE
      AMERICAN RENAISSANCE. Boston: Twayne Publishers,1977, pp.
      1-48.

473. Frothingham, Octavius Brooks. GEORGE RIPLEY. Boston: Houghton,
      Mifflin, 1882. Reprint. New York: AMS Press.

474. ------. TRANSCENDENTALISM IN NEW ENGLAND; A HISTORY. New York:
      G.P. Putnam's Sons, 1876. Reprint. Philadelphia:
      University of Pennsylvania Press, 1972.

475. Fuller, Margaret. MEMOIRS. 2 vols. Boston: Phillips, Sampson,
      and Co., 1852.

476. Gilhooley, Leonard. CONTRADICTION AND DILEMMA: ORESTES BROWNSON
      AND THE AMERICAN IDEA. New York: Fordham University
      Press, 1972.

477. Gohdes, Clarence. "Brook Farm Labor Record." PHILOLOGICAL
      QUARTERLY. 7 (July 1928): 299-302.

478. ------. "Getting Ready for Brook Farm." MODERN LANGUAGE NOTES.
      49 (January 1934): 36-39.

479. ------. PERIODICALS OF AMERICAN TRANSCENDENTALISM. Durham: Duke
      University Press, 1931.

480. ------. "Three Letters by James Kay Dealing with Brook Farm."
      PHILOLOGICAL QUARTERLY. 17 (October 1938): 377-388.

481. Gordon, George Henry. BROOK FARM TO CEDAR MOUNTAIN IN THE WAR
      OF THE GREAT REBELLION. 1861-1862. Boston: J.R. Osgood;
      Houghton, Mifflin, 1883, 1885.

482. Hall, Lawrence Sargent. HAWTHORNE CRITIC OF SOCIETY. New
      Haven: Yale University Press, 1944.

483. Haraszti, Zoltan. "Brook Farm Letters." MORE BOOKS. 12
      (1937): 49-68, 93-114.

484. ------. THE IDYLL OF BROOK FARM; AS REVEALED IN LETTERS IN THE
      BOSTON PUBLIC LIBRARY. Boston: Public Library, 1937.

485. THE HARBINGER, DEVOTED TO SOCIAL AND POLITICAL PROGRESS.
      Vols.1-8. Boston; New York.   June 14, 1845--February 10,
      1849. Reprint. New York: AMS Press, 1971.

486. Hawthorne, Manning. "Hawthorne and Utopian Socialism." THE NEW
      ENGLAND QUARTERLY. 12 (October 1939): 726-730.

487. Hawthorne, Nathaniel. THE BLITHEDALE ROMANCE. Boston: Ticknor,
      Reed, and Fields, 1852.

488.   ------. PASSAGES FROM THE AMERICAN NOTEBOOKS OF NATHANIEL
         HAWTHORNE. Boston: Ticknor and Fields, 1868, pp. 75ff.

489.   Hecker, Isaac Thomas. ISAAC HECKER: THE DIARY: ROMANTIC
         RELIGION IN ANTE-BELLUM AMERICA. Ed. by John Farina. New
         York: Paulist Press, 1988.

490.   ------. "The Transcendental Movement in New England." CATHOLIC
         REVIEW. 23 (1876): 528-537.

491.   Hedge, F.H. CHRISTIAN EXAMINER. 14 (1833): 108-128.

492.   Higginson, Thomas Wentworth. MARGARET FULLER OSSOLI. Boston;
         New York: Houghton, Mifflin & Co., 1884.

493.   Holden, Vincent F. THE EARLY YEARS OF ISAAC THOMAS HECKER
         (1819-1844). Washington, D.C.: Catholic University of
         America Press, 1939.

494.   Hudspeth, Robert N. THE LETTERS OF MARGARET FULLER. Ithaca:
         Cornell University Press, 1984- .

495.   Kirby, Georgianna (Bruce). "Before I Went to Brook Farm." OLD
         AND NEW. 3 (February 1871): 175-185.

496.   ------. "My First Visit to Brook Farm." OVERLAND MONTHLY. 5
         (July 1870): 9-19.

497.   ------. MY FIRST VISIT TO BROOK FARM. San Francisco, 1870.

498.   ------. "Reminiscences of Brook Farm." OLD AND NEW. 3 (April
         1871): 425-438; 4 (September 1871): 347-358; 5 (May
         1872): 517-530.

499.   ------. YEARS OF EXPERIENCE, AN AUTOBIOGRAPHICAL NARRATIVE. New
         York; London: G.P. Putnam's Sons, 1887. Reprint. New
         York: AMS Press 1979.

500.   Knortz, Karl. BROOK FARM UND MARGARET FULLER: VORTRAG GEHALTEN
         IM DEUTSCHEN GESELLIG-WISSENSCHAFTLICHEN VEREIN VON NEW
         YORK AM 11 MARZ 1885. New York: Druck von H. Bartzch,
         1886.

501.   Lane, Charles. "Brook Farm." THE DIAL. 4 (January 1844):
         351-357.

502.   ------. "Social Tendencies." DIAL. 4 (July 1843): 65-86.

503.   ------, and Bronson Alcott. "Bronson Alcott's Works." (1843)
         Unidentified article reprinted in Henry Steele Commager,
         editor, ERA OF REFORM, 1830-1860. Princeton: D. Van
         Nostrand, 1960. First published in DIAL. 3 (April 1843):
         417-454.

504.   Lennon, Florence Becker.   "Three Movements from the Yankee
          Pastoral Symphony."   THOREAU JOURNAL QUARTERLY.   2
          (October 15, 1970):   11-19.

505.   Levy, Leo B.   "The Blithedale Romance, Hawthorne's Voyage
          Through Chaos."   STUDIES IN ROMANTICISM.   8 (August 1968):
          1-15.

506.   McGinley, A.A.   "Brook Farm Today."   CATHOLIC WORLD.   61 (April
          1895): 14-25.

507.   Mathews, James W.   "An Early Brook Farm Letter."   NEW ENGLAND
          QUARTERLY.   53 (June 1980): 226-230.

508.   Metzdorf, Robert F.   "Hawthorne's Suit Against Ripley and Dana."
          AMERICAN LITERATURE.   12 (May 1940): 125-140.

509.   Meyerson, Joel.   "James Burrill Curtis and Brook Farm."   NEW
          ENGLAND QUARTERLY.   51 (September 1978): 396-423.

510.   ------.   "Two Unpublished Reminiscences of Brook Farm [with
          text]."   NEW ENGLAND QUARTERLY. 48 (June 1975): 253-260.

511.   Nelson, Truman John.   THE PASSION BY THE BROOK.   Garden City,
          NY.: Doubleday, 1953. (Fiction)

512.   Orvis, Marianne (Dwight).   LETTERS FROM BROOK FARM, 1844-1847.
          Amy Louise Reed, ed. Poughkeepsie: Vassar College, 1928.
          Reprint. Philadelphia: Porcupine Press, 1972.

513.   Parrington, Vernon Louis.   "Brook Farm."   ENCYCLOPAEDIA OF THE
          SOCIAL SCIENCES.   Edwin R.A. Seligman, Editor-in-Chief.
          New York: Macmillan, 1930. s.v.

514.   Peabody, Elizabeth Palmer.   "A Glimpse of Christ's Idea of
          Society."   DIAL.   2 (October 1841): 222.

515.   ------.   "Plan of the West Roxbury Community."   DIAL.   2 (1842):
          361-372.

516.   Newcomb, C.K.   "Dolton."   DIAL.   3 (July 1842): 112-123.

517.   Ripley, George.   "Brownson's Writings."   DIAL.   1 (July 1840):
          22-46.

518.   ------.   "The Commencement of Association."   THE HARBINGER.   1
          (August 16, 1845): 159-160.

519.   ------.   DISCOURSES OF THE PHILOSOPHY OF RELIGION. Boston: James
          Monroe & Co., 1836.

520.   Russell, Amelia.   "Home Life of the Brook Farm Association."
          ATLANTIC MONTHLY.   42 (October-November, 1878): 458-466;
          556-563.

521. Salisbury, Annie Maria. BROOK FARM. Marborough, MA.: Smith, 1898.

522. Sams, Henry W., ed. AUTOBIOGRAPHY OF BROOK FARM. Englewood Cliffs, NJ: Prentice-Hall, 1952.

523. Saxton, F. Willard. "A Few Reminiscences of Brook Farm." POCUMTUCK VALLEY MEMORIAL ASSOCIATION. HISTORY AND PROCEEDINGS. 6 (1912-1920): 371-386.

524. Schlesinger, Arthur M., Jr. ORESTES A. BROWNSON: A PILGRIM'S PROGRESS. New York: Octagon Books, 1963, c. 1939.

525. Sears, John van der Zee. MY FRIENDS AT BROOK FARM. New York, NY.: Desmond Fitzgerald, 1912. Reprint. New York: AMS Press, 1975.

526. Sedgwick, Ora. "Girl of Sixteen at Brook Farm." ATLANTIC MONTHLY. 85 (March 1900): 394-404.

527. Smart, George K. "A New England Experimentation in Idealism." TRAVEL. 84 (November 1939): 14-16.

528. Sotheran, Charles. HORACE GREELEY AND OTHER PIONEERS OF AMERICAN SOCIALISM. New York: M. Kennerley, 1915.

529. Stoehr, T. "Art vs. Utopia: The Case of Nathaniel Hawthorne and Brook Farm." ANTIOCH REVIEW. 36 (Winter 1978): 89-102.

530. Sumner, Arthur. "A Boy's Recollections of Brook Farm." NEW ENGLAND MAGAZINE. 16 (March-August 1894): 309-313.

531. Swift, Lindsay. BROOK FARM; ITS MEMBERS, SCHOLARS, AND VISITORS. New York: Macmillan, 1900. Reprint. Secaucus, NJ.: The Citadel Press, 1961.

532. Tarbell, Arthur Wilson. "The Brook Farm Experiment." NATIONAL MAGAZINE. 7 (June 1897): 197-203.

533. Wennersten, John R. "Park Godwin Utopian Socialism, and the Politics of Antislavery." NEW YORK HISTORICAL SOCIETY QUARTERLY. 60 (July/October 1976): 107-127.

534. Wilson, James Harrison. LIFE OF CHARLES A. DANA. New York: Harper & Bros., 1907.

COAL CREEK COMMUNITY (1825-1832)

Located in Stonebluff, Fountain County, Indiana, under the leadership of William Ludlow. Originated in Warren County, Ohio.

535.   Whicker, John Wesley. HISTORICAL SKETCHES OF THE WABASH VALLEY.
       Attica, IN.: The Author, 1916, pp.116-125.

COMMUNIA (1847-1856)

A community founded in Clayton County, Iowa, by German
socialists. Later merged with Wilhelm Weitling's group to form
Communia Working Men's League.

536. Armstrong, Gary W. "Utopians in Clayton County, Iowa." ANNALS
      OF IOWA. 41 (Spring 1972): 923-938.

537. Barnikol, Ernst. WEITLING DER GEFANGENE UND SEINE
      "GERECHTIGKEIT": EINE KRITSCHE UNTERSUCHUNG UBER WERK UND
      WESEN DES FRUHSOZIALISTICHEN MESSIAS. Kiel: W.G. Muhlau,
      1929.

538. ------, ed. GESCHICHTE DES RELIGIOSEN UND ATHEISTISCHEN
      FRUHSOZIALISMUS NACH DER DARSTELLUNG AUGUST BECKERS VOM
      JAHRE 1847. Kiel: W.G. Muhlau, 1932.

539. Eiboeck, Joseph. DIE DEUTSCHEN VON IOWA UND DEREN
      ERRUNGENSCHAFTEN. EINE GESCHICHTE DES STAATES, DESSEN
      DEUTSCHER PIONIERE UND IHRER NACHKOMMEN. Des Moines:
      Druck und verlag des Iowa Staats-Anzeiger, 1900, pp.
      96-101.

540. Grant, H. Roger. "Utopia at Communia." THE PALIMPSEST. 61
      (January/February 1980): 12-17.

541. Mielcke, Karl. DEUTSCHE FRUHSOZIALISMUS. GESELLSCHAFT UND
      GESCHICHTE IN DEN SCHRIFTEN VON WEITLING UND HESS.
      Stuttgart: Druck der Union Deutsche Verlags Gesellschaft,
      1931.

542. Muhlestein, Hans. "Marx and the Utopian Wilhelm Weitling." In
      A CENTENARY OF MARXISM. Samuel Bernstein, ed. New York:
      Science and Society, 1948.

543. REPUBLIK DER ARBEITER. New York. April 18, 1851-December 16,
      1854. W. Weitling, editor. Microfilm. Madison: State
      Historical Society of Wisconsin.

544. Schulz-Behrend, George. "Andreas Dietsch and New Helvetia,
      Missouri." In Vol. 2 of the SWISS RECORD, YEARBOOK OF THE
      SWISS AMERICAN HISTORICAL SOCIETY. Madison: The Society,
      1950.

545. ------. "Communia, Iowa, A Nineteenth-Century German-American
      Utopia." IOWA JOURNAL OF HISTORY. 48 (January 1950):
      27-54.

546.   Shanahan, William O. GERMAN PROTESTANTS FACE THE SOCIAL
        QUESTION. Volume 1. Notre Dame: University of Notre Dame
        Press, 1954. pp. 168-177.

547.   Weitling, Wilhelm Christian. DIE BIBLIOTHEK DER ARBEITER.
        ENTHALTEND WILHELM WEITLINGS SAEMMTLICHE WERKE, NEBST
        EINER AUSWAHL DER BEKANNTESTEN UND WIRKSAMSTEN ALLER IN
        DIESEM GEISTE ERSCHIENENEN SCHRIFTEN. New York: Druckerei
        des "Arbeiterbundes," 1854.

548.   ------. DAS EVANGELIUM EINES ARMEN SUNDERS. Bern: Jenni, sohn,
        1845, 1897.

549.   ------. GARANTIEN DER HARMONIE UND FREIHEIT. Hamburg: Verlag des
        Verfassers, 1849. Reprint. Berlin: Akademie-Verlag,
        1955.

550.   ------. DER KATECHISMUS DER ARBEITER. New York: Druckerei der
        Republik der Arbeiter, 1854.

551.   ------. KLASSIFIKATION DES UNIVERSUMS; EINE FRUHSOZIALISTISCHE
        WELTANSCHAUUNG. Keil: W.G. Muhlau, 1931.

552.   ------. DIE MENSCHHEIT, WIE SIE IST UND WIE SIE SEIN SOLLTE.
        Bern: Jenni, sohn, 1845.

553.   ------. DES SELIGEN SCHNEIDER'S WEITLING LEHRE VOM SOCIALISMUS
        UND COMMUNISMUS. New York: Deutsche verlagsanstalt, 1879.

554.   Wittke, Carl. THE UTOPIAN COMMUNIST: A BIOGRAPHY OF WILHELM
        WEITLING, NINETEENTH-CENTURY REFORMER. Baton Rouge:
        Louisiana State University Press, 1950.

COMMUNITY OF UNITED CHRISTIANS (1836-1837)

This community of abolitionists and temperance supporters developed in Berea, Ohio.

ARCHIVAL MATERIALS

555.   Baldwin, John.   "Manuscript History."   Unpublished manuscript now in Western Reserve Historical Society, Cleveland, Ohio.

ARTICLES AND BOOKS

556.   CONSTITUTION OF THE COMMUNITY OF UNITED CHRISTIANS. Berea, 1837.

557.   Gilruth, Robert A.   "The Community of United Christians at Berea, Ohio, in 1836."   Bachelor's thesis, Princeton University, 1946.

558.   Lindsey, David.   "A `Backwoods Utopia': The Berea Community of 1836-1837."   THE OHIO HISTORICAL QUARTERLY.   65 (July 1956): 272-296.

559.   Shaw, Willard H., comp.   HISTORICAL FACTS CONCERNING BEREA AND MIDDLEBURGH TOWNSHIP.   Berea, Ohio: Mohler Printing Co., 1938.

560.   Webber, Amos Richard.   LIFE OF JOHN BALDWIN, SR. OF BEREA, OHIO. Cincinnati: Printed by the Caxton Press, 1925.

CONCORDIA (1825-1831)

Founded by a German Lutheran, Henry Kurtz, as the "German Christian Industrial Community," later named Concordia. While organized in Western Pennsylvania, the colony actually located in Stark County, Ohio. Another colony, named Teutonia in Columbiana County (later Mahoning County), Ohio, 1827, was under the leadership of Peter Kaufman.

561. Durnbaugh, Donald F. "Henry Kurtz: Man of the Book." OHIO HISTORY. 76 (Summer 1967): 115-131. Reprint. BRETHREN LIFE AND THOUGHT. 16 (Spring 1971): 103-121.

562. DER FRIEDENSBOTE VON CONCORDIA (The Peace Messenger of Concordia), 1827.

563. Oda, W.H. "Reverend Henry Kurtz and His Communal Plans." THE PENNSYLVANIA DUTCHMAN. 3 (April 1, 1952): 1, 5-6.

DORRILITES (1798-1799)

Formed by an Englishman, Joseph Dorril in Leydon, Franklin County, Massachusetts, and Guilford, Windham County, Vermont.

564. Ludlum, David M. SOCIAL FERMENT IN VERMONT, 1791-1850 Columbia Studies in American Culture, vol.5. New York: Columbia University Press,1939. pp.239-240, 242-244.

565. Tyler, Edward. "Saints and Sensation Seekers." RURAL VERMONTER. 1 (Summer 1963): 8-12.

EPHRATA COLONY (1732-1770)

Founded by Johann Conrad Beissel, a German mystic, it was also known as the Solitary Brethren of the Community of the Seventh Day Baptists. The community located in Antietam County, Pennsylvania.

ARCHIVAL MATERIALS

566. Ephrata Community. Notes Written in 1749 by the Sisters of the Sisterhood in the Sisterhouse of the Seven Day Baptists at Ephrata in Lancaster County, Pennsylvania. Library of Congress, Manuscript Division, Washington, D.C.

567. Ephrata Community. Records, 1786-1894. Free Library of Philadelphia.

BIBLIOGRAPHIES

568. Doll, Eugene Edgar, and Anneliese Marckwald Funke, eds. THE EPHRATA CLOISTERS: AN ANNOTATED BIBLIOGRAPHY. Bibliographies on German American History, no. 3. Philadelphia: Carl Schurz Memorial Foundation, 1944.

569. Meynen, Emil. BIBLIOGRAPHIE DES DEUTSCHTUMS DER KOLONIALZEITLICHEN EINWANDERUNG IN NORDAMERIKA, INSBESONDERE DER PENNSYLVANIEN DEUTSCHEN UND IHRER NACHKOMMEN, 1683-1933. Leipzig: O. Harrassowitz, 1937.

ARTICLES AND BOOKS

570. Acrelius, Israel. A HISTORY OF NEW SWEDEN; OR THE SETTLEMENTS ON THE RIVER DELAWARE. Tran. William M. Reynolds. Philadelphia: The Historical Society of Pennsylvania, 1874. pp. 373-401.

571. Alderfer, E. Gordon. "Conrad Beissel and the Ephrata Experiment." AMERICAN-GERMAN REVIEW. 21 (August-September 1955): 23-25.

572. ------. THE EPHRATA COMMUNE: AN EARLY AMERICAN COUNTERCULTURE. Pittsburgh: University of Pittsburgh Press, 1985.

573. Aurand, Ammon Monroe, Jr. HISTORICAL ACCOUNT OF THE EPHRATA CLOISTER AND THE SEVENTH DAY BAPTIST SOCIETY. Harrisburg, PA.: Private Print, The Aurand Press, 1940.

574. Beissel, Johann Conrad. DELICIAE EPHRATENSES...ODER DES EHRWURDIGEN VATTERS FRIEDSAM GOTTRECHT, WEYLAND STIFFTERS

UND FUHRERS DES CHRISTLICHEN ORDENS DER EINSAMEN IN
EPHRATA IN PENNSYLVANIA, GEISTLICHEN REDEN... 2 vols. in
one. Ephrata: Typis Societatis, 1773.

575.   ------. A DISSERTATION ON MAN'S FALL. Trans. Prior Jaches [i.e.
Johann Peter Miller]. Ephrata, 1765.

576.   ------. DAS GESANG DER EINSAMEN UND VERLASSENEN TURTEL--TAUBE,
NEMLICHE DER CHRISTLICHEN KIRCHE. ODER GEISTLICHE UND
ERFAHRUNGS-VOLLE LEIDENS UND LIEBES-GETHONE, ALS DARINNEN
BEYDES DIE VORKOST DER NEUEN WELT ALS AUCH DIE DARZWISCHEN
VORKOMMENDE CREUTZES-UND LEIDENS-WEGE NACH IHRER WURDE
DARGESTELLT, UND IN GEISTLICHE REIMEN GEBRACHT VON EINEM
FRIEDSAMEN UND NACH DER STILLEN EWIGKERT WALLENDEN PILGER.
UND NUN ZUM GEBRAUCH DER EINSAMEN UND VERLASSENEN ZU ZION
GESAMMLET UND ANS LICHT GEGEBEN. Ephrata: Drucks der
Bruderschaft, 1747 [i.e. 1749].

577.   ------. JACOBS KAMPFF- UND RITTER-PLATZ ALLWO DER NACH SEINEM
URSPRUNG SICH SCHNENDE GEIST DER IN SOPHIAM VERLIEBTEN
SEELE MIT GOTT UM DEN NEUEN NAMEN GERUNGEN, UND DEN SIEG
DAVON GETRAGEN. ENTWORFFEN IN UNTERSCHIDLICHEN
GLAUBENS-UND LEIDENS-LEIDERN U. EHRFAHRUNGS VOLLEN
AUSTRUCKUNGEN DES GEMUTHS DARINNEN SICH DARSTELLT, SO WOL
AUFF SEITEN GOTTES SEINE UNERMUEDETE ARBEIT ZUR REINIGUNG
SOLCHER SEELEN DIE SICH SEINER FUERUNG ANVERTRAUT. ALS
SUCH AUFF SEITEN DES MENSCHEN DER ERNST DES GEISTES IM AUS
HALTEN UNTER DEM PROCESS DER LAUTERUNG UND ABSCHMELTZUNG
DES MENSCHEN DER SUNDERS SAMT DEM DARAUS ENTSPRINGENDEN
LOBES-GETHON. ZUR GEMUTHLICHEN ERWECKUNG DERER, DIE DAS
HEIL JERUSALEMS LIEB HABEN. VERLOGET VON EINEM LIEBHABER
DER WAHRHEIT, DIE IM VERBORGENEN WOHNT. Philadelphia: B.
Franklin, 1736.

578.   ------. MYSTERION ANOMIAS, THE MYSTERY OF LAWLESNESS: OR LAWLESS
ANTICHRIST DISCOVERED AND DISCLOSED SHEWING ALL THOSE DO
BELONG TO THAT LAWLESS ANTICHRIST, WHO WILFULLY REJECT THE
COMMANDMENTS OF GOD, AMONGST WHICH, IS HIS HOLY, AND BY
HIMSELF BLESSED SEVENTH DAY SABBATH OR HIS HOLY REST, OF
WHICH THE SAME IS A TYPE. WRITTEN TO THE HONOUR OF THE
GREAT GOD AND HIS HOLY COMMANDS. BY CUNRAD BEYSELL.
Translated out of the High-Dutch, by H.W. Philadelphia,
printed by Andrew Bradford, 1729.

579.   ------. MYSTICHE ABHANDLUNG UBER DIE SCHOPFUNG UND VON DES
MENSCHEN FALL UND WIEDERBRINUNG DURCH WEIBES SAAMEN.
Ephrata: Druckt der Bruderschaft, 1745.

580.   ------. MYSTISCHE UND SEHR GEHEYME SPRUECHE, WELCHE IN DER
HIMLISCHEN SCHULE DES HEILIGEN GEISTES ERLERNET. UND DAN
FOLGENS, EINIGE POETISCHE GEDICHTE. AUFGESETZT. DEN
LIEBHABERN UND SCHULERN DER GOTTLICHEN UND HIMMLISCHEN
WEISZHEIT ZUM DIENST. VOR DIE SAU DIESER WELT ABER, HABEN
WIR KEINE SPEISE, WERDEN IHNEN AUCH WOHL EIN

VERSCHLOSSENER GARDEN, UND VERSIEGELTER BRUNNE BLEIBEN.
Philadelphia: B. Franklin, 1730. Reprint. 1896.

581.   ------. PARADISCHES WUNDER-SPIEL WELCHES SICH IN DIESEN LETZTEN
ZEITEN UND TAGEN IN DENEN ABENDLANDISCHEN WELT THEILEN ALS
EIN VORSPIEL DER NEUEN SELT HERVORGETHAN BESTEHEND IN
EINER NEUEN SAMMLUNG ANDACHTICHER UND ZUM LOB DES GROSEN
GOTTES EINGERICHTETER GEISTLICHER/UND EHEDESSEN ZUM THEIL
PUBLICIRTER LIEDER. Ephrata: Typis & Consenser
Societatis, 1754, 1766.

582.   ------. A UNIQUE MANUSCRIPT BY REV. PETER MILLER (BROTHER JABEZ)
PRIOR OF THE EPHRATA COMMUNITY IN LANCASTER COUNTY,
PENNSYLVANIA; WRITTEN FOR BENJAMIN FRANKLIN; TOGETHER WITH
A FACSIMILE AND TRANSLATION OF BEISSEL'S 99 MYSTICAL
PROVERBS, ORIGINALLY PRINTED BY BENJAMIN FRANKLIN IN 1730.
Compiled at the request of the executive committee of the
Pennsylvania-German Society by Julius F. Sachse.
Lancaster, PA.: The Society, 1912.

583.   ------. UNTER DEM PROCESS DER LAEUTERUNG UND ABSCHNELTZUNG DES
MENSCHEN DER SUNDEN SAMT DEM DARAUS ENTSPRINGENDEN
LOBESGETHON, ZUR GEMUTLICHEN ER WECKUNG DERER DIE DAS HEIL
JERUSALEMS LIEB HABEN. VERLEGET VON EINEM LIEBHABER DER
WAHRHEIT DIE IM VERBORGENEN WOHNT. Philadelphia: B.
Franklin, 1736.

584.   ------. VORSPIEL DER NEUEN-WELT ... Philadelphia, 1732.

585.   ------. ZIONITSCHE ROSEN GARTEN. Ephrata, 1754.

586.   ------. ZIONITSCHEN STIFFTS I.-II. THEIL. ODER EINE WOLRICHENDE
NARDE, DIE...HAT UNTER DEN KINDERN DER WEISSHEIT EINEN
BALSAMISCHEN GERUCH VON SICH GEGEBEN. DES...THEOLOGI DEN
MYSTISCHEN GOTTES-GELARTHEIT. IRENICI THEODICAI...
BESTEHEND IN EINER SAMMLUNG GEISTLICHER GEMUTS-BEWEGUNGEN
UND ERFAHRUNGS-VOLLER THEOSOPHISCHER SENDSCHREIBEN...
Ephrata: Drucks und Verlags der Bruderschaft, 1745.

587.   Benz, Ernst. "Litterature du Desert chez les Evangeliques
allemands et les Pietistes de Pennsylvanie." IRENIKON. 51
(1978): 338-357.

588.   Blakely, Lloyd G. "Johann Conrad Beissel and the Music of the
Ephrata Cloister." JOURNAL OF RESEARCH IN MUSIC
EDUCATION. 15 (Summer 1967): 120-138.

589.   Borneman, Henry Stauffer. PENNSYLVANIA GERMAN ILLUMINATED
MANUSCRIPTS; A CLASSIFICATION OF FRAKTUR-SCHRIFTEN AND AN
INQUIRY INTO THEIR HISTORY. Proceedings of the
Pennsylvania German Society, vol. 46. Norristown, PA.:
Pennsylvania German Society, 1937.

590.   Bracht, Tieleman Jansvan. DER BLUTIGE SCHAU-PLATZ, ODER
        MARTYRED SPIEGEL DER TAUFFS GESINTEN ODER
        WEHRLOSEN-CHRISTEN, DIE UM DES ZEUGNUSS JESU IHRES
        SELIGMACHERS WILLEN GELITTEN HABEN, UND SEYND GETODTET
        WORDEN, VON CHRISTI ZEIT AN BIS AUF DAS JAHR 1660.
        VORMALS AUS UNTERSCHIEDLICHEN GLAUBWURDIGEN CHRONICKEN,
        NACHRICHTEN UND ZEUGNUSSEN GESAMLET UND IN HOLLAND ISCHER
        SPRACH HERAUS GEGEBEN VON T.J.V. BRAGHT. NUN ABER
        SORGFALTIGST INS HOCHTEUTSCHE UBERSETZT UND ZUM ERSTENMAL
        ANS LICHTGEBRACHT. Ephrata: Drucks und verlags der Bruder
        Schafft, 1758-1759.

591.   Briner, Andres. "Conrad Beissel and Thomas Mann."
        AMERICAN-GERMAN REVIEW. 26 (December 1959-January 1960):
        24-25, 32.

592.   Brumbaugh, Martin Grove. AN OUTLINE FOR HISTORICAL ROMANCE.
        Proceedings of Pennsylvania German Society, vol. 46.
        Norristown, PA.: Pennsylvania German Society, 1937.

593.   Carlson, Charles Howard. "The Ephrata Cloister's Music of
        Yesteryear." MUSIC JOURNAL. 22 (January 1964): 52+.

594.   Church of the Brethren. HISTORY OF THE CHURCH OF THE BRETHREN
        OF THE EASTERN DISTRICT OF PENNSYLVANIA. Lancaster, PA.:
        The New Era Printing Co., 1915. pp.32-43.

595.   Coleman, John M., John B. Frantz and Robert G. Crist.
        PENNSYLVANIA RELIGIOUS LEADERS. University Park:
        Pennsylvania Historical Association, 1986.

596.   Conynghan, Redmond. AN ACCOUNT OF THE SETTLEMENT OF THE DUNKERS
        AT EPHRATA, IN LANCASTER COUNTY, PENNSYLVANIA, TO WHICH IS
        ADDED A SHORT HISTORY OF THAT RELIGIOUS SOCIETY. By the
        late Rev. Christian Endress of Lancaster. Philadelphia,
        1827.

597.   Croll, Philip Columbus. "The Oley Conference." LUTHERAN
        QUARTERLY. 56 (January 1926): 84-108.

598.   David, Hans Theodore. "Hymns and Music of the Pennsylvania
        Seventh-Day Baptists." AMERICAN-GERMAN REVIEW. 9 (June
        1943): 4-6, 36.

599.   ------. "Musical Composition at Ephrata." AMERICAN-GERMAN
        REVIEW. 10 (June 1944), 4-5.

600.   Diffenderffer, Frank Ried. "The Ephrata Community 120 Years Ago
        as Described by an Englishman." Lancaster County
        Historical Society. HISTORICAL PAPERS AND ADDRESSES. 9
        (January 1905): 127-146.

601.   ------. "Ephrata Community 125 Years Ago." Lancaster County
       Historical Society. HISTORICAL PAPERS AND ADDRESSES. 3
       (September 1898): 3-13.

602.   Doll, Eugene Edgar. THE EPHRATA CLOISTER; AN INTRODUCTION.
       Ephrata, PA.: Ephrata Cloister Associates, 1958.

603.   ------. "Historical Guide to the Seventh Day German Baptist
       Cloister at Ephrata, Pennsylvania." PENNSYLVANIA
       INSTRUCTION. 9 (January 1942): 22-26.

604.   ------. "Rebirth at Ephrata." Reading TIMES. (November 16 & 18,
       1942).

605.   ------. "Social and Economic Organization in Two Pennsylvania
       German Religious Communities." THE AMERICAN JOURNAL OF
       SOCIOLOGY. 57 (September 1951): 168-177.

606.   Dorfman, Mark H. "The Ephrata Cloister." EARLY AMERICAN LIFE.
       10 (January, 1979): 38-41; 64-65.

607.   Duche, Jacob. OBSERVATIONS ON A VARIETY OF SUBJECTS; LITERARY,
       MORAL AND RELIGIOUS; IN A SERIES OF ORIGINAL LETTERS,
       WRITTEN BY A GENTLEMAN OF FOREIGN EXTRACTION, WHO RESIDED
       SOMETIME IN PHILADELPHIA. Revised by a friend, to whose
       hands the manuscript was committed for publication.
       Philadelphia: John Dunlap, 1772.

608.   Durnbaugh, Donald F., ed. THE BRETHREN IN COLONIAL AMERICA.
       Elgin, IL.: Brethren Press, 1967.

609.   Ellis, Franklin, and Samuel Evans. HISTORY OF LANCASTER COUNTY,
       PENNSYLVANIA, WITH BIOGRAPHICAL SKETCHES OF MANY OF ITS
       PIONEERS AND PROMINENT MEN. Philadelphia: Everts & Peck,
       1883. pp. 836-843.

610.   "Ephrata and the Cloister Music." In National Society of the
       Colonial Dames of America. Pennsylvania. CHURCH MUSIC
       AND MUSICAL LIFE IN PENNSYLVANIA IN THE EIGHTEENTH
       CENTURY. 3 vols. Philadelphia: The Society, 1926-1927.
       II, pp. 26-84.

611.   Ephrata Community. EIN ANGENEHMER GERUCH DER ROSEN UND LILIEN
       DIE IM THAI DER DEMUTH UNTER DEN DORNEN HERVOR GEWACHSEN.
       Ephrata, 1756.

612.   ------. DIE BITTRE GUTE, ODER DAS GESAENG DER EIN SAMER
       TURTEL-TAUBE, DER CHRISTLICHEN KIRCHE HIER AUF ORDEN, DIE
       AN NOCH IM TRAUERTHAL AUF DEN DUERREN AESTEN UND ZWEIGEN
       DEN STAND IHRER WITTENSCHAFFT BEKLAGET, UND DABEY IN
       HOFFNUNG SINGEL VON EINER ANDERN UND NOCH MALIGEN
       VERMAELUNG. Ephrata: The Society, 1766.

613.   ------. CHORAL BOOK OF THE EPHRATA CLOISTER. A NEATLY EXECUTED
        MANUSCRIPT VOLUME OF THE MUSIC TO WHICH THE HYMNS WERE
        SUNG, WITH PRINTED INDEX. Ephrata, ca. 1745.

614.   ------. ERNSTHAFTE CHRISTEN-PFLICT, DARINNEN SCHONE GEISTREICHE
        GEBETTER, DARMIT SICH FROMME CHRISTEN-HERTZEN ZU ALLEN
        ZEITEN UND IN ALLEN NOHTEN TRUSTEN KONNEN NEBST EINEN
        ANHANG EINER AUS DEM BLUTIGEN SCHAU-SPIEL UBERSETZTER
        GESCHICHTE ZWEYER BLUTZEUGEN DER WARHEIT. Han von Oberdam
        u. Valerius des Schulmeisters. Ephrata, 1745.

615.   ------. ERSTER THEIL DER THEOSOPHISCHEN LECTIONEN, BETREFFENDE
        DIE SCHULEN DES EINSAMEN LEBENS. Ephrata, 1752.

616.   ------. DAS LIED DER LIEDEREN, WELCHES IST SALOMONS. Ephrata,
        1750?

617.   ------. MUSIC BOOK OF THE EPHRATA CLOISTER, IN NEAT MANUSCRIPT
        WITH COLORED ORNAMENTATION, written by one of the Sisters;
        and with Printed Register. Ephrata, 1772?

618.   Erb, Peter C., ed. JOHANN CONRAD BEISSEL AND THE EPHRATA
        COMMUNITY: MYSTICAL AND HISTORICAL TEXTS. Lewiston, NY.:
        Edwin Mellen Press, 1985.

619.   Ernst, James Emanuel. EPHRATA: A HISTORY. Posthumously edited
        with an introduction by John Joseph Stoudt. Pennsylvania
        German Folklore Society Yearbook, vol. 25 (1961).
        Allentown, PA.: Pennsylvania German Folklore Society,
        1963.

620.   Fahnestock, William H. "An Historical Sketch of Ephrata."
        HAZARD'S REGISTER OF PENNSYLVANIA. 15 (March 14 & 28,
        1835): 161-167, 208. Partially reprinted in I.D. Rupp.
        AN ORIGINAL HISTORY OF THE RELIGIOUS DENOMINATIONS AT
        PRESENT EXISTING IN THE UNITED STATES. 1844.

621.   Franke, Ira. THE EPHRATA STORY [Ephrata, PA]: Hacking
        Printing Co., 1964.

622.   Getz, Russell Paul, ed. EPHRATA CLOISTER CHORALES. New York:
        G. Schirmer, 1971.

623.   ------. "Ephrata Cloister Music." THE NEW GROVE'S DICTIONARY OF
        MUSIC AND MUSICIANS. London: Macmillan, 1980. s.v.

624.   ------. "Music in the Ephrata Cloister." COMMUNAL SOCIETIES. 2
        (Autumn, 1982): 27-38.

625.   Gibbons, Phebe H. (Earle) "PENNSYLVANIA DUTCH," AND OTHER
        ESSAYS. Philadelphia: J.B. Lippincott, 1872, 1882. pp.
        138-172.

626.   Gleim, Elmer Q. "Ephrata Community and the Brethren." BRETHREN
        LIFE AND THOUGHT. 15 (Summer 1970): 159-165.

627.   Hantzsch, Viktor. "Johann Konrad Beissel." ALLGEMEINE DEUTSCHE
        BIOGRAPHIE. Vol. 46. Berlin: Duncker & Humblot, 1971.
        pp. 341-344.

628.   Heinicke, Milton H. HISTORY OF EPHRATA. Arranged for
        publication by Ralph M. Hartrauft. The Historical Society
        of The Cocalico Valley, n.d.

629.   Hildebrand, Johannes. MYSTISCHES UND KIRCHLICHES ZEUCHNUSS DER
        BRUDERSCHAFT IN ZION. Germantown, PA, 1743.

630.   Hocker, E. W. "A Plain People." ERA. 11 (April 1903): 347-366.

631.   Hollyday, Guy T., and Christoph E. Schweitzer. "The Present
        Status of Conrad Beissel/Ephrata Research." MONATSHEFTE.
        68 (Summer 1976): 171-178.

632.   Jacoby, John M. TWO MYSTIC COMMUNITIES IN AMERICA. Paris: Les
        Presses Universitaires de France, 1931. Reprint.
        Westport, CT.: Hyperion Press, 1975.

633.   Jayne, Horace Howard Furness. "Cloisters at Ephrata." AMERICAN
        MAGAZINE OF ART. 29 (September 1936): 594-598.

634.   Kiliam, Oskar. "Konrad Beisel (1691-1768): Founder of the
        Ephrata Cloister in Pennsylvania." BACH 7 AND 8
        (1976-77).

635.   Kissinger, W.S. "Ephrata Cloister: The History and Output of
        Its Press." BRETHREN LIFE AND THOUGHT. 13 (1968):
        162-169.

636.   Klein, Walter Conrad. JOHANN CONRAD BEISSEL, MYSTIC AND
        MARTINET, 1690-1768. Philadelphia: University of
        Pennsylvania Press, 1942. Reprint. Philadelphia:
        Porcupine Press, 1972.

637.   Kraft, John L. FURNITURE OF THE EPHRATA CLOISTER.
        Ephrata, PA.: Journal of the Historical Society of the
        Cocalico Valley, 1978.

638.   Lamech, Brother. CHRONICON EPHRATENSE, ENTHALTEND DEN LEBENS
        TAUF DES EHRWURDIGE VATERS IN CHRISTO FRIEDSAM
        GOTTRECAT...ZUSAMMEN GETRAGEN VON BR. LAMECH [I.E. JACOB
        GASS?] U. AGRIPPA [I.E. JOHANN PETER MILLER ALSO KNOWN AS
        PRIOR JABEZ...] Ephrata, 1786.

639.   ------. CHRONICON EPHRATENSE, A HISTORY OF THE COMMUNITY OF
        SEVENTH DAY BAPTISTS AT EPHRATA, LANCASTER COUNTY, PENN'A,
        BY "LAMECH AND AGRIPPA." Trans. J. Max Hark. Lancaster,

PA.: S.H. Zahm & Co., 1889. Reprint. New York: Burt
Franklin, 1972.

640.   Loher, Franz von. GESCHICHTE UND ZUSTANDE DER DEUTSCHEN IN
       AMERIKA. Cincinnati: Eggers und Wulkop, 1847. pp.55,
       119-124.

641.   McCort, D. "J.C. Beissel, Colonial Mystic Poet."
       GERMAN-AMERICAN STUDIES. 8 (1974): 1-26.

642.   Mann, Thomas. DOCTOR FAUSTUS; THE LIFE OF THE GERMAN COMPOSER,
       ADRIA LEVERKUEHN, AS TOLD BY A FRIEND. Trans. H.T.
       Lowe-Porter. New York: Knopf, 1948.

643.   Martin, Betty Jean. "The Ephrata Cloister and Its Music,
       1732-1785." PhD diss., University of Maryland, 1974.

644.   Pennybacker, Samuel W. HISTORICAL AND BIOGRAPHICAL SKETCHES.
       Philadelphia: R.A. Tripple, 1883. pp. 157-173.

645.   Pyle, Howard. "A Peculiar People." HARPER'S NEW MONTHLY
       MAGAZINE. 79 (October 1889): 776-785. Reprint as A
       PECULIAR PEOPLE: A TALE OF THE EPHRATA CLOISTER. The
       Aurand Press, n.d.

646.   Pugh, Ann Eloise. "The Old Cloister at Ephrata, PA." DAUGHTERS
       OF THE AMERICAN REVOLUTION MAGAZINE. 51 (September 1917):
       146-149.

647.   Randolph, Corliss Fitz. "The German Seventh-Day Baptists," In
       Seventh Day Baptists. General Conference. SEVENTH DAY
       BAPTISTS IN EUROPE AND AMERICA. 2 vols. Plainfield, NJ:
       American Sabbath Tract Society, 1910. II, 933-1257.

648.   Reichmann, Felix, and Eugene Doll. EPHRATA AS SEEN BY
       CONTEMPORARIES. The Pennsylvania German Folklore Society,
       1952, Vol. 17. Allentown, PA.: Schlecter's, 1953.

649.   Richards, Henry, M.M. "The Ephrata Cloister and Its Music."
       PUBLICATIONS OF THE LEBANON COUNTY HISTORICAL SOCIETY. 8
       (1921-24).

650.   Rosenberry, Morris Claude. THE PENNSYLVANIA GERMAN IN MUSIC, In
       Proceedings of the Pennsylvania German Society, Vol. 41.
       Norristown, PA.: Pennsylvania German Society, 1933.

651.   Sachse, Julius Friedrich. THE GERMAN PIETISTS OF PROVINCIAL
       PENNSYLVANIA, 1694-1708. Philadelphia: by the Author,
       1895. Reprint. New York: AMS Press, 1970.

652.   ------. THE GERMAN SECTARIANS OF PENNSYLVANIA, 1708-1800. 2
       vols. Philadelphia, P.C. Stockhausen, 1900. Reprint.
       New York: AMS Press, 1971.

653. ------. THE MUSIC OF THE EPHRATA CLOISTER; ALSO CONRAD BEISSEL'S
     TREATISE ON MUSIC AS SET FORTH IN A PREFACE TO THE "TURTEL
     TAUBE" OF 1747, AMPLIFIED WITH FACSIMILE REPRODUCTIONS OF
     PARTS OF THE TEXT AND SOME ORIGINAL EPHRATA MUSIC OF THE
     WEYRAUCHS HUGEL, 1739; ROSEN UND LILION, 1745; TURTEL
     TAUBE, 1747; CHORAL BUCH, 1754, ETC. Lancaster, PA.:
     Pennsylvania German Society, 1903. Reprint. New York:
     AMS Press, 1971.

654. ------. "A Unique Manuscript by Rev. Peter Miller (Brother
     Jabez), Prior of the Ephrata Community." PROCEEDINGS OF
     PENNSYLVANIA GERMAN SOCIETY. Vol. 21...1910.
     Norristown, PA.: Pennsylvania German Society, 1912. pp.
     69-113.

655. ------. "The Registers of the Ephrata Community." PENNSYLVANIA
     MAGAZINE OF HISTORY AND BIOGRAPHY. 14 (1890): 297-312;
     387-402.

656. Sangmeister, Ezechiel. LEBEN UND WANDEL DES IN GOTTRUHENDEN UND
     SELIGEN BRUDERS EZECHIEL SANGMEISTER, WEILAND EIN
     EINWOHNER VON EPHRATA. 4 vols. Ephrata, PA.: J. Bauman,
     1825-1827.

657. ------. LIFE AND CONDUCT OF THE LATE BROTHER EZECHIEL
     SANGMEISTER. Transl. by Barbara M. Schindler. Ephrata,
     PA: The Historical Society of Cocalico Valley, 1986.

658. Schelbert, Leo. "Die Stimme eines Einsamen in Zion: Ein
     Unbekannter Brief von Bruder Jaebez aus Ephrata,
     Pennsylvanien, aus dem Jahre 1743." ZEITSCHRIFT FUR
     KIRCHENGESCHICHTE. 85 (1974): 77-92.

659. Seidensticker, Oswald W. "A Colonial Monastery." CENTURY
     MAGAZINE. 22 (December 1881): 209-223.

660. ------. EPHRATA, EINE AMERIKANISCHE KLOSTERGESCHICHTE.
     Cincinnati: Druck von Mecklen borg u. Rosenthal, 1883.

661. Seventh Day German Baptists. GOTTLICHE LIEBES UND LOBES
     GETHONE. Philadelphia, 1730.

662. ------. ZIONITISCHER WEYRAUCHS-HUGEL. Germantown, PA.: 1739.

663. Shelley, Donald. THE FRAKTUR WRITINGS OR ILLUMINATED
     MANUSCRIPTS OF THE PENNSYLVANIA GERMANS. Allentown, PA.:
     Pennsylvania German Folklore Society, 1958.

664. Skinner, Charles Montgomery. "Applied Socialism. The Dunkard
     Establishment at Ephrata." Brooklyn EVENING TRANSCRIPT,
     October 27, 1900.

665.   Steirer, William F., Jr. "A New Look at the Ephrata Cloister."
       JOURNAL OF THE LANCASTER COUNTY HISTORICAL SOCIETY. 70
       (Easter 1966): 101-116.

666.   Stoudt, John Joseph. PENNSYLVANIA GERMAN FOLK ART. Allentown,
       PA.: Schlectors, 1948, 1966.

667.   Thompson, D. W. "Oldest American Printing Press." THE
       PENNSYLVANIA DUTCHMAN. 6 (Winter 1954-55): 28-33.

668.   Van Neida, R.D. "The Old Cloister of Ephrata." THE FARM AND
       FIRESIDE (Springfield, OH) (March 1, 1906).

669.   Williams, Edwin M. "The Monastic Orders of Provincial Ephrata."
       In Harry Martin John Klein and Edwin Melvin Williams, eds.
       LANCASTER COUNTY, PENNSYLVANIA; A HISTORY. 4 vols. New
       York; Chicago: Lewis Historical Publishing Co., 1924. I,
       384-476.

670.   Wust, Klaus G. "German Mystics and Sabbatarians in Virginia,
       1700-1764." VIRGINIA MAGAZINE OF HISTORY AND BIOGRAPHY.
       72 (July 1964): 330-347.

671.   ------. THE SAINT-ADVENTURES OF THE VIRGINIA FRONTIER; SOUTHERN
       OUTPOSTS OF EPHRATA. Edinburgh, VA.: Shenandoah History,
       1977.

672.   Zerfass, Samuel Grant. SOUVENIR BOOK OF THE EPHRATA CLOISTER,
       COMPLETE HISTORY FROM ITS SETTLEMENT IN 1728 TO THE
       PRESENT TIME. INCLUDED IS THE ORGANIZATION OF EPHRATA
       BOROUGH AND OTHER INFORMATION OF EPHRATA CONNECTED WITH
       THE CLOISTER. Lititz, PA.: J.G. Zook, 1921. Reprint.
       New York: AMS Press, 1975.

673.   Ziegler, Samuel Hornung. "The Ephrata Printing Press Now in the
       Printshop of Frank R. King, New Enterprise, Bedford
       County, Pennsylvania." PENNSYLVANIA GERMAN FOLKLORE
       SOCIETY. 5. Allentown, PA.: The Society, 1940.

Snow Hill Nunnery (1798-1870)

This group of Seventh Day Baptists located in Franklin County,
Pennsylvania patterned themselves after the Ephrata Cloister and
sought to keep alive the lifestyle of Ephrata.

674.   Seilhamer, Larry. "Remnants of Conrad Beissel's Church."
       BRETHREN LIFE AND THOUGHT. 26 (Summer 1981): 152-153.

675.   Townsend, George Alfred. KATY OF CATOCTIN; OR THE CHAIN-
       BREAKERS; A NATIONAL ROMANCE. New York: D. Appleton and
       Co., 1886. (Fiction)

676.   Treher, Charles M. SNOW HILL CLOISTER. Allentown PA.:
        Pennsylvania German Society, 1968.

FOURIERIST GROUPS

Francois Marie Charles Fourier (1772-1837), was a Frenchman who expounded on the ideal of reorganizing society into small communities, or phalansteries, based on communal sharing of goods. His philosophy found many advocates in the United States, foremost of whom was Albert Brisbane.

ARCHIVAL MATERIALS

677. Alphadelphia Association. Records, 1844-1848. University of Michigan, Michigan Historical Collections. Bentley Historical Library. University of Michigan.

678. Brisbane, Albert. Papers, 1841-1936. University Illinois, Illinois Historical Survey Collections.

679. Fisher, James T. Papers. Massachusetts Historical Society and the Houghton Library. Harvard University.

680. Fourier, Francois Marie Charles. Papers, 1771-1837 Duke University Library, Durham, NC.

681. Godwin, Parke. Papers. Bryant-Godwin and Ford Collections. New York Public Library.

682. Grant, Elijah P. Papers, 1843-1871. University of Chicago Library.

683. North American Phalanx, Phalanx, NJ. Records, 1843-1856. Monmouth County Historical Association Library. Freehold, NJ.

684. Raritan Bay Union, Eagleswood, NJ. Records, ca. 1866-1950. New Jersey Historical Society Collections.

685. Santerre, George Henry. La Reunion Colony, 1766-1962. Papers. Dallas Public Library.

686. Shetterly, Seth K. Papers, 1829-1834. University of Michigan, Michigan Historical Collections.

687. Simonin, Amedee H. Papers, 1854-1874. Library of Congress, Manuscript Division, Washington, D.C.

688. Throop, George Addison. Correspondence, 1803-1939. Cornell University Library. Collection of Regional History and University Archives. Ithaca, NY.

689. Wisconsin Phalanx, Ceresco, Wisconsin. Records, 1844-1870. State Historical Society of Wisconsin.

BIBLIOGRAPHIES

690. Bestor, Arthur Eugene, and Dorothy K.Bestor. FOURIERIST BOOKS
      AND PAMPHLETS PUBLISHED IN GREAT BRITAIN AND THE UNITED
      STATES. [n.p., n.d.].

691. Bo, Giuseppi del. CHARLES FOURIER E LA SCUOLA SOCIETARIA
      (1801-1922), SAGGIO BIBLIOGRAPHICO. Milan: Feltrinelli,
      1957.

ARTICLES AND BOOKS

692. Adair, W. S. "Old French Settlement Near Dallas." DALLAS
      MORNING NEWS, March 26, 1922.

693. Alhaiza, Adolphe. CHARLES FOURIER ET SA SOCIOLOGIE SOCIETAIRE.
      Paris: M. Riviere etc., 1911.

694. Allain, Mathe, ed. FRANCE AND NORTH AMERICA: UTOPIAS AND
      UTOPIANS. Lafayette,LA: University of Southwestern
      Louisiana Press, 1978.

695. American Union of Associationists. ASSOCIATION, AS ILLUSTRATED
      BY FOURIER'S SYSTEM. Printed for the American Union of
      Associationists. Boston: Crosby & Nichols, 1847.
      Microfilm. Harvard College Library, 1942.

696. American Union of Associationists. INDUSTRIAL ASSOCIATION. AN
      ADDRESS TO THE PEOPLE OF THE UNITED STATES, BY THE
      AMERICAN UNION OF ASSOCIATIONISTS. Boston: The
      Association, 1850.

697. Bebel, August. CHARLES FOURIER, SEIN LEBEN UND SEINE THEORIEN.
      Stuttgart: J.H.W. Dietz, 1888.

698. Beecher, Jonathan F. "Charles Fourier and His Early Writings,
      1800-1820." M.A. Thesis, Harvard, 1968.

699. ------. CHARLES FOURIER; THE VISIONARY AND HIS WORLD. Berkeley:
      University of California Press, 1986.

700. Beecher, Jonathan, and Richard Bienvenu, eds. THE UTOPIAN
      VISION OF CHARLES FOURIER: SELECTED TEXTS ON WORK, LOVE,
      AND PASSIONATE ATTRACTION. Boston: Beacon Press, 1971.
      Reprint. Columbia, MO.: University of Missouri Press,
      1983.

701. Bell, Daniel. "Charles Fourier: Prophet of Eupsychia." THE
      AMERICAN SCHOLAR. 38 (Winter 1968-69): 41-58.

702. Bell, Herman J. "The North American Phalanx: Experiment in
       Socialism." NEW JERSEY HISTORY. 81 (October 1963):
       215-246.

703. Bernard, Luther L., and Jessie Bernard. "The Associationist
       Phase of Social Science." In their ORIGINS OF AMERICAN
       SOCIOLOGY. New York: Thomas Y. Crowell, 1943. pp. 59-
       112.

704. Bestor, Arthur Eugene, Jr. "Albert Brisbane -Propagandist for
       Socialism in the 1840's." NEW YORK HISTORY. 28 (April
       1947): 128-158.

705. ------. "American Phalanxes, A Study of Fourierist Socialism in
       the United States (with special reference to the movement
       in western New York)." Ph.D. diss. Yale University,
       1938. Microfilm. Wisconsin Historical Society,1938.

706. ------. "Fourierism in Northampton: A Critical Note." NEW
       ENGLAND QUARTERLY. 13 (March 1940): 110-122.

707. Birney, Catherine H. THE GRIMKE SISTERS: SARAH AND ANGELINA
       GRIMKE, THE FIRST AMERICAN WOMEN ADVOCATES OF ABOLITION
       AND WOMAN'S RIGHTS. Boston: Lee and Shepard; New York:
       C.T. Dillingham, 1885.

708. Boulanger, Francois Louis Florimond. AUX DISCIPLES DE FOURIER:
       PROJET DE SOLIDARITE ENTRE LES DISCIPLES DE FOURIER ET D'
       REALISATION PROCHAINE D'UN ESSAI SOCIETAIRE PAR
       L'ASSOCIATION DE LEURS INTERETS IMMEDIATS. Paris:
       Librairie des sciences sociales, 1872.

709. Bourgin, Hubert. FOURIER: CONTRIBUTION A L' ETUDE DU SOCIALISME
       FRANCAIS. Paris: Societe nouvelle de librairie et
       d'edition, 1905.

710. Bremer, Fredericka. THE HOMES OF THE NEW WORLD: IMPRESSIONS OF
       AMERICA. Trans. Mary Howitt. 2 vols. New York: Harper &
       Bros., 1853. pp. 71-104; 611-624.

711. Breton, Andre. ODE A FOURIER. Paris: Fontaine, 1947, 1961.
       (Poetry).

712. Briancourt, Mathieu. L'ORGANISATION DU TRAVAIL ET
       L'ASSOCIATION. Paris: A la librairie societaire, 1845.

713. ------. THE ORGANIZATION OF LABOR AND ASSOCIATION. Trans.
       Francis George Shaw. New York: W.H. Graham, 1847.

714. ------. VISITE AU PHALANSTERE. Paris: Librairie
       Phalansterienne, 1848.

715.   Brisbane, Albert. ALBERT BRISBANE, A MENTAL BIOGRAPHY WITH A
        CHARACTER STUDY BY HIS WIFE REDELIA BRISBANE. Boston:
        Arena Publishing Co., 1893.

716.   ------. "Association." Series of articles, New York TRIBUNE,
        irregular intervals, 1842-1855.

717.   ------. ASSOCIATION; OR A CONCISE EXPOSITION OF THE PRACTICAL
        PART OF FOURIER'S SOCIAL SCIENCE. New York: Greeley &
        McElrath, 1843.

718.   ------. A CONCISE EXPOSITION OF THE DOCTRINE OF ASSOCIATION. OR
        PLAN FOR A REORGANIZATION OF SOCIETY WHICH WILL SECURE TO
        THE HUMAN RACE, INDIVIDUALLY AND COLLECTIVELY, THEIR
        HAPPINESS AND ELEVATION. (BASED ON FOURIER'S THEORY OF
        DOMESTIC AND INDUSTRIAL ASSOCIATION.) 2d. ed. New York:
        J.S. Redfield, 1843. Pub. in 1843 under title:
        Association; or A concise exposition of the practical part
        of Fourier's social science.

719.   ------. GENERAL INTRODUCTION TO SOCIAL SCIENCES. PART
        FIRST--INTRODUCTION TO FOURIER'S THEORY OF SOCIAL
        ORGANIZATION. PART SECOND--SOCIAL DESTINIES. Charles
        Fourier. New York: C.P. Somerby, 1876.

720.   ------. PHILOSOPHY OF MONEY: A NEW CURRENCY AND A NEW CREDIT
        SYSTEM. n.p., 1863.

721.   ------. SOCIAL DESTINY OF MAN; OR ASSOCIATION AND REORGANIZATION
        OF INDUSTRY. Philadelphia: C.F. Stollmeyer, 1840.
        Reprint. New York: Burt Franklin, 1969. Microfilm.
        University Microfilm, Ann Arbor, 1967.

722.   ------. THEORY OF THE FUNCTIONS OF THE HUMAN PASSIONS, FOLLOWED
        BY AN OUTLINE VIEW OF THE FUNDAMENTAL PRINCIPLES OF
        FOURIER'S THEORY OF SOCIAL SCIENCE. New York: Miller,
        1856.

723.   ------. TREATISE ON THE FUNCTIONS OF HUMAN PASSIONS; AN OUTLINE
        OF FOURIER'S SYSTEM. New York, n.p., 1857.

724.   Brisbane, Albert, and Osborne Macdaniel. "Exposition of Views
        and Principles." THE PHALANX. 1 (October 5, 1843).

725.   Brownson, Orestes. "Church Unity and Social Amelioration."
        BROWNSON'S QUARTERLY REVIEW. (July 1844): 310-327.

726.   ------. "Fourierism Repugnant to Christianity." BROWNSON'S
        QUARTERLY REVIEW. (October 1844): 450-487.

727.   Bruckner, Pascal. FOURIER. Seuil: Ecrivains de Toujours, 1975.

728.   BULLETIN DU MOUVEMENT SOCIETAIRE EN EUROPE ET EN AMERIQUE.
        Brussels. 1-33, Octobre 1857-Decembre 1860?

729. Cantagrel, Felix Francois Jean. THE CHILDREN AT THE
      PHALANSTERY. A FAMILIAR DIALOGUE ON EDUCATION. Trans.
      Francis Geo. Shaw. New York: W.H. Graham, 1848.
      Microfilm. New York Public Library, 1942; University
      Microfilms, Ann Arbor, 1967. Published in 1844 under
      title: Les enfants au Phalanstere; dialogue familier sur
      l' education, Paris: A la Librairie Societaire.

730. Carlson, Oliver. BRISBANE: A CANDID BIOGRAPHY. New York:
      Stackpole Sons, 1937.

731. Channing, William H. "Charles Fourier." THE PRESENT.
      1 (September 1843): 28-29.

732. Chase, Warren. THE LIFE-LINE OF THE LONE ONE. Boston: B.
      Marsh, 1857.

733. ------. "The Wisconsin Phalanx." THE HARBINGER. 7 (January 8,
      1848).

734. Clark, D.W. "Fourierism." METHODIST QUARTERLY REVIEW. 22
      (October 1845): 545-594.

735. Clermont Phalanx, Clermont Co., Ohio. CONSTITUTION OF THE
      CLERMONT PHALANX, ADOPTED MARCH 16, 1844. TO WHICH IS
      ADDED A STATEMENT OF THE CONDITION AND PROSPECTS OF THE
      ASSOCIATION [WITH CAPTION; TO FRIENDS OF ASSOCIATION.]
      Cincinnati: Printed by L'Hommedieu, 1845. Microfilm.
      Harvard College Library, 1951.

736. Clifton, Thomas A. PAST AND PRESENT OF FOUNTAIN AND WARREN
      COUNTIES, INDIANA. Indianapolis: B.F. Bowen, 1913.

737. Commons, John Rogers. A DOCUMENTARY HISTORY OF AMERICAN
      INDUSTRIAL SOCIETY. 10 vols. New York: Russell, 1958.
      VII, pp. 19-44; 185-206; 240-284; 323-343.

738. Considerant, Victor Prosper. AU TEXAS. Paris: La Librairie
      Phalansterienne, 1854; Bruxelles: Societe de colonisation
      [etc.], 1855.

739. ------. DESCRIPTION DU PHALANSTERE ET CONSIDERATIONS SOCIALES SUR
      L'ARCHITECTONIQUE. Paris: Librairie societaire, 1848.

740. ------. DESTINEE SOCIALE. 3 vols. Paris: Bureau de la
      Phalange, 1835.

741. ------. DU TEXAS; PREMIER RAPPORT A MES AMIS. Paris: Librairie
      societaire, 1857.

742. ------. EUROPEAN COLONIZATION IN TEXAS: AN ADDRESS TO THE
      AMERICAN PEOPLE. New York: Baker, Godwin & Co., 1855.

743.   ------. EXPOSITION ABREGEE DU SYSTEME PHALANSTERIEN DE FOURIER.
        Paris: Librairie societaire, 1840.

744.   ------. THE GREAT WEST. A NEW SOCIAL AND INDUSTRIAL LIFE IN ITS
        FERTILE REGIONS. New York: DeWitt & Davenport, 1854.

745.   ------. PRINCIPES DU SOCIALISME; MANIFESTE DE LA DEMOCRATIE AU
        XIX SIECLE. Paris: Librairie Phalansterienne, 1847.

746.   ------. THEORIE DE L'EDUCATION NATURELLE ET ATTRAYANTE; DEDIEE
        AUX MERES. Paris: Librairie de l'Ecole Societaire, 1844.

747.   COUNTIES OF LAGRANGE AND NOBLE, INDIANA. Chicago: Battley,
        1882.

748.   Crawford, Mary Caroline. "A Country Church Industrial."
        OUTLOOK. 73 (February 21, 1903): 448-451.

749.   Crowe, Charles R. "Christian Socialism & 1st Church Humanity."
        CHURCH HISTORY. 35 (March 1966): 93-106.

750.   ------. "Fourierism and the Founding of Brook Farm." BOSTON
        PUBLIC LIBRARY QUARTERLY. 12 (April 1960): 79-88.

751.   ------. "The Religious History of a Christian Socialist: Joseph
        J. Cooke's `A Personal Relation'." RHODE ISLAND HISTORY.
        23 (July 1964): 81-89.

752.   ------. "Utopian Socialism in Rhode Island, 1845-1850." RHODE
        ISLAND HISTORY. 18 (January 1959): 20-26.

753.   ------. "This Unnatural Union of Phalansteries and
        Transcendentalists." JOURNAL OF THE HISTORY OF IDEAS. 20
        (October-December 1959): 495-502.

754.   Dailey, H. "Fourierist Colony in Iowa." ANNALS OF IOWA. 17
        (January 1930): 233-236.

755.   Debout-Oleszkiewicz, Simone. "L'Analogie ou `le poeme
        mathematique' de Charles Fourier." REVUE INTERNATIONALE
        DE PHILOSOPHIE. 16,no. 60 (1962): 176-199.

756.   ------. "La Terre permise ou l'analyse selon Charles Fourier et
        la theorie des groupes." LES TEMPS MODERNES. 22 (July
        1966): 1-55.

757.   Debu-bridel, Jacques. L'ACTUALITE DE FOURIER. Paris: Editions
        France-Empire, 1978.

758.   LA DEMOCRATIE PACIFIQUE. Paris. v. 1-13, no. 70, August 1,
        1843-Novembre 30, 1851. Superseded LaPhalange, journal de
        la science sociale.

759. Desroche, Henri. LA SOCIETE FESTIVE: DU FOURIERISME ECRIT AUX FOURIERISMES PRACTIQUES. Paris: Editions du Seuil, 1975.

760. Di Forti, Massimo. FOURIER E L'ARCHITETTURA DELLA FELICITA SOCIALIZZATA. Bari: Dedalo Libri, 1978.

761. Doherty, Hugh. FALSE ASSOCIATION AND ITS REMEDY; OR A CRITICAL INTRODUCTION TO THE LATE CHARLES FOURIER'S THEORY OF ATTRACTIVE INDUSTRY, AND THE MORAL HARMONY OF THE PASSIONS. TO WHICH IS PREFIXED, A MEMOIR OF FOURIER. London: Office of the London Phalanx, 1841.

762. Dommanget, Maurice. VICTOR CONSIDERANT; SA VIE, SON OEUVRE. Paris: Editions sociales internationales, 1929.

763. Dwight, John S. "Association the Body of Christianity." THE HARBINGER. 2 (February 21, 1846).

764. ------. "The American Review's Account of the Religious Union of Associationists." THE HARBINGER. 5 (June 19, 1847).

765. Ekrich, Arthur A. THE IDEA OF PROGRESS IN AMERICA, 1815-1860. New York: P. South, 1952. pp. 132-165.

766. Emerson, Ralph Waldo. "Fourierism and the Socialists." In UNCOLLECTED WRITINGS, ESSAYS, ADDRESSES, POEMS, REVIEWS AND LETTERS. New York: Lamb Publishing Co., 1912. pp. 71-76.

767. Elias, Joan. "The Wisconsin Phalanx: An Experiment in Association." M.A. thesis, University of Wisconsin, 1968.

768. Ellsworth, Richard C. "Northern New York's Early Cooperative Union." New York State Historical Association, PROCEEDINGS. 28 (October 1929): 328-332.

769. EXPOSE OF THE CONDITION AND PROGRESS OF THE NORTH AMERICAN PHALANX: IN REPLY TO THE INQUIRIES OF HORACE GREELEY, WITH AN INTRODUCTION BY NORMAN L. SWAN. New York: DeWitt & Davenport, 1853. Reprint. Philadelphia: Porcupine Press, 1975.

770. Felix, Armand. FOURIER. 2 vols. Paris: Edition Sociales Internationales, 1937.

771. Fourier, Francois Marie Charles. ANALYSE DU MECANISME DE L'AGIOTAGE ET DE LA METHODE MIXTE EN ETUDE DE L'ATTRACTION. Paris: Librairie Phalansterienne, 1848.

772. ------. L'ASSOCIATION ET LE TRAVAIL ATTRAYANT. Paris: Librairie de la bibliotheque democratique, 1873.

773. ------. L'AVENIR, APERCU DU SYSTEME D'ASSOCIATION DOMESTIQUE, AGRICOLE ET INDUSTRIEL, D'APRES LA THEORIE DE CHARLES

FOURIER... Bordeaux: de l'imprimerie et lithographie de
Henry Faye, 1837.

774.   ------. DE L'ANARCHIE INDUSTRIELLE ET SCIENTIFIQUE. Paris:
Librarie phalansterienne, 1847.

775.   ------. DICTIONNAIRE DE SOCIOLOGIE PHALANSTERIENNE. GUIDE DES
OEUVRES COMPLETES DE CHARLES FOURIER. Paris: M. Riviere,
etc., 1911. Reprint. New York: Burt Franklin, 1965.

776.   ------. FOURIER, 1772-1837. Geneve: Traits, 1947.

777.   ------. HARMONIAL MAN. Ed. Mark Poster. Garden City, NY:
Doubleday, 1971.

778.   ------. LE NOUVEAU MONDE AMOUREUX. Ed. Simone
Debout-Oleszkiewicz. Paris: Editions Anthropos, 1967.

779.   ------. LE NOUVEAU MONDE INDUSTRIEL ET SOCIETAIRE, OU INVENTION
DU PROCEDE D'INDUSTRIE ATTRAYANTE ET NATURELLE DISTRIBUEE
EN SERIES PASSIONNEES. Paris: Bossange pere [etc] 1829.

780.   ------. OEUVRES COMPLETES DES CHARLES FOURIER. Introduction par
Simone Debout Oleszkiewicz. 6 vols. Paris: Editions
Anthropose, 1966.

781.   ------. THE PASSIONS OF THE HUMAN SOUL AND THEIR INFLUENCE ON
SOCIETY AND CIVILIZATION. Translated from the French.
With critical annotations, a biography of Fourier, and a
general introduction, by Hugh Doherty. New York: A.M.
Kelley, 1851, 1968.

782.   ------. DIE PHALANX. EINE AUSLESE AUS SEINEN SCHRIFTEN BESORGT
VON PAUL OESTREICH. Munchen: Dreilander, 1919.

783.   ------. DIE HARMONISCHE ERZIEHUNG. AUSGEWAHLT, EINGELETET UND
UBERSELZT VON WALTER APELT. Berlin: Volk und Wissen
Volkseigener, 1958.

784.   ------. POLITICAL ECONOMY MADE EASY. A sketch, by M. Charles
Fourier, exhibiting the various errors of our present
political arrangements. Presented to the London
Co-operative society, by the translator. London: W.A.
Wright [etc.], 1828.

785.   ------. PUBLICATION DES MANUSCRITS DE FOURIER. Paris: Lange Levy
et Comp., 1841-1849.

786.   ------. SELECTIONS FROM THE WORKS OF FOURIER: London: S.
Sonnenschein & Co., 1901. Reprinted under title: DESIGN
FOR UTOPIA; SELECTED WRITINGS OF CHARLES FOURIER. New
York: Schocken Books, 1971.

787.   ------. THE SOCIAL DESTINY OF MAN; OR, THEORY OF THE FOUR
        MOVEMENTS. Trans. Henry Clapp, Jr. With a treatise on
        the functions of the human passions, and an outline of
        Fourier's system of social science, by Albert Brisbane.
        New York: R.M. Dewitt, 1857. Microfilm. Ann Arbor:
        University Microfilms, 1966.

788.   ------. SOCIAL SCIENCE. THE THEORY OF UNIVERSAL UNITY. With
        notes and appendix by A. Brisbane. New York: American
        News Co., 185?

789.   ------. THEORIE DES QUATRE MOUVEMENS ET DES DESTINEES GENERALS.
        PROSPECTUS ET ANNONCE DE LA DECOUVERTE. Lyon, 1808.

790.   ------. TRAITE DE L'ASSOCIATION DOMESTIQUE-AGRICOLE. 2 vols.
        Paris: Bossange, 1822.

791.   THE FUTURE; DEVOTED TO THE CAUSE OF ASSOCIATION AND A
        REORGANIZATION OF SOCIETY. New York, Fourier Association,
        v. 1, no. 1-8, January 30-July 10, 1841. Ed. Albert
        Brisbane.

792.   Gatti de Gamond, Zoe Charlotte (de Gamond). FOURIER ET SON
        SYSTEME. Parid: L. Desessart, 1838.

793.   ------. FOURIER AND HIS SYSTEM. Trans. C.T. Wood, Jr. With a
        short biographical sketch, extracted from "The London
        Phalanx." London: J.H. Young, 1842.

794.   ------. THE PHALANSTERY; OR ATTRACTIVE INDUSTRY AND MORAL
        HARMONY. Trans. by an English lady. London: Whittaker &
        Co., 1841.

795.   ------. REALISATION D'UN COMMUNE SOCIETAIRE, D'APRES LA THEORIE
        DE CHARLES FOURIER. Paris: Capelle, 1841-42.

796.   Gide, Charles. COMMUNIST AND CO-OPERATIVE COLONIES. Trans.
        Ernest F. Row. New York: Thomas Y. Crowell; London:
        Harrap & Co., Ltd., 1930.

797.   ------. L'ECOLE DE FOURIER ET LES EXPERIMENTATIONS FOURIERISTES;
        DEUX LECONS DU COURS SUR LA COOPERATION AU COLLEGE DE
        FRANCE. Paris: Association pour l'enseignement de la
        cooperation, 1922.

798.   ------. FOURIER, PRECURSEUR DE LA COOPERATION. Paris:
        Association pour l'enseignement de la cooperation, 1925.

799.   ------. INTRODUCTION TO FOURIERS OEUVRES CHOISIES. Paris, 1890.

800.   Giles, Julia Bucklin. "Address to the Monmouth County
        Historical Association." Unpublished manuscript in
        possession of the Historical Association, 1922.

801.   Gladish, Robert Willis. SWEDENBORG, FOURIER AND THE AMERICAS OF
       THE 1840S. Bryn Athyn, PA: Swedenborg Scientific
       Association, 1983.

802.   Godwin, Parke. "The Christian Examiner on the Doctrine of
       Fourier." THE PHALANX. 1 (August 24, 1844).

803.   ------. A POPULAR VIEW OF THE DOCTRINE OF CHARLES FOURIER, WITH
       THE ADDITION OF DEMOCRACY, CONSTRUCTIVE AND PACIFIC. New
       York: J.S. Redfield, 1844. Reprint. Philadelphia:
       Porcupine Press, 1972.

804.   ------. "The Univercoelum." THE HARBINGER. 6 (February 26,
       1848)

805.   Goret, Jean. LA PENSEE DE FOURIER. Vendome: Presses
       Universitaires de France, 1974.

806.   Greeley, Horace. AUTOBIOGRAPHY; OR RECOLLECTIONS OF A BUSY
       LIFE. TO WHICH ARE ADDED MISCELLANEOUS ESSAYS AND PAPERS.
       New York: E.G. Treat, 1868.

807.   ------. "The Social Architects--Fourier." In HINTS TOWARDS
       REFORMS. New York: Harper & Brothers, 1850.

808.   ------. WHAT HORACE GREELEY KNOWS ABOUT FOURIERISM-FREE
       LOVE-FINANCE-LAGER BEER-WOMEN'S RIGHTS...&C., &C., &C.
       New York, 1871?

809.   Greene, Maud Honeyman. "Raritan Bay Union, Eagleswood, New
       Jersey." PROCEEDINGS OF THE NEW JERSEY HISTORICAL
       SOCIETY. 67 (January 1950): 2-19.

810.   Greenough, Horatio. "Fourier et Hoc Genus Omne." THE CRAYON.
       1 (June 13, 1855): 371-372.

811.   Guarneri, Carl J. "The Associationists: Forging a Christian
       Socialism in Antebellum America." CHURCH HISTORY. 52
       (March 1983): 36-49.

812.   ------. "Importing Fourierism to America," JOURNAL OF THE
       HISTORY OF IDEAS. 43 (October-December, 1982): 581-594.

813.   ------. "Utopian Socialism and American Ideas: The Origins and
       Doctrines of American Fourierism, 1832-1848." Ph.D. diss.
       Johns Hopkins University, 1979.

814.   ------. "Who Were the Utopian Socialists? Patterns of Membership
       in American Fourierist Communities." COMMUNAL SOCIETIES.
       5 (1985): 65-81.

815.   Hammond, William Jackson. "La Reunion, a French Colony in
       Texas." THE SOUTHWESTERN SOCIAL SCIENCE QUARTERLY. 17
       (September 1936): 197-206.

816. Hammond, William Jackson, and Margaret Hammond. LA REUNION; A
     FRENCH SETTLEMENT IN TEXAS. Dallas: Royal Publishing Co.,
     1958.

817. THE HARBINGER. Boston and New York. 1-8, 1845-1849. Weekly.

818. Hennequin, Victor Antoine. LOVE IN THE PHALANSTERY. New York:
     Dewitt and Davenport, 1849. Microfilm. Photographic
     Services, University of Illinois Library.

819. Jordan, Philip D. "The Iowa Pioneer Phalanx." THE PALIMPSEST.
     16 (July 1935): 211-225.

820. Kirchmann, George. "Unsettled Utopias: The North American
     Phalanx and the Raritan Bay Union." NEW JERSEY HISTORY.
     97 (Spring 1979): 25-36.

821. Lehouck, Emile. FOURIER AUDOURD'HUI. Paris: Denoel, 1966.

822. ------. VIE DE CHARLES FOURIER. Paris: Denoel/Gonthier, 1978.

823. Lerner, Gerda. THE GRIMKE SISTERS FROM SOUTH CAROLINA: PIONEERS
     FOR WOMAN'S RIGHTS AND ABOLITION. New York: Schocken,
     1967.

824. Lloyd-Jones, I.D. "Charles Fourier, the Realistic Visionary."
     HISTORY TODAY. 12 (March 1962): 198-205.

825. THE LONDON PHALANX, London. no. 1-69, April 3, 1841-May 1843.

826. Louvancour, Henri. DE HENRI DE SAINT SIMON A CHARLES FOURIER;
     ETUDE SUR LE SOCIALISME ROMANTIQUE FRANCAIS DE 1830.
     Chartres: Imprimerie Durand, 1913.

827. Lumpkin, Katharine Du Pres. THE EMANCIPATION OF ANGELINA
     GRIMKE. Chapel Hill: University of North Carolina Press,
     1974.

828. Lutz, Eusibia. "Almost Utopia." SOUTHWEST REVIEW. 14 (Spring
     1929): 321-330.

829. MacKaye, Percy. EPOCH, THE LIFE OF STEELE. McKaye. 2 vols.
     New York: Bone and Liveright, 1927.

830. Madison, Charles Allen. CRITICS AND CRUSADERS: A CENTURY OF
     AMERICAN PROTEST. 2d ed. New York: Ungar, 1959. pp. 83-
     133.

831. McLaren, Donald Campbell. BOA CONSTRICTOR, OR FOURIER
     ASSOCIATION SELF-EXPOSED AS TO ITS PRINCIPLES AND AIMS.
     Rochester, NY.: Printed by Canfield and Warren, 1844.

832. Mason, Edward. "Fourier and Anarchism." THE QUARTERLY JOURNAL
     OF ECONOMICS. 42 (February 1928): 228-262.

833.   ------. "Fourier and Fourierism." ENCYCLOPAEDIA OF THE SOCIAL
        SCIENCES. Editor in chief, Edwin R.A. Seligman. New
        York: Macmillan, 1930; reissued 1937. s.v.

834.   Morgenroth, Kate. CHARLES FOURIER UND DER SOZIALISMUS. Berlin:
        P. Cassirer, 1920.

835.   ------. DIE LEHRE CHARLES FOURIERS. Jena: G. Fischer, 1914.

836.   THE MORNING STAR; OR, PHALANSTERIAN GAZETTE. London: B.C.
        Cousins, no. 1-9, October 21, 1840-January 6, 1841.

837.   "New Clairvaux." COUNTRY TIME AND TIDE. 6 (1904): 65-75.

838.   Olmsted, Frederick Law. "(An American Farmer) The Phalanstery
        and the Phalansterians.'" Letter to the New York TRIBUNE.
        July 24, 1852.

839.   Ontario Phalanx. New York. LABOR'S WRONGS, AND LABOR'S REMEDY.
        Rochester, NY., 1843. Microfilm. Columbia University
        Libraries, 1951.

840.   Peabody, Elizabeth P. "Fourierism." DIAL. 4 (April 1844):
        473-483.

841.   Pedrick, S.M. "The Wisconsin Phalanx at Ceresco." PROCEEDINGS
        OF THE STATE HISTORICAL SOCIETY OF WISCONSIN. (1902):
        190-226.

842.   Pellarin, Charles. THE LIFE OF CHARLES FOURIER. 2nd ed.
        Trans. Francis George Shaw. New York: Graham, 1848.

843.   LA PHALANGE, REVUE DE LA SCIENCE SOCIALE... Paris: Bureaux de
        la Phalange, 1845-49.

844.   LE PHALANSTERE, See Phalange.

845.   PHALANSTERIAN RECORD. Cincinnati, O. 1. 2-5 (January-April
        1858). Continued as SOCIAL RECORD. Dearborn Co., IN.
        (September 1858).

846.   THE PHALANX: ORGAN OF THE DOCTRINE OF ASSOCIATION. New York, 1
        (no. 1-23), October 5, 1843--May 28, 1845. Continued as
        THE HARBINGER. Reprint. CHARLES FOURIER'S THE PHALANX,
        OR JOURNAL OF SOCIAL SCIENCE. New York: Burt Franklin,
        1967.

847.   Philadelphia Unitary Building Association. CONSTITUTION, WITH A
        LITHOGRAPHIC OUTLINE OF THE PROPOSED EDIFICE.
        Philadelphia: United States Job Printing Office, 1849.

848.   Pinloche, A. FOURIER ET LE SOCIALISME. Paris: Librairie Felix
        Alcan, 1933.

849. Poisson, E. FOURIER. Paris: Librairie Felix Alcan,
      1932.

850. Poulat, Emile. LES CAHIERS MANUSCRITS DE FOURIER. ETUDE
      HISTORIQUE ET INVENTAIRE RAISONNE. Paris: Entente
      communautaire, 1957.

851. Quaife, Milo M. LAKE MICHIGAN. Indianapolis, IN: Bobbs-Merrill
      Company, 1944. pp. 231-47.

852. Reybaud, Louis. ETUDES SUR LES REFORMATEURS CONTEMPORAINS ON
      SOCIALISTES MODERNES. SAINT-SIMON, CHARLES FOURIER,
      ROBERT OWEN. 2nd ed. Paris: Guillaumin, 1841.

853. Raisanovsky, Nicholas V. THE TEACHINGS OF CHARLES FOURIER.
      Berkeley: University of California Press, 1969.

854. Santerre, Eloise. "Reunion: A Translation of Dr. Savardan's 'Un
      Naufrage au Texas,' with an Introduction to Reunion and a
      Biographical Dictionary of the Settlers." M.A. thesis,
      Southern Methodist University, 1936.

855. Savardan, Augustin. UN NAUFRAGE AU TEXAS; OBSERVATIONS ET
      IMPRESSIONS RECUEILLIES PENDANT DEUX ANS ET DEMI AU TEXAS
      ET A TRAVERS LES ETATS-UNIS D'AMERIQUE. Paris: Garnier
      freres, 1858. Microfilm. Yale University.

856. Schafer, Joseph. "The Wisconsin Phalanx." THE WISCONSIN
      MAGAZINE OF HISTORY. 19 (June 1936): 454-474.

857. Scherer, Rene. CHARLES FOURIER. Paris: Editions Seghers, 1970.

858. Schirber, Eric. "The North American Phalanx, 1843-1855." M.A.
      thesis, Princeton University, 1972.

859. Sears, Charles. EXPOSE OF THE CONDITION AND PROGRESS OF THE
      NORTH AMERICAN PHALANX: IN REPLY TO THE INQUIRIES OF
      HORACE GREELEY, AND IN ANSWER TO THE CRITICISMS OF FRIENDS
      AND FOES DURING THE PAST YEAR. INTENDED TO SET FORTH THE
      PRINCIPLES, AIMS, AND CHARACTER OF THE PHALANX IN ITS
      RELATIONS TO THE GENERAL SUBJECT OF SOCIAL REFORM. New
      York: Dewitt & Davenport, 1853.

860. ------. THE NORTH AMERICAN PHALANX, AN HISTORICAL AND DESCRIPTIVE
      SKETCH. Prescott, WI.: J.M. Pryse, 1886.

861. ------. SOCIALISM AND CHRISTIANITY: BEING A RESPONSE TO AN
      INQUIRER CONCERNING RELIGION AND THE OBSERVANCE OF
      RELIGIOUS FORMS AT THE NORTH AMERICAN PHALANX. Monmouth
      Co., NJ.: The Phalanx, 1854. Microfilm. New York Public
      Library, 1942.

862. Semler, Heinrich. GESCHICHTE DES SOZIALISMUS UND COMMUNISMUS IN
      NORDAMERIKA. Leipzig: F.A. Brockhaus, 1880.

863.   Shaw, William B. "A Forgotten Socialism." NEW ENGLAND
       MAGAZINE. 3 (August 1893): 773-776.

864.   Sheffield, C.A. HISTORY OF FLORENCE, MASSACHUSETTS; INCLUDING A
       COMPLETE ACCOUNT OF THE NORTHAMPTON ASSOCIATION OF
       EDUCATION AND INDUSTRY. Florence: MA., 1895.

865.   Silberling, E. DICTIONAIRE DE SOCIOLOGIE PHALANSTERIENNE: GUIDE
       DES OEUVRES COMPLETES DE CHARLES FOURIER. New York: B.
       Franklin, 1911.

866.   Smart, George K. "Fourierism in Northampton: Two Documents."
       THE NEW ENGLAND QUARTERLY. 12 (June 1939): 370-374.

867.   Smith, Carlton. "Elijah Grant and the Ohio Phalanx." M.A.
       thesis, University of Chicago, 1950.

868.   SOCIAL RECORD. v. 1-3, December 1857-January 1859. Cincinnati.
       Title varies: December 1857-August 1858, PHALANSTERIAN
       RECORD.

869.   Sokolow, Jayme A. "Culture and Utopia: The Raritan Bay Union."
       NEW JERSEY HISTORY. 94 (Summer-Autumn 1976): 89-100.

870.   Spencer, Michael C. CHARLES FOURIER. Boston: G.K. Hall,
       Twayne, 1981.

871.   Spurlin, Paul M. "On France and North America: A Review."
       FRENCH-AMERICAN REVIEW. 4 (Spring 1980): 42-45.

872.   Stellhorn, Paul A., ed. PLANNED AND UTOPIAN EXPERIMENTS: FOUR
       NEW JERSEY TOWNS. Trenton: New Jersey Historical
       Commission, 1980.

873.   Swann, Norma Lippincott. "The North American Phalanx."
       MONMOUTH COUNTY HISTORICAL ASSOCIATION BULLETIN. 1 (May
       1935): 35-65.

874.   Thibert, Marguerite. LE FEMISME DANS 6 SOCIALISME FRANCAIS DE
       1830 A 1850. Paris: M. Girard. 1926.

875.   Thomas, Benjamin Platt. THEODORE WELD, CRUSADER FOR FREEDOM.
       New Brunswick, NJ.: Rutgers University, Press, 1950. pp.
       225-235.

876.   Transon, Able Louis Etienne. CHARLES FOURIER'S THEORY OF
       ATTRACTIVE INDUSTRY, AND THE MORAL HARMONY OF THE
       PASSIONS. Trans.Hugh Doherty. London: Office of the
       London Phalanx, 1841.

877.   TWO ESSAYS ON THE SOCIAL SYSTEM OF CHARLES FOURIER, BEING AN
       INTRODUCTION TO THE CONSTITUTION OF THE FOURIER SOCIETY OF
       NEW YORK. FIRST ESSAY - A SIMPLE AND SUCCINCT EXPOSITION

OF THE THEORY'S PRESUMPTIONS. SECOND ESSAY - MECHANICAL MEANS, OR THE MODE OF ITS ORGANIZATION. New York: H.D. Robinson, 1838.

878. Union of Associationists. Philadelphia, CONSTITUTION OF THE GROUP OF ACTUATION. Philadelphia, 1850? Microfilm. Harvard College Library.

879. Vincent, Louella Styles. "The Story of Old Frenchtown." Dallas MORNING NEWS. November 23, 1919.

880. Warren, Dale. "Uncle Marcus." NEW ENGLAND GALAXY. 9 (Summer 1967): 16-26.

881. "A Week in the Phalanstery." LIFE ILLUSTRATED. Part 1 (August 11, 1855); Part 2 (August 18, 1855).

882. Weld, Angelina Emily Grimke. APPEAL TO THE CHRISTIAN WOMEN OF THE SOUTH. New York: American Anti-Slavery Society, 1836.

883. ------. LETTERS TO CATHERINE E. BEECHER. Boston: Printed by I. Knapp, 1838.

884. Williams, John S. THE DETRIMENTS OF CIVILIZATION, AND BENEFITS OF ASSOCIATION; ALSO PLEDGES AND RULES FOR THE INTEGRAL PHALANX, PRECEDED BY OBSERVATIONS ON THE SAME. WITH OBJECTIONS TO THE COMMON PROPERTY SYSTEM OF OWEN, RAPP, AND OTHERS. Cincinnati: The Integral Phalanx, 1844.

885. Wolski, Kalikst. "A Visit to the North American Phalanx." Trans. Marion Moore Colemen. PROCEEDINGS OF THE NEW JERSEY HISTORICAL SOCIETY, 83 (July 1965): 149-160.

886. Zeldin, David. THE EDUCATIONAL IDEAS OF CHARLES FOURIER (1771-1837). London: Cass, 1969.

887. Zilberfarb, Ioganson Isaakovich. SOTSIALNAIA FILOSOFIIA SHARLIA FUR'E. Moscow: Hayka, 1964.

FRUITLANDS (1843-1844)

Organized by New England transcendentalists Bronson Alcott and
Charles Lane at Harvard, Massachusetts.

888. Alcott, Amos Bronson. THE JOURNALS OF BRONSON ALCOTT. Ed.
Odell Shepard. Boston: Little, Brown, 1938. Reprint.
Port Washington, NY.: Kennikat, 1966.

889. Cheyney, Ednah D., ed. LOUISA MAY ALCOTT; HER LIFE, LETTERS AND
JOURNALS. Boston: Roberts Bros., 1890. pp. 32-55.

890. Clark, Annie M.L. THE ALCOTTS IN HARVARD. Lancaster, MA.:
J.C.L. Clark, 1902.

891. Edgell, David P. "Charles Lane at Fruitlands." NEW ENGLAND
QUARTERLY. 33 (September 1960): 374-377.

892. Francis, Richard. "Circumstances and Salvation: the Ideology of
the Fruitlands Utopia." AMERICAN QUARTERLY. 35 (May
1973): 202-234.

893. McCuskey, Dorothy. BRONSON ALCOTT, TEACHER. New York:
Macmillan, 1940.

894. O'Brien, Harriet E. LOST UTOPIAS; A BRIEF DESCRIPTION OF THREE
QUESTS FOR HAPPINESS, ALCOTT'S FRUITLANDS, OLD SHAKER
HOUSE, AND AMERICAN INDIAN MUSEUM, RESCUED FROM OBLIVION,
RECORDED AND PRESERVED BY CLARA ENDICOTT SEARS ON PROSPECT
HILL IN THE OLD TOWNSHIP OF HARVARD, MASSACHUSETTS.
Boston: Perry Walton, 1929.

895. Sanborn, F. B. BRONSON ALCOTT AT ALCOTT HOUSE, ENGLAND, AND
FRUITLANDS, NEW ENGLAND (1842-1844). Cedar Rapids, IA.:
Torch Press, 1908.

896. Sanborn, F.B., and William T. Harris. A. BRONSON ALCOTT: HIS
LIFE AND PHILOSOPHY. Boston: Roberts Bros., 1893.

897. Sears, Clara Endicott, compiler. BRONSON ALCOTT'S FRUITLANDS.
WITH TRANSCENDENTAL WILD OATS BY LOUISA M. ALCOTT. New
York; Boston: Houghton-Mifflin Co., 1915. Reprint.
Philadelphia: Porcupine Press, 1975.

898. Shepard, Odell. PEDLAR'S PROGRESS: THE LIFE OF BRONSON ALCOTT.
Boston: Little, Brown, 1937.

899. Thoreau, Henry David. "The Library at Fruitlands: Catalogue of
Books." THE DIAL. 3 (April 1843): 545-548.

900.   Walker, Robert Howland. "Charles Lane and the Fruitlands
        Utopia." Ph.D. diss. University of Texas, 1967.

901.   Willis, Frederick D.H. ALCOTT MEMOIRS POSTHUMOUSLY COMPILED
        FROM PAPERS, JOURNALS, AND MEMORANDA OF THE LATE DR.
        FREDERICK D.H. WILLIS. Boston: Richard G. Badger, 1915.

GRAND PRAIRIE HARMONIAL COMMUNITY (1845-1847)

Established in Rainsville, Warren County, Indiana by a group of
communitarians from The First Community of Man's Free
Brotherhood (1833-1835), Covington, Indiana. Andreas Smolnikar
apparently was a member of this group.

902.   Shoemaker, Alfred L. "Andreas Bernadus Smolnikar, God's
        Ambassador Extraordinary." THE PENNSYLVANIA DUTCHMAN.
        (March 15, 1952).

903.   Smolnikar, Andreas Bernardus. DENKWURDIGE EREIGNISSE IM LEBEN
        DES ANDREAS BERNARDUS SMOLNIKAR. 3 vols. Cambridge: Mit
        stereotypen gedruckt in der buchdruckerei der herrn
        Folsom, Wells und Thurston, 1838-1840.

904.   ------. GRAND PREPARATIONS FOR THE PROMISED, PEACEABLE REIGN OF
        CHRIST, WHICH WILL BE THE REPUBLIC OF TRUTH,
        RIGHTEOUSNESS, UNION, AND PEACE OF NATIONS, COMMONLY,
        ALTHOUGH IMPROPERLY CALLED MILLENNIUM. Baltimore:
        Peace-Union Trustees, 1866.

905.   ------. THE ONE THING NEEDFUL, NAMELY, TO SPREAD AS RAPIDLY AS
        POSSIBLE THE GLORIOUS MANIFESTATION OF OUR LORD JESUS
        CHRIST. Philadelphia: Barrett & Jones, 1841.

906.   ------. REDEMPTION OF OPPRESSED HUMANITY. Cincinnati: Ben
        Franklin, 1856.

907.   ------. SECRET ENEMIES OF TRUE REPUBLICANISM. Donnally's Mill,
        PA.: Published by Robert D. Eldridge, 1859.

908.   ------. TO THE REFORMERS OF THE UNITED STATES AND ELSEWHERE, A
        MOST IMPORTANT CONVENTION OF REFORMS OF EVERY DESCRIPTION
        WILL BE HELD AT THE TRUMBULL PHALUX, TRUMBULL COUNTY,
        OHIO, TO COMMENCE ON THE 12TH OF AUGUST [1847] FOR
        INSTRUCTION AND INITIATING THE MESSENGERS OF JESUS CHRIST
        INTO THE POINTS AND METHODS BY WHICH THE NEW ERA OF
        UNIVERSAL PEACE IS TO BE REALIZED UPON EARTH. n.p., 1847.

909.   ------. TREATISE ON THE WORK WHICH HAS NOW APPEARED IN THE GERMAN
        LANGUAGE IN THREE VOLUMES COMPLETE, AND OF WHICH THE THIRD
        VOLUME HAS THE FOLLOWING TITLE: "MEMORABLE EVENTS IN THE
        LIFE OF ANDREAS BERNARDUS SMOLNIKAR." New York: Printed
        with stereotype, 1840.

HARMONY SOCIETY (1805-1898)

Begun in 1805 in Butler County, Pennsylvania, by George Rapp, a
Separatist who left Wurttemburg, Germany with a large following.
The first village was sold in 1814, and the group established
Harmony on the Wabash River in Indiana. In 1825 these lands
were in turn sold to Robert Owen who established his New Harmony
experiment. The Rapp followers returned to Pennsylvania, near
Pittsburg to establish Economy.

ARCHIVAL MATERIALS

910.   Harmony Society. Economy, PA., Records, 1837-1935. Pennsylvania
        State University Library, University Park, PA.

911.   Harmony Society. Records, 1790-1950. Pennsylvania Historical
        And Museum Commission, Harrisburg, PA.

BIBLIOGRAPHIES

912.   Demorest, Rose. THE HARMONISTS: A BIBLIOGRAPHY OF THE
        COLLECTION ON THE HARMONY SOCIETY IN THE CARNEGIE LIBRARY
        OF PITTSBURGH. Pittsburgh: Carnegie Library of
        Pittsburgh, 1940.

913.   Federal Writers Project. THE HARMONY SOCIETY IN PENNSYLVANIA.
        Philadelphia: William Penn Association, 1937.

914.   Illinois Historical Survey. University of Illinois. RECORDS OF
        THE NEW HARMONY COMMUNITY. Publication No. 2. Urbana,
        IL., 1950.

915.   Pennsylvania Historical and Museum Commission. BIBLIOGRAPHY
        RELATING TO VARIOUS ASPECTS OF THE HISTORY OF THE HARMONY
        SOCIETY. Ambridge, PA.; Pennsylvania Historical and
        Museum Commission, 1963.

916.   ------. GUIDE TO THE MICROFILMED HARMONY SOCIETY RECORDS,
        1786-1951 (MANUSCRIPT GROUP 185) IN THE PENNSYLVANIA STATE
        ARCHIVES. Compiled by Robert M. Dructor. Harrisburg,
        PA.: Pennsylvania Historical and Museum Commission, 1983.

917.   Reibel, Daniel B. BIBLIOGRAPHY OF ITEMS RELATED TO THE HARMONY
        SOCIETY WITH SPECIAL REFERENCE TO OLD ECONOMY, AND MANY
        WORKS ON COMMUNITIES AND UTOPIAS WHICH ALSO DISCUSS THE
        HARMONY SOCIETY. Ambridge, PA.: Pennsylvania Historical
        and Museum Commission, 1969.

ARTICLES AND BOOKS

918.   Andressohn, John C. "The Arrival of the Rappites at New
       Harmony." INDIANA MAGAZINE OF HISTORY. 42 (December
       1946): 395-409.

919.   ------. "Three Additional Rappite Letters." INDIANA MAGAZINE OF
       HISTORY. 42 (December 1946): 395-409; 44 (March 1948):
       82-108; 45 (June 1949): 184-188.

920.   ------. "Twenty Additional Rappite Manuscripts." INDIANA
       MAGAZINE OF HISTORY. 44 (March 1948): 83-108.

921.   Arndt, Karl John Richard. "Bismarck's Socialist Law of 1878 and
       the Harmonists." WESTERN PENNSYLVANIA HISTORY MAGAZINE.
       59 (January 1976): 55-69.

922.   ------, compiler and editor. A DOCUMENTARY HISTORY OF THE INDIANA
       DECADE OF THE HARMONY SOCIETY, 1814-1824. 2 Vols.
       Indiana Historical Society, 1975-1978.

923.   ------, compiler and editor. ECONOMY ON THE OHIO, 1826-1834: THE
       HARMONY SOCIETY DURING THE PERIOD OF ITS GREATEST POWER
       AND INFLUENCE AND ITS MESSIANIC CRISIS: GEORGE RAPP'S
       THIRD HARMONY: A DOCUMENTARY HISTORY= OKONOMIE AM OHIO:
       DIE HARMONIE GESELLSCHAFT DER ZEIT IHRES HOCHSTEN INTER
       NATIONALEN EIN FLUSSES UND IHRER MESSIAS KRISE.
       Worcester, MA.: Harmony Society Press, 1984.

924.   ------. "George Rapp Discovers the Wabash." WESTERN PENNSYLVANIA
       HISTORICAL MAGAZINE. 26 (September-December 1943):
       109-116.

925.   ------. "George Rapp's Harmonists and the Beginnings of Norwegian
       Migration to America." WESTERN PENNSYLVANIA HISTORICAL
       MAGAZINE. 60 (July 1977): 241-263.

926.   ------. GEORGE RAPP'S HARMONY SOCIETY, 1785-1847. Philadelphia:
       University of Pennsylvania Press, 1965. Rev. ed.
       Rutherford, NJ.: Fairleigh Dickinson University Press,
       1972.

927.   ------. "George Rapp's Petition to Thomas Jefferson."
       AMERICAN-GERMAN REVIEW. 7 (October 1940): 5-9, 35.

928.   ------. GEORGE RAPP'S SEPARATISTS, 1700-1803: THE GERMAN PRELUDE
       TO RAPP'S AMERICAN HARMONY SOCIETY, A DOCUMENTARY HISTORY
       // GEORG RAPPS SEPARATISTEN, 1700-1703: DIE DEUTSCHE
       VORGESCHICHTE VON RAPPS AMERIKANISCHER HARMONIE-
       GESELLSCHAFT. Worcester, MA.: Harmony Society Press,
       1980.

929.   ------. GEORGE RAPP'S SUCCESSORS AND MATERIAL HEIRS, 1847-1916.
       Teaneck, NJ.: Fairleigh Dickinson University Press, 1971.

930.   ------.   GEORGE RAPP'S YEARS OF GLORY: ECONOMY ON THE OHIO 1834-
       1847 // OKONOMIE AM OHIO.   New York: Peter Lang, 1988.

931.   ------.   "The Harmonists and the Hutterians."   AMERICAN-GERMAN
       REVIEW.   10 (August 1944): 24-27.

932.   ------.   "The Harmonists and the Mormons."   AMERICAN-GERMAN
       REVIEW.   10 (June 1944): 6-9.

933.   ------, compiler and editor.   HARMONY ON THE CONNOQUENESSING,
       1803-1815: GEORGE RAPP'S FIRST AMERICAN HARMONY: A
       DOCUMENTARY HISTORY // HARMONIE AM CONNOQUENESSING: GEORGE
       RAPPS ERSTE AMERIKANISCHE HARMONIE.   Worcester, MA.:
       Harmony Society Press, 1980.

934.   ------.   HARMONY ON THE WABASH IN TRANSITION, 1824-1826:
       TRANSITIONS TO GEORGE RAPP'S DIVINE ECONOMY ON THE OHIO,
       AND ROBERT OWEN'S NEW MORAL WORLD AT NEW HARMONY ON THE
       WABASH: A DOCUMENTARY HISTORY // HARMONIE AM WABASCH IM
       UBERGANG, 1824-1826: UBERGANGE ZU GEORGE RAPPS GOTTLICHE
       OKONOMIE AM OHIO UND ROBERT OWENS NEUE MORALISCHE WELT ZU
       NEW HARMONIE AM WABASCH.   Worcester, MA.: Harmony Society
       Press, 1982.

935.   ------.   "Harmony Society and Wilhelm Meisters Wanderjahre."
       COMPARATIVE LITERATURE.   10 (Summer 1958): 193-202.

936.   ------.   "The Indiana Decade of George Rapp's Harmony Society,
       1814-1824."   PROCEEDINGS OF THE AMERICAN ANTIQUARIAN
       SOCIETY.   80, part 2 (October 21, 1970): 299-323.

937.   ------.   "Pious Fraud: Rapp's 1805 Harmony Society Articles of
       Association."   WESTERN PENNSYLVANIA HISTORICAL MAGAZINE.
       68 (July 1985): 277-286.

938.   ------.   "Rapp's Harmony Society as an Institution 'calculated to
       Undermine and Destroy Those Fundamental Principles of Free
       Government,Which Have Conspiculously Distinguished Us From
       All the Nations of the Earth.'"   WESTERN PENNSYLVANIA
       HISTORICAL MAGAZINE.   63 (October 1980): 359-366.

939.   ------.   "Review of John S. Duss; THE HARMONISTS."   WESTERN
       PENNSYLVANIA HISTORICAL MAGAZINE.   26 (September-December
       1943): 109-116.

940.   ------.   "The Strange and Wonderful New World of George Rapp and
       His Harmony Society."   WESTERN PENNSYLVANIA HISTORICAL
       MAGAZINE. 57 (April 1974): 141-166.

941.   ------, and Patrick R. Brostowin.   "Pragmatists and Prophets:
       George Rapp and J.A. Roebling versus J.A. Etzler and Count
       Leon."   WESTERN PENNSYLVANIA HISTORICAL MAGAZINE.   52
       (January 1969): 1-27; (April 1969): 171-198.

942.   ------, and Richard D. Wetzel. "Harmonist Music and Pittsburgh
        Musicians in Early Economy." THE WESTERN PENNSYLVANIA
        HISTORICAL MAGAZINE. 54 (April 1971): 125-157; (July
        1971): 284-311; (October 1971): 391-413.

943.   Baker, Romelius L. "Another Rappite Letter." Ed. John C.
        Andressohn. INDIANA MAGAZINE OF HISTORY. 51 (December
        1955): 359-360.

944.   ------. "Description of Economy, Beaver County, Pennsylvania."
        Historical Society of Pennsylvania. MEMOIRS. 4, Part 2.
        Philadelphia, 1850. pp 183-187.

945.   Bausman, Joseph Henderson. HISTORY OF BEAVER COUNTY,
        PENNSYLVANIA AND ITS CENTENNIAL CELEBRATION. New York:
        The Knickerbocker Press, 1904. 2 vols., II, 1004-1030.

946.   Bernhard, Karl, Duke of Saxe-Weimar Eisenach. TRAVELS THROUGH
        NORTH AMERICA, DURING THE YEARS 1825 AND 1826. 2 vols. in
        1. Philadelphia: Carey, Lea & Carey, 1828. II, pp.
        106-123.

947.   Birkbeck, Morris. NOTES ON A JOURNEY IN AMERICA. London:
        Severn & Co., 1818. Reprint. Clifton, NJ.: A.M. Kelley,
        1971.

948.   Blair, Don. HARMONIST CONSTRUCTION PRINCIPALLY AS FOUND IN THE
        TWO-STORY HOUSES BUILT IN HARMONIE, INDIANA 1814-1824.
        Indianapolis: Indiana Historical Society, 1964.

949.   ------. THE NEW HARMONY STORY. New Harmony, IN.: Publications
        Committee, 1967.

950.   Bole, John Archibald. THE HARMONY SOCIETY: A CHAPTER IN GERMAN
        AMERICAN CULTURE HISTORY. Philadelphia: Americana
        Germanica Press, 1904. Reprint. New York: AMS Press,
        1973.

951.   Brauns, Ernst Ludwig. AMERIKA UND DIE MODERNE VOLKER WANDERUNG.
        NEBSTEINER DARSTELLUNG DER GEGENWARTIG ZU OKONOMIE--
        ECONOMY AM OHIO ANGESIEDELTEN HARMONIE--GESELLSCHAFT UND
        EINEM KUPFER GEORG RAPP, LEITER DER HARMONIE--
        GESELLSCHAFT, VORSTELLAND. Potsdam: H. Vogler, 1833.

952.   Buckingham, James Silk. THE EASTERN AND WESTERN STATES OF
        AMERICA. 3 vols. London: Fisher, Son & Co., 1842. II,
        205-236. Microfilm. Ann Arbor: University Microfilms,
        1960.

953.   Byrd, Cecil K. "The Harmony Society and Thoughts on the Destiny
        of Man." THE INDIANA UNIVERSITY BOOKMAN. 1 (January
        1956): 5-15.

954. CHRISTIAN POLICY IN FULL PRACTICE AMONG THE PEOPLE OF HARMONY, A
      TOWN IN THE STATE OF PENNSYLVANIA, NORTH AMERICA; AS
      DESCRIBED IN MELISH'S TRAVELS THROUGH THE UNITED STATES,
      AND BIRKBECK'S NOTES ON A JOURNEY IN AMERICA. TO WHICH
      ARE SUBJOINED, A CONCISE VIEW OF THE SPENCEAN SYSTEM OF
      AGRARIAN FELLOWSHIP AND SOME OBSERVATIONS ON THE MANIFEST
      SIMILARITY BETWEEN THE PRINCIPLES OF THAT SYSTEM AND OF
      THE TRULY FRATERNAL AND CHRISTIANLY ESTABLISHMENT OF THE
      HARMONITES. BY A SPENCEAN PHILANTHROPIST. London: 1818.

955. CONTEMPORARY EDUCATION. 58 (Winter 1987).

956. Davis, W. G. "The Passing of the Rappists." GUNTON'S MAGAZINE.
      25 (July 1903): 20-26.

957. Denehie, Elizabeth Smith. "The Harmonist Movement." INDIANA
      MAGAZINE OF HISTORY. 19 (June 1923): 188-200.

958. Douglas, Paul H. "The Material Culture of the Harmony Society."
      PENNSYLVANIA FOLKLIFE. 24 (Autumn 1975): 2-16.

959. Duncan, James. ANIMADVERSIONS ON THE PRINCIPLES OF THE NEW
      HARMONY SOCIETY. Indianapolis: Printed for the author,
      by Douglass and Maguire, 1826.

960. Duss, John Samuel. "The Dawn of Economy's Golden Day." WESTERN
      PENNSYLVANIA HISTORICAL MAGAZINE. 52 (March-June 1942):
      37-46.

961. ------. GEORGE RAPP AND HIS ASSOCIATES (THE HARMONY SOCIETY).
      Address Delivered by J.S. Duss, June 4, Nineteen Hundred
      Fourteen, at the Centennial Celebration at New Harmony,
      Ind. Indianapolis: The Hollenback Press, 1914.

962. ------. THE HARMONISTS; A PERSONAL HISTORY. (Harrisburg, PA.:
      Pennsylvania Book Service, 1943.)

963. ------. THE MARCH OF TIME, SOUVENIR OF OLD ECONOMY. Words and
      Music by J.S. Duss. n.p. 1921.

964. Flesher, Tonya K., and Dale L. Flesher. "The Contributions of
      Accounting to the Early Success of the Harmonists."
      COMMUNAL SOCIETIES. 4 (Fall 1984): 109-120.

965. Friesen, Gerhard K. "An Additional Source on the Harmony
      Society of Economy, Pennsylvania." WESTERN PENNSYLVANIA
      HISTORICAL MAGAZINE. 61 (October 1978): 301-314.

966. Gormley, Agnes, M. Hays. "Economy--A Unique Community."
      WESTERN PENNSYLVANIA HISTORICAL MAGAZINE. 1 (July 1918):
      113-131.

967. ------. OLD ECONOMY. Sewickley, PA.: George Hays Printer, 1966.

968.   Hall, Ben. "Old Economy: `The Silent Village.'" CARNEGIE
        MAGAZINE. 31 (1957): 185-190.

969.   HARMONISCHES GESANGBUCH. THEILS VON ANDEREN AUTHOREN, THEILS
        NEU VERFASST. ZUM GEBRAUCH FUR SINGEN UND MUSIK, FUR ALTE
        UND JUNGE. NACH GESCHMACK UND UMSTANDEN ZU WAHLEN
        GEWIDMET. Oekonomie, Beaver County, im Staat
        Pennsylvanien, 1827.

970.   "The Harmonists." ATLANTIC MONTHLY. 17 (May 1866): 529-538.

971.   Harmony Society. GEDANKEN UBER DIE BESTIMMUNG DES MENSCHEN,
        BESONDERS IN HINSICHT DER GEGENWARTIGEN ZEIT; VON DER
        HARMONIE GESELLSCHAFT IN INDIANA. New Harmony: 1824.

972.   Harmony Society. THOUGHTS ON THE DESTINY OF MAN, PARTICULARLY
        WITH REFERENCE TO THE PRESENT TIMES, BY THE HARMONY
        SOCIETY IN INDIANA. New Harmony, 1824.

973.   Hays, George A. THE CHURCHES OF THE HARMONY SOCIETY. Ambridge,
        PA.: Old Economy, 1964.

974.   ------. EARLY AMERICAN PRINTING AND THE 1822 HARMONY WOOD PRESS.
        Ambridge, PA.: Old Economy, 1961.

975.   ------. FOUNDERS OF THE HARMONY SOCIETY. Ambridge, PA.: Old
        Economy, 1959.

976.   ------. GERTRUD RAPP. Ambridge, PA.: Old Economy, 1959.

977.   ------. THE GROTTO AT OLD ECONOMY. 2nd ed. Ambridge, PA.: Old
        Economy, 1963.

978.   ------. THE SILK INDUSTRY AND OTHER CRAFTS OF THE HARMONIE
        SOCIETY. Ambridge, PA.: Old Economy, 1964.

979.   Hebert, William. A VISIT TO THE COLONY OF HARMONY, IN INDIANA
        IN THE UNITED STATES OF AMERICA. London: George Mann,
        1825.

980.   Heuss, Theodor. SCHATTENBESCHWORUNG: RANDFIGUREN DER
        GESCHICHTE. Stuttgart and Tubingen: R. Wunderlich, 1947,
        pp. 117-128.

981.   Holliday, John H. "An Indiana Village, New Harmony." INDIANA
        HISTORICAL SOCIETY PUBLICATIONS. 5, No. 4 (1914):
        201-229.

982.   Hulme, Thomas. "A Journal Made During a Tour in the Western
        Countries of America, September 30, 1818--August 7, 1819."
        EARLY WESTERN TRAVELS, Reuben Gold Thwaites, ed. Vol. 10.
        Cleveland: A.H. Clark Co., 1904, pp. 50, 53-61.

983. Johns, H. "Economy, Pennsylvania Today." HARPERS WEEKLY. 37
     (February 25, 1893): 173-175.

984. Knoedler, Christina F. THE HARMONY SOCIETY; A
     NINETEENTH-CENTURY AMERICAN UTOPIA. New York: Vantage
     Press, 1954.

985. Knortz, Karl. DIE CHRISTLICH-KOMMUNISTISCHE KOLDER RAPPISTEN IN
     PENNSYLVANIEN UND NEUE MITTEILUNGEN UBER NIKOLAUS LENEAU'S
     AUFENTHALT UNTER DEN RAPPISTEN. Leipzig: E. Wiest, 1892.

986. Knox, Julie Le Clerc. "The Unique Little Town of New Harmony."
     INDIANA MAGAZINE OF HISTORY. 32 (March 1936): 52-58.

987. Kring, Hilda Adam. THE HARMONISTS: A FOLK-CULTURAL APPROACH.
     Metuchen, NJ.: The Scarecrow Press and The American
     Theological Library Association, 1973.

988. Larner, John. "Nails and Sundrie Medicines: Town Planning and
     Public Health in the Harmony Society, 1805-1840." WESTERN
     PENNSYLVANIA HISTORICAL MAGAZINE. 45 (June 1962):
     115-138; (September 1962): 209-227.

989. Leffel, John C., ed. HISTORY OF POSEY COUNTY, INDIANA.
     Chicago: Goodspeed Publishing Co., 1886. Reprint.
     Owensboro, KY.: McDowell Publishers, 1982.

990. Lindley, Harlow, ed. INDIANA AS SEEN BY EARLY TRAVELERS: A
     COLLECTION OF REPRINTS. Indianapolis: Indiana Historical
     Commission, 1916. pp. 360-417.

991. Lockridge, Ross F. THE LABYRINTHE: A HISTORY OF THE NEW HARMONY
     LABYRINTHE, INCLUDING SOME SPECIAL STUDY OF THE SPIRITUAL
     AND MYSTICAL LIFE OF ITS BUILDERS, THE RAPPITES, AND A
     BRIEF SURVEY OF LABYRINTHS GENERALLY. New Harmony, IN.:
     The New Harmony Memorial Commission, 1941.

992. Macartney, Clarence Edward. NOT FAR FROM PITTSBURGH.
     Pittsburgh: Gibson Press, 1936.

993. ------. "The Passing of the Harmonites: A Story of a Successful
     Communistic Venture." PENNSYLVANIA MAGAZINE OF HISTORY
     AND BIOGRAPHY. 39, no. 3 (1915): 337-344.

994. [MacDonald, Donald]. THE DIARIES OF DONALD MACDONALD,
     1824-1826. Introduction by Caroline D. Snedeker. INDIANA
     HISTORICAL SOCIETY PUBLICATIONS, Vol. 14, no. 2, pp.
     147-379. Indianapolis: Indiana Historical Society, 1942.
     Reprint. Clifton, NJ.: A.M. Kelley, 1973.

995. Mason, Harrison D. OLD ECONOMY AS I KNEW IT. IMPRESSIONS OF
     THE HARMONITES, THEIR VILLAGE AND ITS SURROUNDING, AS SEEN
     ALMOST A HALF-CENTURY AGO. Crafton, PA.: Cramer Printing
     & Publishing Co., 1926.

996. Matter, Evelyn. "The Baker House." Ambridge, PA.: Old Economy,
      1968. (Mimeographed).

997. Maximilian, Prince of Wied. "Travels in the Interior of North
      America, 1832-1834." R.G. Thwaites, editor. EARLY
      WESTERN TRAVELS. Vol. 22. Cleveland: A.H. Clark Co.,
      1906.

998. Melish, John. ACCOUNT OF A SOCIETY AT HARMONY (TWENTY-FIVE
      MILES FROM PITTSBURGH) PENNSYLVANIA, UNITED STATES OF
      AMERICA. Taken from "Travels in the United States of
      America in the Years 1806 and 1807, and 1809, 1810, and
      1811." London, 1812.

999. ------. TRAVELS IN THE UNITED STATES OF AMERICA. Philadelphia,
      1818.

1000. Nevin, D.E. "The Late George Rapp and the Harmonists."
      SCRIBNER'S MONTHLY. 17 (March 1879): 703-712.

1001. "New Harmony." In INDIANA AND INDIANANS. Ed. Jacob Pratt Dunn.
      Chicago; New York: The American Historical Society, 1919.
      pp. 1071-1120.

1002. New York Society for Promoting Communities. AN ESSAY ON COMMON
      WEALTHS. New York: The New York Society for Promoting
      Communities, 1822.

1003. Passavant, William A. "A Visit to Economy in the Spring of
      1840." WESTERN PENNSYLVANIA HISTORICAL MAGAZINE. 4 (July
      1921): 144-149.

1004. Pelham, William. "Letters to William Creese Pelham 1825 and
      1826." INDIANA HISTORICAL COLLECTIONS. 3 (1916):
      360-417.

1005. Pennsylvania Historical and Museum Commission. OLD ECONOMY.
      Harrisburg: The Commission, 1947.

1006. Pitzer, Donald E. "The Harmonist Heritage of Three Towns."
      HISTORICAL PRESERVATION. 29 (October-December 1977):
      4-10.

1007. ------, and Josephine M. Elliott. "New Harmony's First Utopians,
      1814-1824." INDIANA MAGAZINE OF HISTORY. 75 (September
      1979): 224-300.

1008. Rauscher, Julian. "Des Separatisten G. Rapp Leben und Treiben."
      THEOLOGISCHE STUDIEN AUS WURTTEMBURG. 6 (1885): 253-313.

1009. Reibel, Daniel B. A GUIDE TO OLD ECONOMY. Harrisburg, PA.: The
      Pennsylvania Historical and Museum Commission, 1972.

1010. ------. "It All Came From Cloth." CARNEGIE MAGAZINE. 41 (1967): 203-207.

1011. ------. "Old Economy." CARNEGIE MAGAZINE. 38 (1965): 207-209, 212.

1012. Ritter, Christine C. "Life in Early America: Father Rapp and the Harmony Society." EARLY AMERICAN LIFE. 9 (February 1978): 40-43; 71-72.

1013. Schneck, Jacob, and Richard Owen. THE RAPPITES: INTERESTING NOTES ABOUT EARLY NEW HARMONY; GEORGE RAPP'S REFORM SOCIETY. Evansville, IN., 1890.

1014. Schott, Theodor. "Johann Georg Rapp." ALLGEMEINE DEUTSCHE BIOGRAPHIE. Vol. 27. Berlin: Duncker & Humblot, 1970. s.v.

1015. Sluder, Claude K. "Music in New Harmony Indiana, 1825-1865: A Study of the Music and Musical Activities of Robert Owen's Community of Equality (1825-1827) and Its Cultural Afterglow (1827-1865)." PhD. Diss. Indiana U., 1987.

1016. Stewart, Arthur I., and Loran W. Veith, compilers. HARMONY. Harmony, PA., 1955.

1017. Stewart, Arthur I., and Loran W. Veith. HARMONY, COMMEMORATING THE SESQUICENTENNIAL OF HARMONY, PENNSYLVANIA, 1805-1955. n.p. 1956.

1018. Stotz, Charles Morris. "Threshold of the Golden Kingdom: The Village of Economy and Its Restoration." WINTERTHUR PORTFOLIO 8. Edited by Ian M.G. Quimby. Charlottesville: Published for the Henry Francis du Pont Winterthur Museum by the University Press of Virginia, 1973. pp. 133-169.

1019. Stuart, Emily. "The Silent Village Lives Again." CARNEGIE MAGAZINE. 32 (1958): 133-135.

1020. Taylor, Ann. VISIONS OF HARMONY: A STUDY IN NINETEENTH CENTURY MILLENARIANISM. New York: Oxford University Press, 1987.

1021. Van Way, John Frank. "The Economic Systems of the New Harmony Communities." Urbana, IL.: 1940. (Typescript).

1022. Wetzel, Richard D. "Frontier Music-Makers." CARNEGIE MAGAZINE. 42 (1968): 343-347.

1023. ------. FRONTIER MUSICIANS ON THE CONNOQUENESSING, WABASH AND OHIO: A HISTORY OF THE MUSIC AND MUSICIANS OF GEORGE RAPP'S HARMONY SOCIETY (1805-1906). Athens, O.: Ohio University Press, 1976.

1024. ------. "Harmonist Music Between 1827 and 1832: A Reappraisal."
       COMMUNAL SOCIETIES. 2 (Autumn 1978): 65-84.

1025. ------. "J.C. Muller & W.C. Peters at Economy: A Reappraisal."
       COMMUNAL SOCIETIES. 3 (Fall 1983): 158-174.

1026. Whicker, John Wesley. HISTORICAL SKETCHES OF THE WABASH VALLEY.
       Attica, IN.: The Author, 1916. pp. 116-125.

1027. Williams, Aaron. THE HARMONY SOCIETY AT ECONOMY, PENN'A,
       FOUNDED BY GEORGE RAPP, A.D. 1805. Pittsburgh: W.S.
       Haven, 1866. Reprint. New York: AMS Press, 1971.

1028. Wilson, William Edward. THE ANGEL AND THE SERPENT; THE STORY OF
       NEW HARMONY. Bloomington, IN.: Indiana University Press,
       1964.

1029. Woods, John. "Two Years' Residence in the Settlement on the
       English Prairie in the Illinois Country." EARLY WESTERN
       TRAVELS. R.G. Thwaites, editor. Vol. 10, Cleveland, O.:
       1904. pp. 312-314.

1030. Yelland, John Hornstein. "The Garden Grotto at Old Economy."
       Ambridge, PA.: Old Economy, 1959. Mimeographed.

1031. Young, Marguerite. ANGEL IN THE FOREST, A FAIRY TALE OF TWO
       UTOPIAS. New York: Reynal & Hitchcock,1945. 2d ed. New
       York: Scribners, 1966.

1032. Young, Norman C., comp. and ed. OLD ECONOMY-AMBRIDGE
       SESQUICENTENNIAL HANDBOOK. Ambridge, PA: The Author,
       1974.

1033. Young, Otis E. "Personnel of the Rappite Community of Harmony,
       Indiana, in the Year 1824." INDIANA MAGAZINE OF HISTORY.
       47 (September 1951): 313-319.

Blooming Grove (1805- ?)

Friedrich Conrad Haller, a Wurttemburg dissenter left   the
Rapp community with a group of separatists to form the Blooming
Grove Colony of Dunkers.

1034. Durnbaugh, D. F. "Blooming Grove Colony." THE BRETHREN
       ENCYCLOPEDIA. Philadelphia; Oak Brook, IL.: The Brethren
       Encyclopedia, Inc., s.v.

1035. ------. "Blooming Grove Colony." PENNSYLVANIA DUTCHMAN. 25
       (Spring 1976): 18-23.

1036. Gilbert, Russell Wieder. "Autobiography of Ernst Max Adam,
       M.D." SUSQUEHANNA UNIVERSITY STUDIES. 5 (1953): 17-49.

1037. ------. "Blooming Grove, the Dunker Settlement in Central
       Pennsylvania." PENNSYLVANIA HISTORY. 20 (January-October
       1953): 22-39.

1038. McMinn, Joseph H. BLOOMING GROVE, A HISTORY OF THE CONGREGATION
       OF GERMAN DUNKERS WHO SETTLED IN LYCOMING COUNTY,
       PENNSYLVANIA, 1805. Williamsport, PA.: Scholl Bros.,
       1901.

1039. Royer, Galen B., ed. A HISTORY OF THE CHURCH OF THE BRETHREN IN
       THE MIDDLE DISTRICT OF PENNSYLVANIA. [n.p.]: District
       Conference, 1925.

1040. Ulmer, D. C. BRIEF HISTORICAL SKETCH OF THE BLOOMING GROVE
       COLONY. n.d.

The Count Leon (Bernhard Muller) Colonies

       Bernhard Muller, a religious mystic from Germany, travelled in
       the U.S. under the alias Count Leon. He visited Economy, Pa.,
       where he tried to usurp the leadership of George Rapp. He
       succeeded in taking a group of Harmonist secessionists with him
       to form the New Philadelphia Society (1832-1833) just ten miles
       away. When this colony dissolved he led a group to Louisiana to
       form Grand Encore (1834-1833) in Natchitoches Parish. Following
       his death in 1834 his followers organized Germantown (1836-1871)
       in Webster Parish, Louisiana.

                          ARCHIVAL MATERIALS

1041. New Philadelphia Society (Louisiana). Records, 1832-1837.
       Library of Congress, Manuscript Division, Washington, D.C.

                          ARTICLES AND BOOKS

1042. Arndt, Karl J. R. "The Genesis of Germantown, Louisiana: or the
       Mysterious Past of Louisiana's Mystic, Count de Leon."
       LOUISIANA HISTORICAL QUARTERLY. 24 (April 1941): 378-433.

1043. ------. "The Life and Mission of Count Leon." AMERICAN-GERMAN
       REVIEW. 6 (June 1940): 5-8; 36-37; (August 1940): 15-19.

1044. DER CHRISTEN-BOTE: EINE ALLGEMEINE CHRISTLICHE ZEITSCHRIFT, ed.
       Johann Christian Friederich Burk. Stuttgart, 1852.

1045. Jennings, Pauline. "Eliza Leon: First Lady of the Germantown
       Colony." NORTH LOUISIANA HISTORICAL ASSOCIATION JOURNAL.
       8 (1977): 43-51.

1046. Koch, Carl G. LEBENSERFAHRUNGEN. Cleveland, O.: Gedruckt im
       verlagshaus der Evangelischen gemeinschaft. 1871.

1047. Pennybacker, S. W. "The Settlement of Germantown,"
           PENNSYLVANIA-GERMAN SOCIETY, PROCEEDINGS AND ADDRESSES. 9
           (1898): 229-263.

1048. Wagner, Jonathan. GESCHICHTE UND VERHALTNISSE DER
           HARMONIE-GESELLSCHAFT IN NORD-AMERIKA. Ed. W.G.
           Deininger. Vailhinger: C. Burkhart, 1883.

1049. DERWUNDERMANN DES NEUNZEHNTEN JAHRHUNDERTS. Trans. J.
           Kreideburg. Hanau, 1833.

HARRIS, THOMAS LAKE, AND COLONIES

Born May 15, 1823 in Fenny Stratford, England, his family moved
to upstate New York. Coming under the influence of
Swedenborgian spiritualism, Harris founded and led the
spiritualist colonies of Mountain Cove Community (1851-1853) in
Fayette County, Virginia (now West Virginia); the Brotherhood of
New Life (1863-1867) in Dutchess County, New York; Brocton
Community (1867-1881), Chautauqua County, New York; and Fountain
Grove (1876-1900), in Sonoma County, California.

ARCHIVAL MATERIALS

1050. Harris, Thomas Lake. Records, 1854-1942. Special Collections
       Library, Columbia University, New York, and Wagner College
       Library, Staten Island, New York. Microfilm. Glen Rock,
       NJ.: Microfilming Corporation of America, 1974.

ARTICLES AND BOOKS

1051. Cuthbert, Arthur A. THE LIFE AND WORLD-WORK OF THOMAS LAKE
       HARRIS, Written From Direct Personal Knowledge. Glasgow:
       C.W. Pearce, 1908.

1052. Harris, Thomas Lake. AIMS AND ISSUES OF THE NEW CHURCH.
       Glasgow: James Fowler, 1863.

1053. ------. ARCANA OF CHRISTIANITY: AN UNFOLDING OF THE CELESTIAL
       SENSE OF THE DIVINE WORD, THROUGH T.W. HARRIS. 2 vols.
       New York: New Church Publishing Association, 1858-1867.
       Reprint. New York: AMS Press, 1976.

1054. ------. APPENDIX TO THE ARCANA OF CHRISTIANITY. New York: New
       Church Publishing Association, 1858.

1055. ------. THE BREATH OF GOD WITH MAN: AN ESSAY ON THE GROUNDS AND
       EVIDENCES OF UNIVERSAL RELIGION. New York: Brotherhood of
       New Life, 1867.

1056. ------. BRIDAL HOURS. Santa Rosa, CA.: Fountaingrove Press,
       1878.

1057. ------. BROTHERHOOD OF THE NEW LIFE: ITS FACT, LAW, METHOD, AND
       PURPOSE; LETTER FROM THOMAS LAKE HARRIS WITH PASSING
       REFERENCE TO RECENT CRITICISMS. Santa Rose, CA.:
       Fountaingrove Press; London: E.W. Allen, 1891.

1058. ------. CAME THE CYCLONE YESTERDAY... [n.p.], 1894.

1059. ------. THE CONCEPTS OF THE WORD. n.p., [1878].

1060. ------. CONVERSATION IN HEAVEN, A WISDOM SONG. Santa Rosa, CA.:
       Fountaingrove, Priv. print., 1894.

1061. ------. DECLARATIONS OF THE DIVINE ONE-TWAIN. Santa Rosa, CA.:
       1882.

1062. ------. DEDICATION ODE FOR THE HOUSE OF JESUS AND YESSA. Santa
       Rosa, CA.: 1878.

1063. ------. DIVINE CHARITY. London: White, 1859.

1064. ------. AN EPIC OF THE STARRY HEAVEN. New York: Partridge &
       Brittan, 1854.

1065. ------. EXTEMPORANEOUS SERMONS; PREACHED IN THE MARYLEBONE
       INSTITUTE, LONDON, IN THE YEAR, 1860, BY THOMAS L. HARRIS.
       Collated and edited by Thomas Robinson... Manchester:
       Ratcliffe & Co., printers, 1879.

1066. ------. FIRST BOOK OF THE CHRISTIAN RELIGION. New York: New
       Church Publishing Association, 1858.

1067. ------. FRAGMENTS. 1896.

1068. ------. GOD'S BREATH IN MAN AND IN HUMAN SOCIETY. Santa Rosa,
       CA.: Fountaingrove Press, The Author, 1891.

1069. ------. THE GOLDEN CHILD; A DAILY CHRONICLE. Santa Rosa, CA.:
       Fountaingrove Press, 1878.

1070. ------. THE GREAT REPUBLIC: A POEM OF THE SUN. London: E.W.
       Allen, 1867, 1891.

1071. ------. THE GREAT REPUBLIC: A POEM OF THE SUN. New York; London:
       Brotherhood of the New Life, 1867.

1072. ------. HE THAT HATH THE BRIDE. [n.p.], August, 1893.

1073. ------. HEART-WANTS OF LONDON. [n.p., 1859?]

1074. ------. THE HOLY CITY AND THE LIGHT THEREIN. Fountaingrove,
       Santa Rosa, CA.: Priv. Print., 1880.

1075. ------. HYMNS OF SPIRITUAL DEVOTION. New York: New Church
       Publishing Association. 1858.

1076. ------. HYMNS OF SPIRITUAL DEVOTION: FOR THE NEW CHRISTIAN AGE.
       New York: New Church Publishing Association, 1861.

1077. ------. HYMNS OF THE TWO-IN-ONE: FOR BRIDAL WORSHIP IN THE
       KINGDOM OF THE NEW LIFE. PART FIRST. Salem-on-Erie, NY.:
       Brotherhood of the New Life, 1876.

1078. ------. IN DAWNRISE; A SONG OF SONGS. DEDICATED IN FAITH, LOVE
       AND ADORATION TO OUR LADY CHRISTA-YESSA, ONE WITH CHRIST
       JESUS, OUR LIFE AND LORD. Fountaingrove, Santa Rosa, CA.:
       Priv. Print., 1896.

1079. ------. INWARD PRAYER; AND A FEW NOTES. Santa Rosa, CA.:
       Fountaingrove Press, 1896.

1080. ------. THE JOY BRINGER: FIFTY THREE MELODIES OF THE
       ONE-IN-TWAIN. FEBRUARY-MARCH, 1886. A BIRTHDAY GIFT, FROM
       FOUNTAINGROVE. Santa Rosa, CA.: Fountaingrove Press,
       1886.

1081. ------. JUVENILE DEPRAVITY AND CRIME IN OUR CITY. A
       SERMON...PREACHED IN THE STUYVESANT INSTITUTE...JAN. 13TH,
       1850. WITH AN APPENDIX EMBODYING THE RECENT REPORT OF
       THE CHIEF OF POLICE CONCERNING DESTITUTION AND CRIME AMONG
       CHILDREN IN THE CITY. New York: C.B. Norton, 1850.

1082. ------. THE LAST WORDS OF JESUS. London: White, 1859.

1083. ------. LECTURE ON SPIRITUAL MANIFESTATIONS, PAST AND PRESENT,
       AND FUTURE, DELIVERED IN THE PEOPLE'S THEATER, SAINT
       LOUIS, MO., SUNDAY EVENING, MARCH 24, 1853. Reported by
       E.S. Underhill. Boston: Geo. C. Rand, 1853.

1084. ------. A LETTER TO YOUNG MEN WHO, WHILE HAVING TENDER HEARTS,
       DOUBT THAT THERE IS A GOD. August, 1894: reprinted with
       notes, April, 1895.

1085. ------. THE LORD: THE TWO-IN-ONE; DECLARED, MANIFESTED, AND
       GLORIFIED. Salem on Erie, NY.: Brotherhood of the New
       Life, 1876.

1086. ------. THE LUMINOUS LIFE. Fountaingrove, Santa Rosa, CA.: Priv.
       Print., 1882.

1087. ------. LYRA TRIUMHPALIS[!]; PEOPLE SONGS: BALLADS AND MARCHES.
       Santa Rosa, CA.: Fountaingrove Press, 1891.

1088. ------. A LYRIC OF THE GOLDEN AGE. New York: Partridge and
       Brittan, 1856.

1089. ------. A LYRIC OF THE MORNING LAND. New York: Partridge and
       Brittan, 1854.

1090. ------. A LYRIC OF THE MARTYR AGE, BY A CHILD OF THE
       RESURRECTION. Glasgow: John Thomson, 1870.

1091. ------. THE MARRIAGE OF HEAVEN AND EARTH. VERIFIED REALITIES.
       Glasgow: C.W. Pearce & Co., 1903.

1092. ------. THE MILLENNIAL AGE: TWELVE DISCOURSES ON THE SPIRITUAL
       AND SOCIAL ASPECTS OF THE TIMES. EXTEMPORANEOUSLY SPOKEN

BY THOMAS L. HARRIS...IN THE MARYLEBONE INSTITUTE, LONDON,
FEBRUARY AND MARCH, 1860. Phonographically reported by
Mr. T.A. Reed. New York: New Church Publishing
Association, 1860.

1093. ------. THE MISSION OF THE NEW CHURCH, AND HOW IT IS TO BE
ACCOMPLISHED. Glasgow: James Fowler; London: Fred Pitman,
1863.

1094. ------. MODERN SPIRITUALISM. London: 1860.

1095. ------. THE NEW CHURCH: ITS SPIRIT, SCOPE AND MISSION. A LECTURE
DELIVERED IN THE CAIRO STREET SCHOOL-ROOM, WARRINGTON,
NOVEMBER 9, 1859. Manchester: Johnson and Rawson, 1860.

1096. ------. THE NEW CHURCH, SEEN IN ITS DOCTRINE OF REGENERATION. A
SERMON, PREACHED AT THE MARYLEBONE LITERARY AND SCIENTIFIC
INSTITUTION. EDWARDS STREET, PORTMAN SQUARE...MAY 29TH,
1859. London: W. White, 1859.

1097. ------. THE NEW JERUSALEM, THE CROWN OF CHURCHES AND THE GLORY OF
THE WORLD. A SERMON, PREACHED ON WEDNESDAY, MARCH 14TH,
1860, IN THE MECHANICS' HALL, NOTTINGHAM. London: W.
White, 1860.

1098. ------. THE NEW REPUBLIC; A DISCOURSE OF THE PROSPECTS, DANGERS,
DUTIES AND SAFETIES OF THE TIMES, ORIGINALLY ADDRESSED TO
THE SOCIALISTS OF AMERICA, BUT OF UNIVERSAL APPLICATION IN
PRINCIPLE. London: E.W. Allen, 1891.

1099. ------. THE NEW REPUBLIC. A DISCOURSE OF THE PROSPECTS, DANGERS,
DUTIES AND SAFETIES OF THE TIMES. Santa Rosa, CA.:
Fountaingrove Press, 1891.

1100. ------. THE POWER AND GLORY OF THE CHURCH OF CHRIST. London: W.
White, 1860.

1101. ------. PROBABLE GROUNDS OF CHRISTIAN UNION. A LECTURE DELIVERED
IN THE CAIRO STREET SCHOOL-ROOM, WARRINGTON, OCTOBER 19,
1859. Manchester: Johnson and Rawson, 1859.

1102. ------. THE RE-EVOLUTION IN THE LORD'S REDEMPTION. Fountaingrove, CA: Privately printed, 1895.

1103. ------. REGINA: A SONG OF MANY DAYS. London: W. White; New York:
New Church Publishing Association, 1860.

1104. ------. SECOND BOOK OF FRAGMENTS. n.p., 1897.

1105. ------. THE SECOND VISIBILITY OF JESUS ... (SERMON PREACHED ...
FEB. 12, 1860). London: n.p., 1860.

1106. ------. SERMONS, PREACHED IN THE MECHANICS' INSTITUTION, DAVID
STREET. Manchester, n.p., 1859.

1107. ------. SERMONS, PREACHED IN THE STORE STREET MUSIC HALL, LONDON.
       London: W. White; Manchester: Johnson & Rawson, 1860.

1108. ------. THE SONG OF SATAN; A SERIES OF POEMS, ORIGINATING WITH A
       SOCIETY OF INFERNAL SPIRITS, AND RECEIVED DURING
       TEMPTATION-COMBATS. 2nd ed. New York: New Church
       Publishing Association, 1860.

1109. ------. THE SONG OF THEOS. A TRILOGY. PART I. EASTER. PART II.
       EMANCIPATIONS. PART III. AVATAR. Glasgow: C.W. Pearce, &
       Co., 1903.

1110. ------. STAR-FLOWERS, A POEM OF THE WOMAN'S MYSTERY. Santa Rosa,
       CA: Fountaingrove, Priv. print., 1896.

1111. ------. "THEY CHANGE TO ANGELS BY DEGREES ..." In Rogers, E.H.
       NATIONAL LIFE IN THE SPIRIT WORLD. Chelsea, MA: 1891.

1112. ------. THE THREE PRINCIPLES: THE GREATER EVIL-THE LESSER EVIL-
       NO EVIL. Santa Rosa, CA: 1878.

1113. ------. THE TRIUMPH OF LIFE. Glasgow: C.W. Pearce & Co., 1903

1114. ------. TRUTH AND LIFE IN JESUS. PREACHED IN THE MECHANICS'
       INSTITUTION, DAVID STREET, MANCHESTER, OCTOBER, NOVEMBER
       AND DECEMBER, 1859. Manchester: T. Robinson, 1860.

1115. ------. "TRUTH AND LOVE WILL TRIUMPH." THE GNOSTIC. 1 (July
       1881): 301.

1116. ------. VERITAS, A WORD-SONG. Glasgow: C.W. Pearce & Co., 1910.

1117. ------. A VOICE FROM HEAVEN... Fountaingrove, Santa Rosa, CA:
       Priv. Print., 1879.

1118. ------. THE WEDDING-GUEST: JESUS-IN-YESSA. Fountaingrove, CA:
       Printed and published for the Brotherhood of the New Life,
       1877-1888.

1119. ------. WHITE ROSES FOR THE PASS. 2 vols. Glasgow: C.W. Pearce &
       Co., 1910.

1120. ------. THE WISDOM OF ANGELS. New York: New Church Publishing
       Association, 1857.

1121. ------. THE WISDOM OF THE ADEPTS. ESOTERIC SCIENCE IN HUMAN
       HISTORY. Fountaingrove, Santa Rosa, CA: Priv. print.,
       1884.

1122. Henderson, Philip. THE LIFE OF LAURENCE OLIPHANT: TRAVELER,
       DIPLOMAT AND MYSTIC. London: R. Hale, 1956. Reprint.
       Arden Library, 1981.

1123. THE HERALD OF LIGHT: A MONTHLY JOURNAL OF THE LORD'S NEW CHURCH.
       v. 1-6; May 1857-Aug. 1, 1861. New York: New Church
       Publishing Association, 1857-1861.

1124. Howells, William Dean. REVIEW OF REVIEWS. (London) September
       1909.

1125. Kagan, Paul. NEW WORLD UTOPIAS. New York: Penguin Books, 1975.

1126. McCully, Richard. THE BROTHERHOOD OF THE NEW LIFE AND THOMAS
       LAKE HARRIS: A HISTORY AND EXPOSITION BASED UPON THEIR
       PRINTED WORKS AND UPON OTHER PUBLIC DOCUMENTS. Glasgow:
       J. Thomson, 1893. Reprinted and revised as THE
       BROTHERHOOD OF THE NEW LIFE: AN EPITOME OF THE WORK AND
       TEACHING OF THOMAS LAKE HARRIS. 3rd ed. Glasgow: J.
       Thomson, 1914.

1127. ------. TRIBUTE TO SIR THOMAS LAKE HARRIS. Santa Rosa, CA: Santa
       Rosa Commandory, Knights Templar, 1906.

1128. Oliphant, Laurence. MASOLLAM; A PROBLEM OF THE PERIOD. 3 vols.
       Edinburgh; London: W. Blackwood and Sons, 1886.
       (Fiction).

1129. Oliphant, Margaret Oliphant Wilson. MEMOIR OF THE LIFE OF
       LAURENCE OLIPHANT AND OF ALICE OLIPHANT, HIS WIFE. 2
       vols. New York: Harper & Brothers; Edinburgh: William
       Blackwood and Sons, 1891.

1130. Schneider, Herbert Wallace, and George Lawton. A PROPHET AND A
       PILGRIM: BEING THE INCREDIBLE HISTORY OF THOMAS LAKE
       HARRIS AND LAWRENCE OLIPHANT; THE SEXUAL MYSTICISM AND
       UTOPIAN COMMUNITIES AMPLY DOCUMENTED TO CONFOUND THE
       SKEPTIC. New York: Columbia University Press, 1942.
       Reprint. New York: AMS Press, 1970.

1131. Swainson, W.P. THOMAS LAKE HARRIS AND HIS OCCULT TEACHINGS.
       London: William Rider & Son, 1922.

1132. Taylor, Anne. "Darkness Into Light: Laurence Oliphant's
       Experience of Communal Discipline in the United States and
       Palestine." COMMUNAL SOCIETIES. 4 (Fall 1984): 87-96.

1133. ------. LAURENCE OLIPHANT, 1829-1888. New York: Oxford, 1982.

HOPEDALE (1842-1867)

Founded by Adin Ballou at Milford, Massachusetts, out of a universalist church as an experiment in industrial utopianism.

ARCHIVAL MATERIALS

1134. Hopedale Community. Records. 1821-1938. Bancroft Library, Hopedale, Massachusetts. Microfilm. Glen Rock, NJ: Microfilming Corporation of America, 1976.

BIBLIOGRAPHIES

1135. Ballou, Adin. CATALOGUE OF THE PRIVATE LIBRARY OF THE LATE REV. ADIN BALLOU, HOPEDALE, MASS., FOUNDER OF THE HOPEDALE COMMUNITY. TOGETHER WITH OTHER CONSIGNMENTS INCLUDING BOOKS AND PAMPHLETS RELATING TO THE HOPEDALE COMMUNITY OR PRINTED BY THE HOPEDALE PRESS. Boston: C.F. Libbie & Co., 1916.

ARTICLES AND BOOKS

1136. Ballou, Adin Augustus. ADDRESS DELIVERED BEFORE THE THWING FAMILY ANNUAL GATHERING, AT EBENEZER D. AND ANNA T. DRAPER'S IN HOPEDALE, THANKSGIVING DAY, NOV. 19, 1849. WITH THE ORIGINAL HYMNS SUNG ON THE OCCASION. Hopedale, MA: Community Press; A.G. Spalding, printer, 1849.

1137. ------. AN ADDRESS, DELIVERED IN THE CHAPEL AT HOPEDALE, MASS., FEB. 2, 1870; AT THE FUNERAL OF MRS. ANNA T. DRAPER, WIFE OF MR. EBENEZER D. DRAPER; WHO PASSED TO THE HIGHER LIFE, SUNDAY, JAN. 30, PRECEDING, AFTER A LONG AND DISTRESSING SICKNESS IN THE FULL ASSURANCE OF A BLISSFUL IMMORTALITY. Hopedale, MA: 1870.

1138. ------. AUTOBIOGRAPHY OF ADIN BALLOU, 1830-1890. CONTAINING AN ELABORATE RECORD AND NARRATIVE OF HIS LIFE FROM INFANCY TO OLD AGE. Ed. by his son-in-law, William S. Heywood. Lowell MA: The Vox Populi Press, 1896. Reprint. Philadelphia: Porcupine Press, 1975.

1139. ------. CHRISTIAN NON-RESISTANCE DEFENDED AGAINST REV. HENRY WARD BEECHER, IN HIS DISCOURSE ON EPHES. IV:13, PUBLISHED IN "THE INDEPENDENT", OF MARCH 14, 1861, BEING A REVIEW, IN PART, OF SAID DISCOURSE. Hopedale, MA: 1862. Reprint. New York: Garland, 1972.

1140. ------. CHRISTIAN NON-RESISTANCE, IN ALL ITS IMPORTANT BEARINGS, ILLUSTRATED AND DEFENDED. Philadelphia: J.M. M'Kim, 1846.

Reprint. New York: Da Capo Press, 1970. New York: J.S. Ozer, 1972.

1141. ------. CHRISTIAN SOCIALISM. Hopedale and New York, 1854.

1142. ------. CONCISE EXPOSITION OF THE HOPEDALE COMMUNITY: DESCRIPTIVE, STATISTICAL, HISTORICAL AND CONSTITUTIONAL. Hopedale, MA: 1853.

1143. ------. CONSTITUTION OF THE PRACTICAL CHRISTIAN MINISTRY. Hopedale, MA: 1848.

1144. ------. A DISCOURSE OF THE SUBJECT OF AMERICAN SLAVERY, DELIVERED IN THE FIRST CONGREGATIONAL MEETING HOUSE, IN MENDON, MASS., JULY 4, 1837. Boston: Printed by I. Knapp, 1837.

1145. ------. A DISCOURSE ON CHRISTIAN NON-RESISTANCE IN EXTREME CASES. Hopedale, Milford, MA: 1860. Reprint. New York: Garland, 1972.

1146. ------. AN ELABORATE HISTORY AND GENEALOGY OF THE BALLOUS IN AMERICA, CAREFULLY COMPILED AND EDITED BY ADIN BALLOU ... ARIEL BALLOU ... AND L.W. BALLOU ... PROPRIETARY PUBLISHERS. Providence, RI: Press of E.L. Freeman, & Son, 1888.

1147. ------. EPISTLE TO THE PRACTICAL CHRISTIAN COMMUNION: LEGAL AND POLITICAL ACTION. Hopedale, MA: 1849.

1148. ------. AN EXPOSITION OF VIEWS RESPECTING THE MODERN SPIRIT MANIFESTATIONS: TOGETHER WITH INTERESTING PHENOMENAL STATEMENTS AND COMMUNICATIONS. Boston: B. Marsh, 1852.

1149. ------. HISTORY OF THE HOPEDALE COMMUNITY FROM ITS INCEPTION TO ITS VIRTUAL SUBMERGENCE IN THE HOPEDALE PARISH. William S. Heywood, ed. Lowell, MA: Thompson & Hill--THE VOX POPULI PRESS, 1897. Reprint. Philadelphia: Porcupine Press, 1972. New York: AMS Press, 1974.

1150. ------. HISTORY OF THE TOWN OF MILFORD, WORCESTER COUNTY, MASSACHUSETTS, FROM ITS FIRST SETTLEMENT TO 1881. Boston: Franklin Press; Rand, Avery & Co., 1882.

1151. ------. THE HOPEDALE COLLECTION OF HYMNS AND SONGS FOR THE USE OF PRACTICAL CHRISTIANS. Hopedale, MA: 1849.

1152. ------. HUMAN PROGRESS IN RESPECT TO RELIGION: TWO DISCOURSES, DELIVERED IN THE CHAPEL AT HOPEDALE, MASS., MAY 26TH AND JUNE 9TH, 1867. I. ON THE TENDENCY OF THE AGE TO DISPENSE WITH THE SPECIALTIES AND PERSONAL RESPONSIBILITIES OF RELIGION. II. ON THE ULTIMATE CONVINCEMENT OF PROGRESSIVE MINDS IN FAVOR OF PURE CHRISTIAN RELIGION AND CHURCH. Hopedale, MA: 1867.

1153. ------. MEMOIR OF ADIN AUGUSTUS BALLOU: WRITTEN AND COMPILED BY HIS FATHER. Hopedale, MA: Community Press, 1853.

1154. ------. MONITORIAL GUIDE FOR THE USE OF INDUCTIVE CONFERENCES, COMMUNITIES, ETC., ETC., IN THE PRACTICAL CHRISTIAN REPUBLIC. Hopedale, MA: Spiritual Reformer Office, 1862.

1155. ------. NON-RESISTANCE IN RELATION TO HUMAN GOVERNMENTS. Boston: Non-Resistance Society, 1839.

1156. ------. ORATION DELIVERED BEFORE THE CITIZENS OF BLACKSTONE VILLAGE AT MENDON, MASS. July 5, 1830.

1157. ------. AN ORATION, DELIVERED JULY 4TH, A.D., 1827, BEFORE THE REPUBLICAN CITIZENS OF MILFORD, AND THE NEIGHBORING TOWNS AT THE UNIVERSALIST MEETING HOUSE, IN SAID MILFORD. Boston: True and Greene, Printers, 1827.

1158. ------. PRACTICAL CHRISTIAN SOCIALISM: A CONVERSATIONAL EXPOSITION OF THE TRUE SYSTEM OF HUMAN SOCIETY; IN THREE PARTS, VIZ: I. FUNDAMENTAL PRINCIPLES. II. CONSTITU-TIONAL POLITY. III. SUPERIORITY TO OTHER SYSTEMS. Hopedale, MA; New York: Fowlers and Wells, 1854. Reprint. New York: AMS Press, 1974.

1159. ------. PRACTICAL CHRISTIANITY AND ITS NON-RESISTANCE IN RELATION TO HUMAN GOVERNMENTS. Boston, 1839.

1160. ------. PRACTICAL CHRISTIANITY IN RELATION TO DIFFERENT CHRISTS AND CHRISTIANITIES. Hopedale, MA: 186?

1161. ------. PRACTICAL CHRISTIANITY IN RELATION TO THE DOGMA OF ENDLESS PUNISHMENT; PRESENTING THREE GRAND REASONS FOR ITS REJECTION. Hopedale, MA: Spiritual Reformer Office, 1860.

1162. ------. PRACTICAL CHRISTIANITY IN RELATION TO THE SUPERIORITY OF MORAL OVER POLITICAL POWER. Hopedale, MA: 186?

1163. ------. PRIMITIVE CHRISTIANITY AND ITS CORRUPTIONS ... DISCOURSES DELIVERED IN HOPEDALE MASS. 3 vols. Boston: Universalist Publishing House, 1870; Lowell: Thompson and Hull-Vox Populi Press, 1899. Vols. 2 and 3 ed. by William S. Heywood.

1164. ------. REPORT OF A PUBLIC DISCUSSION, BETWEEN THE REVS. ADIN BALLOU, AND DANIEL D. SMITH; ON THE QUESTION, "DO THE HOLY SCRIPTURES TEACH THE DOCTRINE, THAT MEN WILL BE PUNISHED AND REWARDED SUBSEQUENTLY TO THIS LIFE, OR AFTER DEATH, FOR THE DEEDS DONE IN THIS LIFE?" HELD IN BOSTON, ON TUESDAY, MARCH 18, A.D. 1834, AND CONTINUED THROUGH WEDNESDAY AND THURSDAY. Mendon, MA: G.W. Stacy, printer, 1834.

1165. ------. THE TOUCHSTONE EXHIBITING UNIVERSALISM AND RESTORATIONISM
       AS THEY ARE MORAL CONTRARIES. BY A CONSISTENT RESTORA-
       TIONIST. Providence: Cranston & Co., 1837.

1166. ------. THE TRUE SCRIPTURAL DOCTRINE OF THE SECOND ADVENT; AN
       EFFECTUAL ANTIDOTE TO MILLERISM, AND OTHER KINDRED ERRORS.
       Hopedale, MA: Community Press, 1843.

1167. ------. VIOLATIONS OF THE FEDERAL CONSTITUTION IN THE
       "IRREPRESSIBLE CONFLICT" BETWEEN THE PROSLAVERY AND THE
       ANTI-SLAVERY SENTIMENTS OF THE AMERICAN PEOPLE; A LECTURE
       DELIVERED IN SUNDRY PLACES DURING JANUARY AND FEBRUARY,
       1861. Hopedale, Milford, MA: Spiritual Reformer Office,
       1861.

1168. ------. THE VOICE OF DUTY. AN ADDRESS DELIVERED AT THE
       ANTI-SLAVERY PICNIC AT WESTMINSTER, MASS., JULY 4, 1843.
       Hopedale, Milford, MA: Community Press, 1843.

1169. Cary, George L. "Adin Ballou and the Hopedale Community." NEW
       WORLD: A QUARTERLY REVIEW OF RELIGION ETHICS AND THEOLOGY.
       7 (December 1898): 670-683.

1170. Coffey, David M. "The Hopedale Community." HISTORY JOURNAL OF
       WESTERN MASSACHUSETTS. 4 (Winter 1975): 16-26.

1171. Faulkner, Barbara Louise. "Adin Ballou and the Hopedale
       Community." PhD diss. Boston University, 1965.

1172. THE FRATERNAL COMMUNION. CONSTITUTION ... WITH AN EXPOSITION OF
       THE SAME; INCLUDING THE FIRST PROCEEDINGS OF FRATERNAL
       COMMUNITY, NO. 1. Mendon, MA: 1841.

1173. Heywood, William Sweetzer. A COLLECTION OF PORTRAITS OF HIS
       FAMILY, AUTOGRAPHS OF HIS FRIENDS AND VIEWS OF HOPEDALE,
       MASS. Hopedale, MA: 186?

1174. HOPEDALE REMINISCENCES: PAPERS READ BEFORE THE HOPEDALE LADIES'
       SEWING SOCIETY AND BRANCH ALLIANCE. Hopedale, MA: School
       Press, 1910.

1175. Hunt, James. "Gandhi, Thoreau, and Adin Ballou." JOURNAL OF THE
       LIBERAL MINISTRY. 9 (Fall 1969): 32-52.

1176. INDEPENDENT MESSENGER. Vol. 1-9, no. 12. Jan. 1, 1831-October
       12, 1839.

1177. MEMORIAL OF ADIN BALLOU. Cambridge, MA: Riverside Press, 1890.

1178. Perry, Lewis. "Adin Ballou's Hopedale Community and the
       Theology of Anti-slavery." CHURCH HISTORY. 39 (September
       1970): 372-389.

1179. THE PRACTICAL CHRISTIAN. Milford, MA: Vol. 1-20, 1840-1860?

1180. Reichert, William O. "The Philosophical Anarchism of Adin Ballou." HUNTINGTON LIBRARY QUARTERLY. 27 (August 1964): 357-374.

1181. Rollins, Richard M. "Adin Ballou and the Perfectionist's Dilemma." JOURNAL OF CHURCH AND STATE. 17 (Autumn 1975): 459-476.

1182. Staples, Carlton Albert. IN MEMORIAM REV. ADIN BALLOU: A SERMON GIVEN IN THE UNITARIAN CHURCH AT MENDON, AUGUST 24, 1890. Boston: G.H. Ellis, printer, 1890.

1183. Wilson, Lewis G. "The Christian Doctrine of Non-Resistance." THE ARENA. 3 (December 1890): 1-12.

1184. ------. "Hopedale and Its Founder." NEW ENGLAND MAGAZINE. New Series. 4 (April 1891): 197-212.

ICARIANS (1848-1886)

This was the inspiration of a French socialist, Etienne Cabet (1788-1858), author of VOYAGE EN ICARIE, 1839. He led a group of workers to America to establish Icarian communities in Texas, Nauvoo, Illinois, and St. Louis. A faction in opposition to Cabet established communities in Iowa and California.

ARCHIVAL MATERIALS

1185. Cabet, Etienne. Papers, 1824-1863. Library. Southern Illinois University, Edwardsville, IL.

1186. Icarian Community. Clayton County, Iowa. 1838-1954. State Department of History and Archives. Iowa Local Miscellaney. Des Moines.

1187. Icarian Community, Corning (Adams County) Iowa. Records, 1853-1947. Formerly Iowa State Historical Department. Housed in Center for Icarian Studies. Western Illinois University Libraries. Macomb, IL.

ARTICLES AND BOOKS

1188. Albrecht, Henry F. GEGENWART UND ZUKUNFT. UNSERE SOZIALEN ZUSTANDE VOR DEM RICHTERSTUHL DER GESUNDEN MENSCHENVERNUNFT, NEBST ANDENTUNGEN, AUF WELCHE WEISE EIN VERNUNFTIG ORGANISIRTES GESELLSCHAFTLEBEN ERREICHBAR IST ... MIT EINEM ANHANG: "DIE SOZIALE ORGANIZATION IKARIENS" von E. Cabet. Philadelphia: F.W. Thomas und Sohne, 1873.

1189. Barnes, Sherman B. "An Icarian in Nauvoo." JOURNAL OF THE ILLINOIS STATE HISTORICAL SOCIETY. 34 (June 1941): 233-244.

1190. Begos, Jane Dupree. "`Icaria', A Footnote to the Peters Colony." COMMUNAL SOCIETIES. 6 (1986): 84-92.

1191. ------, ed. and trans. "Document: Henri Levi's The Perilous Voyage to Icaria (1848)." COMMUNAL SOCIETIES. 3 (Fall 1983): 147-157.

1192. Beluze, Jean Pierre. AUX ICARIENS. Paris: Chez l'auteur, 1856.

1193. ------. CELEBRATION A SAINT-LOUIS, DU NEUVIEME ANNIVERSIARE DE LA FONDATION D'ICARIE. Paris: Chez l'auteur, 1857.

1194. ------. CELEBRATION DU PREMIER ANNIVERSAIRE DE LA NAISSANCE DU FONDATEUR D'ICARIE. Paris, 1857.

1195. ------. CHELTENHAM. Paris: Chez l'auteur, 1858.

1196. ------. LA COLONIE ICARIENNE A SAINT-LOUIS ... Paris: L'auteur,
         1857.

1197. ------. COMPTE-RENDU DE LA GERANCE A LA COMMUNAUTE ICARIENNE, A
         SAINT-LOUIS, SUR LA SITUATION MORALE ET MATERIELLE DE LA
         COMMUNAUTE PENDANT LES MOIS DE NOVEMBRE ET DECEMBRE 1856
         ET LES MOIS DE JANVIER ET FEVRIER, 1857. Paris: Chez
         l'auteur, 1857.

1198. ------. COMPTE-RENDU DE LA SITUATION MORALE ET MATERIELLE DE LA
         COLONIE ICARIENNE, DU MOIS D'AOUT 1857 AU MOIS DE FEVRIER
         1858. Paris: Chez l'auteur, 1858.

1199. ------. EMPRUNT ICARIEN DE UN MILLION DE FRAMES, (LOI DU 21
         JUILLET 1857.) Paris: Chez l'auteur, 1857.

1200. ------. INAUGURATION DU COURS ICARIEN. Paris: Chez l'auteur,
         1858.

1201. ------. LETTRE A MAXIMILLIEN. Paris: 1858

1202. ------. LETTRE SUR LA COLONIE ICARIENNE, PAR UN ICARIEN. Paris:
         Chez l'auteur, 1856.

1203. ------. LETTRES ICARIENNES. A MON AMI EUGENE. Paris: F.
         Malteste et ce, 1859-1860.

1204. ------. MORT DU FONDATEUR D'ICARIE. Paris: Chez l'auteur, 1856.

1205. ------. ORGANISATION DU TRAVAIL DANS LA COMMUNAUTE ICARIENNE.
         Paris: Chez l'auteur, 1857.

1206. ------. PAMPHLETS ON COMMUNISM AND ON THE ICARIAN COLONY. 13
         PAMPHLETS IN 1 VOL. Paris: l'auteur, 1856-1863.

1207. Benguerel, Xavier. ICARIA, ICARIA ...: NOVELA. Barcelona:
         Editorial Planeta, 1974. (Fiction.)

1208. Blick, Boris, and H. Roger Grant. "French Icarians in St.
         Louis." MISSOURI HISTORICAL SOCIETY BULLETIN. 30
         (October 1973): 3-28.

1209. ------. "Life in New Icaria, Iowa: A Nineteenth Century Utopian
         Community." ANNALS OF IOWA. 42 (Winter 1974): 198-204.

1210. Bonnaud, Felix. ETIENNE CABET ET SON OEUVRE; APPEL A TOUS LES
         SOCIALISTES. Paris: Societe libre d'edition des gens de
         lettres, 1900.

1211. Booth, Arthur John. SAINT-SIMON AND SAINT SIMONISM; A CHAPTER
         IN THE HISTORY OF SOCIALISM IN FRANCE. London: Longmans,
         Green, Reader, and Dyer, 1871.

1212. Bradford, W.J.A. "The Icarian Community." CHRISTIAN EXAMINER.
4th series. 18 (November 1852): 372-386.

1213. Brown, Katharine Holland. DIANE; A ROMANCE OF THE ICARIAN
SETTLEMENT ON THE MISSISSIPPI. New York: Doubleday, Page
& Co., 1904. (Fiction.)

1214. ------. "The Icarian Community." HARPER'S MONTHLY MAGAZINE. 110
(December 1904): 141-146.

1215. Bush, Robert D. "Communism, Community, and Charisma: The
Crisis in Icaria at Nauvoo." OLD NORTHWEST. 3 (December
1977): 409-428.

1216. Cabet, Etienne. A BAS LES COMMUNISTES. Paris: 1848.

1217. ------. ADRESSE DU FONDATEUR D'ICARIE AUX ICARIENS. Paris:
L'auteur, 1858.

1218. ------. ALMANACH ICARIEN, ASTRONOMIQUE, SCIENTIFIQUE, PRATIQUE,
INDUSTRIEL, STATISTIQUE, POLITIQUE ET SOCIAL. 7 vols.
Paris: Au Bureau du Populaire, 1843-1852.

1219. ------. BIOGRAPHIE. Paris, 1846.

1220. ------. COLONIE ICARIENNE AUX ETATS-UNIS D'AMERIQUE. SA
CONSTITUTION, SES LOIS , SA SITUATION MATERIELLE ET
MORALE, APRES LE PREMIER SEMESTRE 1855. Paris: Chez
l'auteur, 1856. Reprint. New York: Burt Franklin, 1971.

1221. ------. COLONIE ICARIENNE. GUERRE A MORT DE L'OPPOSITION CONTRE
LE CIT. CABET, FONDATEUR ET PRESIDENT D'ICARIE, ET
MEMORABLE SEANCE DE LA NUIT DU 12 AU 13 MOI 1856 DE 7 1/2
DU SOIR A 6 DU MATIN. Nauvoo, IL: Typographie icarienne,
1856.

1222. ------. COLONIE ICARIENNE. REFORME ICARIENNE. 21 NOVEMBRE 1853.
Paris: L'auteur, 1853.

1223. ------. COLONIE OU REPUBLIQUE ICARIENNE DANS LES ETATS-UNIS
D'AMERIQUE, SON HISTOIRE. Paris: Au Bureau de
l'Emigration Icarienne, rue Baillet, 1853, 1855.

1224. ------. COLONY OR REPUBLIC OF ICARIA IN THE UNITED STATES OF
AMERICA. ITS HISTORY. ICARIAN SYSTEM OR DOCTRINE.
--SOCIAL AND POLITICAL ORGANIZATION. --ICARIAN COMMUNE.
--ADVANTAGES OF COMMUNITY. --ICARIAN CONSTITUTION.
--PRINCIPAL LAWS OF THE COLONY. --MODE AND CONDITIONS OF
ADMISSION. BY MR. CABET, FORMERLY AN ATTORNEY GENERAL AND
DEPUTY IN FRANCE, AND NOW PRESIDENT OF THE ABOVE
COMMUNITY. Nauvoo, IL: Icarian Printing Office, 1852.

1225. ------. COMOTE-RENDU PAR LE PRESIDENT DE LA COMMUNAUTE SUR L'ETAT
       DE LA COLONIE ICARIENNE, APRES LE 1ER SEMESTRE DE 1854.
       Paris: 1854.

1226. ------. COMMENT JE SUIS COMMUNISTE 3 ED. Paris: Impr. de C.B.
       Delanchy, 18-?

1227. ------. DEFENSE DU CITOYEN CABET ACCUSSE D'ESCROGUERIE DEVANT LA
       COUR D'APPEL DE PARIS 11 DECEMBRE, 1850. Paris, 1851.

1228. ------. DEPART DE NAUVOO DU FONDATEUR D'ICARIE AVEC LES VRAIS
       ICARIENS. Paris, 1856.

1229. ------. FAITS DIVERS, 1847-1849. 16 PAMPHLETS IN 1 V. Paris:
       Bureau du Populaire, 1847-1849.

1230. ------. LA FEMME DANS LA SOCIETE ACTUELLE ET DANS LA COMMUNAUTE.
       2.ED. Paris: Prevot, 1841.

1231. ------. LE FONDATEUR D'ICARIE AUX ICARIENS. Paris: Chez
       l'auteur, 1856.

1232. ------. GUERRE DE L'OPPOSITION CONTRE LE CITOYEN CABET, FONDATEUR
       D'ICARIE. Paris, 1856.

1233. ------. "History of the Colony or Republic of Icaria in the
       United States of America," as translated in Thomas Teakle,
       "History and Constitution of the Icarian Community."
       IOWA JOURNAL OF HISTORY AND POLITICS. 15 (April 1917):
       214-286. Reprint. New York: AMS Press, 1975.

1234. ------. ICARIAN COMMUNITY: CONDITIONS OF ADMISSION. Nauvoo, IL:
       Icarian Printing Office, 1854.

1235. ------. INVENTAIRE DE LA COLONIE ICARIENNE 1853. CELEBRATION DE
       L'ANNIVERSAIRE DU 3 FEVRIER 1848. UN JUGEMENT EN ICARIE.
       Paris, 1853.

1236. ------. LETTRE SUR LA REFORME ICARIENNE. DU 21 NOVEMBRE 1853.
       REPONSE DU CITOYEN CABET A QUELQUES OBJECTIONS SUR CETTE
       REFORME. Paris: l'auteur, 1854.

1237. ------. LIGNE DROITE, AU VRAIE CHEMIN DU SALUT POUR LE PEUPLE, ET
       PROPAGANDE COMMUNISTE, OU, QUESTIONS A DUSCUTER OU A
       ECARTER. Paris, 1847.

1238. ------. MANIFESTES DE L'OPPOSITION ET RESPONSE DU CITOYEN CABET.
       Paris, 1856.

1239. ------. OPINION ICARIENNE SUR LE MARIAGE. ORGANISATION
       ICARIENNE. Paris, 1855.

1240. ------. OEUVRES. Pref. de Henri Desroche. Paris: Anthropos
       1970-

1241. ------. PAMPHLETS ON COMMUNISM AND ON ICARIA. Paris: 1845-1856.
Microfilm. New York: New York Public Library, 1966.

1242. ------. PROGRES DE LA COLONIE ICARIENNE ETABLIE A NAUVOO.
(ETATS-UNIS D'AMERIQUE) [PAR] M. CABET A JULIEN, ICARIEN
DISPOSE A VENIR EN ICARIE - Paris: l'auteur, 1854.

1243. ------. PROSPECTUS; GRANDE EMIGRATION AU TEXAS EN AMERIQUE POUR
REALISER LA COMMUNAUTE D'ICARIE. Paris: Au Bureau du
Populaire, 1848.

1244. ------. REALISATION D'ICARIE. no. 1-8; nouveau serie no. 1-6.
Paris: Bureau du Populaire, n.d.

1245. ------. REISE NACH IKARIEN. Paris: Bureau des Popular, 1847.

1246. ------. SUPPLEMENT A L'ALMANACH ICARIEN POUR 1848. AVERTISEMENT.
CE SUPPLEMENT A L'ALMANACH ICARIEN POUR 1848 EST
SPECIALEMENT CONSACRE A LA DESCRIPTION DU TEXAS. Paris:
Au Bureau du Populaire, 1847.

1247. ------. TRAVELS IN ICARIA. Transl. Robert P. Sutton. Macomb,
IL: Western Illinois University, 1985.

1248. ------. VOYAGE ET AVENTURES DE LORD VILLIAM GARISDALL EN ICARIE,
TRADUIT DE L'ANGLAIS DE FRANCIS ADAMS [PSEUD.] PAR TH.
DUFRUIT MAITRE DE LANGUES. 2 VOLS. Paris: H. Souverain,
1840. Second and succeeding editions published under
title: VOYAGE EN ICARIE. Microfilm. Ann Arbor:
University Microfilms, 1968. Reprint. Clifton, NJ: A.M.
Kelley, 1973.

1249. ------. LE VRAI CHRISTIANISME SUIVANT JESUS CHRIST. Paris:
Rousseau, 1846.

1250. Carle, Henri. BIOGRAPHIE DE ETIENNE CABET, FONDATEUR DE L'ECOLE
ICARIENNE. Paris, 1861-1862.

1251. Carre, Paul. CABET DE LE DEMOCRATIE AU COMMUNISME. Lille:
Bigot Freres, 1903.

1252. The Center for Icarian Studies. NEWSLETTER. Macomb, IL:
Western Illinois University Libraries, v. 1-   1979-

1253. Chicomeau, Jacques C. "Etienne Cabet and Icarians." WESTERN
ILLINOIS REGIONAL STUDIES. 2 (Spring 1979): 5-16.

1254. Col. [...], M.A. THE FULFILLMENT!! OR TWELVE YEARS
AFTERWARDS: PARIS, JUNE, 1858: TO TEXAS!! Trans. by James
W. Phillips. Dallas, TX: De Golyer Foundation Library.
Occasional publication no. 2, 1963.

1255. COMMUNITY OF ICARIE. London: Printed by F.J. Watson, 1847.

1256. Cretinon, Jean Francois. VOYAGE EN ICARIE; deux ouvriers
      viennois aux Etats-Unis en 1855. Textes etablis et
      presentes par Fernand Rude. Paris: Presses universitaires
      de France, 1952.

1257. Daughters, Robert. "Icaria-Speranza: The Last Try at Icarian
      Communism." Unpublished paper. Dept. of Architecture,
      University of California, Berkeley, June 6, 1973.

1258. Davidson, Rondel. "Victor Considerant and the Failure of La
      Reunion." SOUTHWESTERN HISTORICAL QUARTERLY. 76 (January
      1973): 277-276.

1259. Gallaher, Ruth Augustus. "Icaria and Icarians." THE
      PALIMPSEST. 2 (April 1921): 97-112.

1260. Gerard, Jean Baptiste. AUX ANCIENS ICARIENS DU TEXAS DE NAUVOO,
      ET DE LA COLONIE DE L'IOWA. Corning, IA: 1880?

1261. Grant, Roger, ed. AN ICARIAN COMMUNIST IN NAUVOO: COMMENTARY BY
      EMILE VALLET. Springfield, IL: Illinois State Historical
      Society, 1971.

1262. Gray, Alexander. THE SOCIALIST TRADITION, MOSES TO LENIN.
      London; New York: Longmans, Green, 1946.

1263. Gray, Charles. "The Icarian Community." ANNALS OF IOWA. 6
      (July 1903): 107-114.

1264. Hepner, Adolf. DIE IKARIER IN NORDAMERIKA; EINE-WARNUNG VOR
      COMMUNISTICHEN COLONIAL-GRUNDUNGEN. New York: Gedruckt
      bei J. Oehler, 1886.

1265. Icarian Community, Corning. Iowa. CONTRAT DE LA COMMUNAUTE
      ICARIENNE D'ADAMS COUNTY, IOWA. Corning, Iowa, 1880.

1266. "Icarian Influence on Temple Square." Nauvoo (Il.) INDEPENDENT.
      (April 5, 1972): p. 8.

1267. Isambert, Alf. "Etienne Cabet." NOUVELLE BIOGRAPHIE BENERALE.
      Paris: Libraires de l'institute de France, 1854, s.v.

1268. Johnson, Christopher H. "Communism and the Working Class Before
      Marx: The Icarian Experience." AMERICAN HISTORICAL
      REVIEW. 76 (June 1971): 642-689.

1269. ------. "Etienne Cabet and the Icarian Communist Movement in
      France, 1839-1848." PhD diss. University of Wisconsin,
      1967.

1270. ------. "Etienne Cabet and the Problem of Class Antagonism."
      INTERNATIONAL REVIEW OF SOCIAL HISTORY. 11 (1966):
      403-443.

1271. ------. UTOPIAN COMMUNITIES IN FRANCE: CABET AND THE ICARIANS
1839-1851. Ithaca; London: Cornell University Press,
1974.

1272. Jones, Russell M. "Victor Considerant's American Experience
(1852-1869)." FRENCH-AMERICAN REVIEW. 1 (1976): 65-94.

1273. Lauer, Jeanette C., and Robert H. Lauer. "Cheltanham: the
Search for Bliss in Missouri." MISSOURI HISTORICAL
REVIEW. 81 (January 1987): 173-183.

1274. Manuel Frank Edward. THE NEW WORLD OF HENRI ST. SIMON.
Cambridge: Harvard University Press, 1956.

1275. ------. THE PROPHETS OF PARIS. Cambridge: Harvard University
Press, 1962.

1276. ------, and P. Fritzie Manuel. FRENCH UTOPIAS: AN ANTHOLOGY OF
IDEAL SOCIETIES. New York: Free Press, 1966.

1277. Miller, I.G. "The Icarian Community of Nauvoo, Illinois."
PUBLICATIONS OF THE HISTORICAL LIBRARY OF ILLINOIS. No.
11 (1906): 23, 103-107.

1278. NOUVELLE REVUE ICARIENNE. St. Louis, 1857-   Vol. 1-43.

1279. Piotrowski, Sylvester A. ETIENNE CABET AND THE VOYAGE EN
ICARIE. A STUDY IN THE HISTORY OF SOCIAL THOUGHT.
Washington, D.C.: Catholic University of America, 1935.
Reprint. Westport, CT: Hyperion Press, 1975.

1280. Prevost, M. "Etienne Cabet." DICTIONNAIRE DE BIOGRAPHIE
FRANCAISE. Paris: Letorizey, 1933. s.v.

1281. Prudhommeaux, Jules Jean. ICARIE ET SON FONDATEUR, ETIENNE
CABET. Paris: Edouard Cornely & Cie., 1907.

1282. Ross, Marie Marchand. CHILD OF ICARIA. New York: City Printing
Co., 1938. Reprint. Westport, CT.: Hyperion Press, 1976.

1283. Shaw, Albert. "Cooperation in the Northwest." HISTORY OF
COOPERATION IN THE UNITED STATES. Johns Hopkins
University Studies in Historical and Political Science.
Vol. 6. Ed. Herbert B. Adams. Baltimore: Johns Hopkins
University Press, 1888. pp. 199-359.

1284. ------. ICARIA, A CHAPTER IN THE HISTORY OF COMMUNISM. New York:
G.P. Putnam's Sons-The Knickerbocker Press, 1884.
Reprint. Philadelphia: Porcupine Press, 1972.

1285. Smith, Martha Browning. "The Story of Icaria." ANNALS OF IOWA.
38 (Summer 1965): 36-64.

1286. ------. "The Story of Icaria" in PATTERNS AND PERSPECTIVES IN
      IOWA'S HISTORY. Dorothy Schwieder, ed. Ames: Iowa State
      University Press, 1973. pp. 231-261.

1287. Snider, Felicie Cottet. "A Short Sketch of the Life of Jules
      Leon Cottet, a Former Member of the Icarian Community."
      ILLINOIS STATE HISTORICAL SOCIETY JOURNAL. 7 (October
      1914): 200-217.

1288. Snyder, Lillian M. "The Contribution of Icarian, Alfred
      Piquenard, to Architecture in Iowa and Illinois."
      COMMUNAL SOCIETIES. 6 (1986): 163-171.

1289. ------, ed. HUMANISTIC VALUES OF THE ICARIAN MOVEMENT.
      Proceedings of a Symposium, Nauvoo, Illinois, July 21-22,
      1979. Cartage, IL: The Country Printer, 1980.

1290. ------, and Robert P. Sutton, eds. IMMIGRATION OF THE ICARIANS TO
      ILLINOIS. Proceedings of Icarian Weekend in Nauvoo, July
      19-20, 1986. Macomb, IL: Yeast Printing, 1987.

1291. Sutton, Robert P. "Etienne Cabet and the Nauvoo Icarians."
      ILLINOIS MAGAZINE: THE MAGAZINE OF THE PRAIRIE STATE.
      (March-April 1985): 29-38.

1292. ------, and Rulon N. Smithson. "'Mon Cher Emile': The
      Cabet-Baxter Letters, 1854-1855." WESTERN ILLINOIS
      REGIONAL STUDIES. 2 (Spring 1979): 20-37.

1293. Tumminelli, Roberto. "Etienne Cabet e le Colonie Icariane Negli
      Stati Uniti." POLITICO. 50 (1985): 67-81.

1294. ------. "Etienne Cabet e il Modello Politico-sociale di Icaria."
      POLITICO. [Italy] 44 (1979): 92-112.

1295. Vallet, Emile. COMMUNISM ... HISTORY OF THE EXPERIMENT AT
      NAUVOO OF THE ICARIAN SETTLEMENT. Nauvoo, IL: Printed by
      the Nauvoo RUSTLER, 1890?

1296. ------. AN ICARIAN COMMUNIST IN NAUVOO. Springfield, IL:
      Illinois State Historical Society, 1971.

1297. Wick, Berthies L. "The Icarian Community-Story of Cabet's
      Experiment in Communism." THE MIDLAND MONTHLY. 3 (1895):
      370-376.

1298. Zelie, John S. "Amiel in Nebraska; Letters, Newly Discovered
      and Translated Addressed to Edward Lyanna of Icaria
      Community." ATLANTIC. 127 (March 1921): 289-300.

JASPER COLONY (1851-1853)

Formed in Jasper, Iowa, by a group of German Swedenborgians from
St. Louis. They gave up the communistic idea and remained in
the area in the New Church.

ARTICLES AND BOOKS

1299. Block, Marguerite Beck. THE NEW CHURCH IN THE NEW WORLD: A
       STUDY OF SWEDENBORGIANISMS IN AMERICA. New York: H. Holt
       & Co., 1932. Reprint. New York: Octagon, 1969.

1300. Hawley, Charles Arthur. "A Communistic Swedenborgian Colony in
       Iowa." THE IOWA JOURNAL OF HISTORY AND POLITICS. 33
       (January 1935): 3-26.

1301. ------. "The New Church in Iowa: the Jasper Colony and Later
       Developments." THE NEW CHURCH REVIEW. 41 (1934):
       193-208.

1302. ------. "Swedenborgianism on the Frontier." CHURCH HISTORY. 6
       (September 1937): 203-223.

JERUSALEM (1788-1820)

Also known as The Society of Universal Friends, it was founded
in Yates County, New York, by Jemima Wilkinson.

ARCHIVAL MATERIALS

1303. Wilkinson, Jemima. Papers, 1772-1849. Library. Cornell
       University, Ithaca, NY.

ARTICLES AND BOOKS

1304. Adams, John Quincy, Rev. "Jemima Wilkinson, the Universal
       Friend." JOURNAL OF AMERICAN HISTORY. 9 (April-July
       1915): 249-263.

1305. Barbe-Marbois, Francois, Marquis de. LETTERS, transl. by Eugene
       Parker Chase under the title OUR REVOLUTIONARY
       FOREFATHERS. New York: Duffield & Co., 1929.

1306. Bronner, Edwin B. "Quakers Labor With Jemima Wilkinson-1794."
       QUAKER HISTORY. 58 (Spring 1969): 41-47.

1307. Cleveland, Stafford Canning. HISTORY AND DIRECTORY OF YATES
       COUNTY, CONTAINING A SKETCH OF ITS ORIGINAL SETTLEMENT BY
       THE PUBLIC UNIVERSAL FRIENDS, THE LESSER COMPANY AND
       OTHERS, WITH AN ACCOUNT OF INDIVIDUAL PIONEERS AND THEIR
       FAMILIES; ALSO OTHER LEADING CITIZENS. INCLUDING CHURCH,
       SCHOOL AND CIVIL HISTORY, AND A NARRATIVE OF THE UNIVERSAL
       FRIEND, HER SOCIETY AND DOCTRINE. Penn Yan, NY: S.C.
       Cleveland, 1873.

1308. Hendricks, Mrs. Walter A., and Arnold Potter, "The Universal
       Friend: Jemima Wilkinson," NEW YORK HISTORY 23. (April
       1942): 159-165.

1309. Hudson, David. HISTORY OF JEMIMA WILKINSON, A PREACHERESS OF
       THE EIGHTEENTH CENTURY; CONTAINING AN AUTHENTIC NARRATIVE
       OF HER LIFE AND CHARACTER, AND OF THE RISE, PROGRESS AND ·
       CONCLUSION OF HER MINISTRY. Geneva, Ontario County, NY:
       Printed by S.P. Hull, 1821. Reprinted as MEMOIRS OF
       JEMIMA WILKINSON. Bath, NY: R.L. Underhill, 1844.
       Reprint. New York: AMS Press, 1972.

1310. Johnson, Colonel. "Jemima Wilkinson, American Prophetess."
       ECLECTIC MAGAZINE. 5 (August 1845): 546 ff.

1311. Marlin, Charles Lowell. "Jemima Wilkinson: Errant Quaker
       Divine." QUAKER HISTORY. 52 (Autumn 1963): 90-94.

1312. St. John, Robert Porter. "Jemima Wilkinson," New York State
          Historical Association, PROCEEDINGS. 28 (April 1930):
          158-175.

1313. ------. JERUSALEM THE GOLDEN: AN HISTORICAL NOVEL OF THE FINGER
          LAKE COUNTRY OF NEW YORK. New York: F.H. Hitchcock, 1926.
          (Fiction.)

1314. Upson, Ruth. "New Jerusalem and the Public Universal Friend."
          NEW YORK FOLKLORE QUARTERLY. 11 (Spring 1955): 20-33.

1315. Wilkinson, Israel. MEMOIRS OF THE WILKINSON FAMILY IN AMERICA.
          Jacksonville, IL: Davis & Penninan, printers, 1869.

1316. Wilkinson, Jemima. THE UNIVERSAL FRIEND'S ADVICE, TO THOSE OF
          THE SAME RELIGIOUS SOCIETY. RECOMMENDED TO BE READ IN
          THEIR PUBLIC MEETINGS FOR DIVINE WORSHIP. Philadelphia:
          Printed by Francis Bailey, 1784. Reprint under title:
          THE PUBLIC UNIVERSAL FRIEND. Penn Yan, NY: Printed by
          A.H. Bennett, for Nathaniel Ingraham and others, 1821.

1317. ------. SOME CONSIDERATIONS, PROPOUNDED TO THE SEVERAL SORTS AND
          SECTS OF PROFESSORS OF THIS AGE. Providence, 1779.

1318. Wisbey, Herbert A., Jr. PIONEER PROPHETESS, JEMIMA WILKINSON,
          THE PUBLICK UNIVERSAL FRIEND. Ithaca: Cornell University
          Press, 1964.

KIANTONE COMMUNITY (1853-1863)

This spiritualist community, which also is known as the Domain, Harmonia, or the Association of Beneficients, was established by John Murray Spear in Kiantone, Chatauqua County, New York. This group also established a colony at Patriot, Indiana, in 1860.

ARCHIVAL MATERIALS

1319. Harmonia. Records, 1853-1865. Library. University of Pittsburgh.

1320. Spear, John Murray. The Sheldon Papers. Library. University of Pittsburgh.

ARTICLES AND BOOKS

1321. Chase, Oliver F. "The Kiantone Movement." CENTENNIAL HISTORY OF CHAUTAUQUA COUNTY. Jamestown: Chautauqua Historical Society, 1904. II, 827-829.

1322. Duino, Russell. "Utopian Theme With Variations: John Murray Spear and His Kiantone Domain." PENNSYLVANIA HISTORY. 29 (April 1962): 140-150.

1323. Hewitt, S.C. MESSAGES FROM THE SUPERIOR STATE; COMMUNICATED BY JOHN M. SPEAR. Boston: Bela Marsh, 1853.

1324. Newton, A.E., ed. THE EDUCATOR, ETC. ... COMPRISED IN A SERIES OF REVEALMENTS ... THROUGH JOHN MURRAY SPEAR. Boston: Office of Practical Spiritualists, 1857.

1325. Spear, John Murray. TWELVE DISCOURSES ON GOVERNMENT PURPORTING TO HAVE BEEN DELIVERED IN BOSTON, MASS., DECEMBER 1852, BY THOMAS JEFFERSON, OF THE SPIRIT WORLD; THROUGH JOHN M. SPEAR, MEDIUM. Ed. by Adin Ballou. Hopedale MA: Community Press, 1853.

1326. ------. TWENTY YEARS ON THE WING. Boston: W. White & Co., 1873.

1327. SPIRITUAL TELEGRAPH, New York, May 1852-1860. Superseded by HERALD OF PROGRESS, New York, 1860-1864.

KINGDOM OF PARADISE, 1736

Established in Georgia by Christian Gottlieb Priber (1697-1744).
Immigrating from Zittau, Germany in 1735 he settled among the
Cherokees around whom he sought to build his colony, based on
liberty and equality. Seen as a threat to the non-Indians of
Georgia and South Carolina, Governor James Oglethorpe arrested
him and Priber died in prison.

ARTICLES AND BOOKS

1328. Crane, Verner Winslow. "A Lost Utopia of the First American
      Frontier." SEWANEE REVIEW. 27 (January-March, 1919):
      48-61.

1329. Mellon, Knox. "Christian Priber and the Jesuit Myth." SOUTH
      CAROLINA HISTORICAL MAGAZINE. 61 (April 1960): 75-81.

1330. ------. "Christian Priber's Cherokee Kingdom of Paradise."
      GEORGIA HISTORICAL QUARTERLY. 57 (Fall 1973): 319-331.

1331. ------. "Christian Gottlieb Priber." DICTIONARY OF GEORGIA
      BIOGRAPHY, ed. Kenneth Coleman and Charles Stephen Gurr.
      Athens: University of Georgia Press, 1983. s.v.

1332. Mereness, Newton. TRAVELS IN THE AMERICAN COLONIES. New York:
      Macmillan, 1916. Pages 239-245 include an English
      translation of Christian Priber's journal.

1333. Williams, Samuel Cole. EARLY TRAVELS IN THE TENNESSEE COUNTRY,
      1540-1800. Johnson City, TN: The Watauga Press, 1928.
      pp. 149-162.

LABADIST COLONY, 1638-1732

Established at Bohemia Manor, Maryland, Cecil County, by Peter
Sluyter and Jasper Danckaerts, Dutch followers of the teachings
of Jean de Labadie (1610-1674), a French reformer, and founder
of a quietistic sect in Amsterdam.

ARTICLES AND BOOKS

1334. Berkum, Hendrikus Van. DE LABADIE EN DE LABADISTEN EENE BLADZIJ
DE UIT DE GESCHIEDENIS DER NEDERLANDISCHE HERVORMDE KERK.
Sneek: Van Druten & Bleeker, 1851.

1335. Birch, Una Constance. ANNA VAN SCHURMAN: ARTIST, SCHOLAR,
SAINT. London: Longmans, Green & Co., 1909.

1336. Bownas, Samuel. AN ACCOUNT OF THE LIFE, TRAVELS AND CHRISTIAN
EXPERIENCES IN THE WORK OF THE MINISTRY OF SAMUEL BOWNAS.
London: William Dunlap, 1759.

1337. Danckaerts, Jasper. JOURNAL OF JASPER DANCKAERTS, 1679-1680,
ed. Bartlett Burleigh James and J. Franklin Jameson. New
York: C. Scribner's Sons, 1913. Reprint. New York:
Barnes & Noble, 1941, 1952.

1338. ------. JOURNAL OF A VOYAGE TO NEW YORK AND A TOUR IN SEVERAL OF
THE AMERICAN COLONIES IN 1679-80. Trans. for the Long
Island Historical Society and ed. by Henry C. Murphy.
Brooklyn: Long Island Historical Society, 1867.
Microfilm. Ann Arbor: University Microfilms, 1969.

1339. Deane, Charles. "Communication Relative to Jasper Danckaerts
and the Indian Bible." PROCEEDINGS OF THE MASSACHUSETTS
HISTORICAL SOCIETY. 13 (1874): 307-311.

1340. Frank, Gustav William. "Labadie, Jean de, Labadists." NEW
SCHAFF-HERZOG ENCYCLOPEDIA OF RELIGIOUS KNOWLEDGE. New
York: Funk and Wagnalls, 1910. s.v.

1341. Green, Ernest J. "The Labadists of Colonial Maryland (1683-
1722)." Unpublished paper presented at National Historic
Communal Societies Conference, Bishop Hill, Illinois,
October 18, 1987. Typescript.

1342. Heck, Earl L.S. AUGUSTINE HERRMAN. Englewood, O: The Author,
1941.

1343. Irwin, J. "Anna Maria van Schurman: From Feminism to Pietism."
CHURCH HISTORY. 46 (March 1977): 48-62.

1344. James, Bartlett Burleigh. THE LABADIST COLONY IN MARYLAND.
Johns Hopkins University Studies in Historical and

133

          Political Science. Vol. 17, no. 6. Baltimore, 1899.
          Reprint. New York: AMS Press, 1978.

1345. Koelman, Jacobus. HISTORISCH VERHAEL NOPENDE DER LABADISTEN
          SCHEURINGH, EN VEELERLEY DWALINGEN, MET DE WEDERLEGGINGH
          DER SELVER. Amsterdam: Johannes Boeckholt, 1683.

1346. Leakin, George A. "Labadists of Bohemia Manor." MARYLAND
          HISTORICAL MAGAZINE. 1 (1906): 337-345.

1347. ------. "A Visit to Bohemia Manor." MARYLAND HISTORICAL
          MAGAZINE. 2 (1907): 143-146.

1348. Lovejoy, David S. RELIGIOUS ENTHUSIASM IN THE NEW WORLD: HERESY
          TO REVOLUTION. Cambridge: Harvard University Press,
          1985.

1349. Mallary, Charles Payson. ANCIENT FAMILIES OF BOHEMIA MANOR.
          Wilmington: Delaware Historical Society, n.d.

1350. Saxby, Trevor John. THE QUEST FOR THE NEW JERUSALEM: JEAN DE
          LABADIE AND THE LABADISTS, 1610-1730. Dordrecht; Boston:
          M. Nijhoff Publishers, 1987.

1351. Schotel, Gilles Dionysius Jacobus. ANNA MARIA VAN SCHURMAN.
          Hertogenbosch: Gebroeders Muller, 1853.

1352. Stoeffler, F. Ernst. THE RISE OF EVANGELICAL PIETISM. Leiden:
          E.J. Brill, 1965. pp. 162-169.

1353. Wilson, James Grant. AUGUSTINE HERMAN, BOHEMIAN. Trenton: New
          Jersey Historical Society, n.d.

1354. ------. "An Old Maryland Manor". A paper read before the Maryland
          Historical Society, March 11th, 1889. Baltimore: Printed
          by J. Murphy, 1890.

MATTHIAS COLONY, 1830-1835

Founded by Robert Matthews, who called himself Matthias, this
colony, also known as Zion Hill Community, was located near Sing
Sing, New York.

ARTICLES AND BOOKS

1355. Fausett, Arthur Huff. SOJOURNER TRUTH: GOD'S FAITHFUL PILGRIM.
       Chapel Hill: University of North Carolina Press, 1938.

1356. Stone, William Leete. MATTHIAS AND HIS IMPOSTURES: OR THE
       PROGRESS OF FANATICISM. ILLUSTRATED IN THE EXTRAORDINARY
       CASE OF ROBERT MATTHEWS, AND SOME OF HIS FORERUNNERS AND
       DISCIPLES. New York: Harper & Bros., 1835. Microfilm.
       Ann Arbor: UMI, 1966.

MEMNONIA INSTITUTE (1856-1857)

Founded by Thomas Low Nichols and Mary Gove Nichols at Yellow
Spring, Ohio. Also known as the School of Life, it followed a
Fourierist pattern.

ARTICLES AND BOOKS

1357. Gleason, Philip. "From Free-Love to Catholicism: Dr. and Mrs.
Thomas L. Nichols at Yellow Springs." OHIO HISTORICAL
QUARTERLY. 70 (October 1961): 283-307.

1358. NICHOLS MONTHLY, A MAGAZINE OF SOCIAL SCIENCE AND PROGRESSIVE
LITERATURE. Cincinnati, v. 1-3, 1854-1856.

1359. Nichols, Thomas Low. ESOTERIC ANTHROPOLOGY: A COMPREHENSIVE AND
CONFIDENTIAL TREATISE ON THE STRUCTURE, FUNCTION,
PASSIONAL ATTRACTIONS AND PERVERSIONS, TRUE AND FALSE
PHYSICAL AND SOCIAL CONDITIONS, AND THE MOST INTIMATE
RELATIONS OF MEN AND WOMEN. Cincinnati: Watkin,
Nicholson, 1853.

1360. ------. FORTY YEARS OF AMERICAN LIFE. London: J. Maxwell and
Company, 1864. Reprint. New York: Stackpole Sons, 1937.

1361. ------, and Mary Gove. MARRIAGE: ITS HISTORY, CHARACTER AND
RESULTS. Cincinnati: V. Nicholson & Co., 1854.
Microfilm. Ann Arbor: University Microfilms (American
Culture Series), 1968.

1362. Noever, Janet Hubly. "Passionate Rebel: The Life of Mary Gove
Nichols, 1810-1884." PhD diss. University of Oklahoma,
1983.

1363. Stearns, Bertha-Monica. "Memnonia: The Launching of Utopia."
NEW ENGLAND QUARTERLY. 15 (June 1942): 280-295.

1364. ------. "Two Forgotten New England Reformers." NEW ENGLAND
QUARTERLY. 6 (March 1933): 59-84.

MODERN TIMES (1851-1863)

A Josiah Warren colony, established on Long Island, New York, on the basis of anarchism.

ARCHIVAL MATERIALS

1365. Warren, Josiah. Papers, 1834-1868. University of Michigan Library. Department of Rare Books and Special Collections, Ann Arbor.

ARTICLES AND BOOKS

1366. Andrews, Stephen Pearl. THE BASIC OUTLINE OF UNIVERSOLOGY. AN INTRODUCTION TO THE NEWLY DISCOVERED SCIENCE OF THE UNIVERSE; ITS ELEMENTARY PRINCIPLES; AND THE FIRST STAGES OF THEIR DEVELOPMENT IN THE SPECIAL SCIENCES. New York: D. Thomas, 1872.

1367. ------. LOVE, MARRIAGE, AND DIVORCE, AND THE SOVEREIGNTY OF THE INDIVIDUAL. New York: Stringer & Townsend, 1853.

1368. ------. THE SCIENCE OF SOCIETY. New York: Fowler and Wells, 1853. Boston: Sarah E. Holmes, 1888. Reprint. Westen, MA: M & S Press, 1970.

1369. Andrusius, PANTARCH, pseud. (Andrews, Stephen Pearl). CONSTITUTION OR ORGANIC BASIS OF THE PANTARCHY. New York: Baker and Godwin, 1860.

1370. Arieli, Yehoshua. INDIVIDUALISM AND NATIONALISM IN AMERICAN IDEOLOGY. Cambridge: Harvard University Press, 1964. pp. 289-296.

1371. Bailie, William. JOSIAH WARREN, THE FIRST AMERICAN ANARCHIST: A SOCIOLOGICAL STUDY. Boston: Small, Maynard & Co., 1906. Reprint. New York: Arno Press & The New York Times, 1972.

1372. Bernard, Luther L., and Jessie Bernard. "The Direct Influence of Comte: the Modern Times Experiment." In their ORIGINS OF AMERICAN SOCIOLOGY. New York: Thomas Y. Crowell, 1943. pp. 161-176; 313-338.

1373. Buckstein, Frederick. "Josiah Warren: The Peaceful Revolutionist." CINCINNATI HISTORICAL SOCIETY BULLETIN. 32 (Spring-Summer 1974): 61-71.

1374. Butler, Anne Caldwell. "Josiah Warren: Peaceful Revolutionist." Ph.D. diss., Ball State U., 1978.

1375. Cress, Kit Firth. "Communitarian Connections: Josiah Warren,
           Robert Smith, and Peter Kaufmann." COMMUNAL SOCIETIES.   7
           (1987): 67-81.

1376. Martin, James J. MEN AGAINST THE STATE: THE EXPOSITORS OF
           INDIVIDUALIST ANARCHISM IN AMERICA, 1827-1908. DeKalb,
           IL: Adrian Allen Associates, 1953.

1377. THE PEACEFUL REVOLUTIONIST. Cincinnati, Utopia, Ohio. v. 1,
           January-April 1833; v. 2, May 1848.

1378. THE PROPAGANDIST, New York, 1850-1851.

1379. Stern, Madeline. THE PANTARCH: A BIOGRAPHY OF STEPHEN PEARL
           ANDREWS. Austin: University of Texas Press, 1968.

1380. ------. "Stephen Pearl Andrews and Modern Times, Long Island."
           JOURNAL OF LONG ISLAND HISTORY.   4 (Fall 1964): 1-15.

1381. Warren, Josiah. EQUITABLE COMMERCE: A NEW DEVELOPMENT OF
           PRINCIPLES, FOR THE HARMONIOUS ADJUSTMENT AND REGULATION
           OF THE PECUNIARY, INTELLECTUAL, AND MORAL INTERCOURSE OF
           MANKIND, PROPOSED AS ELEMENTS OF NEW SOCIETY. New
           Harmony, IA: J. Warren, 1846.

1382. ------. MANIFESTO. New Harmony, IA: J. Warren, 1841. Reprint.
           Berkeley Heights, NJ: Oriole Press, 1952.

1383. ------. PRACTICAL DETAILS IN EQUITABLE COMMERCE, SHOWING THE
           WORKINGS, IN ACTUAL EXPERIMENT, DURING A SERIES OF YEARS,
           OF THE SOCIAL PRINCIPLES EXPOUNDED IN THE WORKS CALLED
           "EQUITABLE COMMERCE." New York: Fowlers and Wells, 1854.

1384. ------. TRUE CIVILIZATION: A SUBJECT OF VITAL AND SERIOUS
           INTEREST TO ALL PEOPLE; BUT MOST IMMEDIATELY TO THE MEN
           AND WOMEN OF LABOR AND SORROW. Princeton, MA: B.R.
           Tucker, 1875.

1385. ------. TRUE CIVILIZATION AN IMMEDIATE NECESSITY, AND THE LAST
           GROUND OF HOPE FOR MANKIND. BEING THE RESULTS AND
           CONCLUSIONS OF THIRTY-NINE YEARS' LABORIOUS STUDY AND
           EXPERIMENTS IN CIVILIZATION AS IT IS, AND IN DIFFERENT
           ENTERPRISES FOR RECONSTRUCTION. Boston: J. Warren, 1863.
           Reprint. New York: Burt Franklin, 1967.

1386. Wunderlich, Roger. "The Three Phases of Modern Times--
           Communitarian, Reform, and Long Island." COMMUNAL
           SOCIETIES.   6 (1986): 50-60.

MORAVIANS

There were brief communal moments in the early years of the
Moravians in America as well as the two Wisconsin Moravian
communitarian settlements known as Ephraim (1850-1853;
1853-1864).

ARCHIVAL MATERIALS

1387. General Economy, Northampton Co., Pa. Records, 1750-1771.
Moravian Archives. Bethlehem, PA.

ARTICLES AND BOOKS

1388. Fries, Adelaide. THE ROAD TO SALEM. Chapel Hill, NC:
University of North Carolina Press, 1944.

1389. Gollin, Gillian Lindt. MORAVIANS IN TWO WORLDS: A STUDY OF
CHANGING COMMUNITIES. New York: Columbia University
Press, 1967.

1390. Hamilton, J. Taylor,and Kenneth G. Hamilton. HISTORY OF THE
MORAVIAN CHURCH. Bethlehem, PA: Interprovincial Board of
Christian Education, Moravian Church of America, 1967.

1391. Hamilton, Kenneth G. "The Moravians and Wachovia." NORTH
CAROLINA HISTORICAL REVIEW. 44 (April 1967): 144-153.

1392. Levering, Joseph Mortimer. A HISTORY OF BETHLEHEM,
PENNSYLVANIA, 1741-1892, WITH SOME ACCOUNT OF ITS FOUNDERS
AND THEIR EARLY ACTIVITY IN AMERICA. Bethlehem, PA: Times
Publishing Co., 1903. Reprint. New York: AMS, 1971.

1393. Mainwaring, W. Thomas. "Communal Ideals, Worldly Concerns, and
the Moravians of North Carolina, 1753-1772." COMMUNAL
SOCIETIES. 6 (1986): 138-162.

1394. RECORDS OF THE MORAVIANS IN NORTH CAROLINA. 11 vols. Raleigh:
North Carolina Archives, 1933-1969.

1395. Sessler, Jacob John. COMMUNAL PIETISM AMONG EARLY AMERICAN
MORAVIANS. New York: H. Holt, 1933. Reprint. New York:
AMS Press, 1970.

1396. Smaby, Beverly Prior. THE TRANSFORMATION OF MORAVIAN BETHLEHEM:
FROM COMMUNAL MISSION TO FAMILY ECONOMY. Philadelphia:
University of Pennsylvania Press, 1988.

1397. TWO CENTURIES OF NAZARETH, 1740-1940. Nazareth, PA: Nazareth
Pennsylvania Bi-centennial, Inc., 1940.

NORTHAMPTON ASSOCIATION OF EDUCATION
AND INDUSTRY (1842-1846)

Located in Hampshire County, Massachusetts, this was a secular, industrial communal group.

ARTICLES AND BOOKS

1398. Bestor, Arthur E., Jr. "Fourierism in Northampton: A Critical Note." NEW ENGLAND QUARTERLY. 13 (March 1940): 110-122.

1399. McBee, Alice Eaton. FROM UTOPIA TO FLORENCE: THE STORY OF A TRANSCENDENTALIST COMMUNITY IN NORTHAMPTON, MASS., 1830-1852. Smith College Studies in History, vol. 32. Northampton, MA: Smith College, 1947.

1400. Northampton, Mass. Tercentenary History Committee. THE NORTHAMPTON BOOK: CHAPTERS FROM 300 YEARS IN THE LIFE OF A NEW ENGLAND TOWN, 1654-1954. Lawrence E. Wiklander, et al. compilers. Northampton, 1954.

1401. Rumsey, Olive. "The Northampton Association of Education and Industry." NEW ENGLAND MAGAZINE. New Series. 12 (1895): 22-32.

1402. Sheffield, Charles Arthur, ed. THE HISTORY OF FLORENCE, MASSACHUSETTS, INCLUDING A COMPLETE ACCOUNT OF THE NORTHAMPTON ASSOCIATION OF EDUCATION AND INDUSTRY. Florence, 1895.

1403. Smart, George K. "Fourierism in Northampton: Two Documents." NEW ENGLAND QUARTERLY. 12 (June 1939): 370-374.

1404. Terry, E. "Sojourner Truth: The Person Behind the Libyan Sibyl; an essay by Esther Terry with a Memoir by Frederick Douglass:What I Found at the Northampton Association." THE MASSACHUSETTS REVIEW. 26 (Summer-Autumn 1985): 425-444.

1405. "Together: Northampton Community." COUNTY TIME AND TIDE. 5 (1903-1904): 37-43, 63-68.

OBERLIN COLONY (1833-1841)

Settled in Lorain County, Ohio by New England families under the
leadership of John Shipherd.

ARTICLES AND BOOKS

1406. Fairchild, Edward Henry. HISTORICAL SKETCH OF OBERLIN COLLEGE.
       Springfield, OH: Printed by Republic Printing Co., 1868.

1407. Fairchild, James Harris. OBERLIN: THE COLONY AND THE COLLEGE.
       Oberlin, OH: E.J. Goodrich, 1883.

1408. Fletcher, Robert Samuel. THE GOVERNMENT OF THE OBERLIN COLONY.
       Cedar Rapids, IA, 1933.

1409. ------. "The Government of the Oberlin Colony." MISSISSIPPI
       VALLEY HISTORICAL REVIEW. 20 (September 1933): 179-190.

1410. ------. ONEIDA AND OBERLIN. Utica, NY, 1931.

1411. Wright, George Frederick. OBERLIN COLLEGE. Boston, 1900.
       Originally published in NEW ENGLAND MAGAZINE (September
       1900).

OCTAGON CITY (1856)

A vegetarian colony on the Neosho River, near Fort Scott,
Kansas, under the guidance of an Englishman, Henry S. Clubb.

ARTICLES AND BOOKS

1412. Colt, Miriam Davis. WEST TO KANSAS: BEING A THRILLING ACCOUNT
OF AN ILL-FATED EXPEDITION TO THAT FAIRY LAND, AND ITS SAD
RESULTS. Watertown, NY: L. Ingalls & Co., 1862.

1413. Clubb, Henry Stephen. THE VEGETARIAN PRINCIPLE. Philadelphia:
Vegetarian Society of America , 1898.

1414. Gambone, Joseph G. "Octagon City." AMERICAN HISTORY
ILLUSTRATED. 10 (August 1975): 10-15.

ONEIDA COMMUNITY (1848-1881)

The Bible Communists, or Perfectionists, organized by John Humphrey Noyes at Oneida Creek, New York, after their group had been driven from Putney, Vermont (1843-1848). In 1880, Oneida ceased to exist as a communal society and became a joint stock company, Oneida Company, Ltd. (in 1935, Oneida, Ltd.).

ARCHIVAL MATERIALS

1415. Barron, Helen M. Memorandum dictated to Hope E. Allen, May 24, 1913. Historical collection, Mansion House Library, Kenwood, NY.

1416. Kinsley, Jessie. Diary, 1914-1918. Private collection of Jane Kinsley Rich. Kenwood, NY.

1417. Nash Family. Oneida Community Papers, 1827. Stanford University Libraries.

1418. Noyes, Harriet A. "History of the Printing Business of the Oneida Community." MS, [1875?]. Historical collection. Mansion House Library, Kenwood, NY.

1419. Noyes, Hilda Herrick, comp. Collection of MSS on the Oneida Community and the Oneida Community, Limited. Private collection of Mrs. Adele Noyes Davies, Toronto, Canada.

1420. Noyes, Holton V. "History of the Oneida Community, Limited: 1880-1925." Taken from the minutes of the board of directors, with annotations by the author. 1930. Private collection of the late Stephen R. Leonard, Jr., Kenwood, NY.

1421. Noyes, John Humphrey. "Niagara Journal." Stone Cottage, Clifton, Ontario. 1881. Private collection of the late Stephen R. Leonard, Sr., and Stephen R. Leonard, Jr., Kenwood, NY.

1422. Oneida Community. Letters, 1849-1877. Amherst College Library, Amherst.

1423. Oneida Community. Papers. George Arents Research Library. Syracuse University.

1424. Oneida Family Register. MS listing names and personal data for the first 111 persons who joined the Oneida Community. Historical collection, Mansion House Library, Kenwood, NY.

1425. Religious Diary, 1851-1854. Author's name withheld. Private
        collection of the late Stephen R. Leonard, Jr., Kenwood,
        NY.

1426. Robertson, Constance (Noyes) Papers, 1837-1851, 1931-1966.
        Syracuse University Library .

                            BIBLIOGRAPHIES

1427. Wells, Lester G. THE ONEIDA COMMUNITY COLLECTION IN THE
        SYRACUSE LIBRARY. Syracuse: The Library, 1961.

                          ARTICLES AND BOOKS

1428. Achorn, Erik. "Mary Cragin, Perfectionist Saint: Noyes' Theory
        and Experiments." THE NEW ENGLAND QUARTERLY. 28 (December
        1955): 490-518.

1429. Bishop, Morris. "The Great Oneida Love-In." AMERICAN HERITAGE.
        20 (February 1969): 14-16, 86-92.

1430. Carden, Maren Lockwood. "The Experimental Utopia in America."
        In Frank E. Manuel, ed. UTOPIAS AND UTOPIAN THOUGHT.
        Boston: Houghton Mifflin, 1966.

1431. ------. ONEIDA: UTOPIAN COMMUNITY TO MODERN CORPORATION.
        Baltimore: The Johns Hopkins University Press, 1969.

1432. Carmer, Carl Lamson. LISTEN FOR A LONESOME DRUM: A YORK STATE
        CHRONICLE; with sketches by Cyrus Leroy Baldridge. New
        York: Blue Ribbon Books, Farrar, & Rinehart; Editions for
        the Armed Services, 1936, 1938. Reprint. New York: D.
        McKay, 1950.

1433. ------. "A Reporter at Large. Children of the Kingdom." THE NEW
        YORKER. 12 (March 21, 1936): 26-36; (March 28, 1936):
        43-49.

1434. Cavan, Ruth Shonle. "The Contrasting Roles of Women at Oneida
        Community, the Midwestern Frontier, and the Urban East in
        the Mid-Nineteenth Century." COMMUNAL SOCIETIES. 1
        (Autumn 1981): 67-79.

1435. Chandler, J.W. "The Communitarian Quest for Perfection." In A
        MISCELLANY OF AMERICAN CHRISTIANITY: ESSAYS IN HONOR OF
        H. SHELTON SMITH. Durham: Duke University Press, 1963.

1436. Church, C. C. "Communism in Marriage: Human Relationships at
        the Oneida Community." THE NATION. 123 (August 11,
        1926): 124-126.

1437. COMMUNITY QUADRANGLE. Kenwood, NY. Vols. 1-5, 1926-1930.

1438. COMMUNITY QUADRANGLE. (2nd Series). Kenwood, NY. January-
      September/October, 1938. (Mimeographed.).

1439. Cragin, George, ed. FAITH-FACTS; OR A CONFESSION OF THE KINGDOM
      OF GOD, AND THE AGE OF MIRACLES. Oneida Reserve, NY:
      Leonard & Co., Printers, 1850. Microfilm. Ann Arbor:
      University Microfilms, 1969.

1440. Cragin, John H. CHRIST CAME AS PROMISED. Kenwood, NY: By the
      author, 1895.

1441. Demaria, Richard. COMMUNAL LOVE AT ONEIDA: A PERFECTIONIST
      VISION OF AUTHORITY, PROPERTY AND SEXUAL ORDER. 2nd ed.
      Lewiston, NY: Edwin Mellen Press, 1978, 1984.

1442. Dixon, William Hepworth. NEW AMERICA. Philadelphia: J.B.
      Lippincott & Co., 1867.

1443. ------. SPIRITUAL WIVES. 2d ed. Philadelphia: J.B. Lippincott &
      Co., 1868.

1444. Eastman, Hubbard. NOYEISM UNVEILED: A HISTORY OF THE SECT OF
      SELF-STYLED PERFECTIONISTS WITH A SUMMARY VIEW OF THEIR
      LEADING DOCTRINES. Brattleboro, VT: By the author, 1849.
      Reprint. New York: AMS Press, 1972. Microfilm. Ann Arbor:
      University Microfilms, 1966.

1445. Easton, Abel. THE DISSOLUTION OF THE ONEIDA COMMUNITY. n.p.,
      n.d. (After 1881).

1446. Edmonds, Walter Dumaux. THE FIRST HUNDRED YEARS: 1848-1948:
      1848, ONEIDA COMMUNITY; 1880, ONEIDA COMMUNITY, LIMITED;
      1935, ONEIDA, LTD. Oneida, NY: Oneida Ltd., 1948.

1447. Estlake, Allan. THE ONEIDA COMMUNITY: A RECORD OF AN ATTEMPT TO
      CARRY OUT THE PRINCIPLES OF CHRISTIAN UNSELFISHNESS AND
      SCIENTIFIC RACE-IMPROVEMENT. London: George Redway, 1900.
      Reprint. AMS Press, New York: 1973.

1448. Fogarty, Robert S. "Oneida: A Utopian Search for Religious
      Security." LABOR HISTORY. 14 (Spring 1973): 202-227.

1449. ------. "A Utopian Literary Canon." NEW ENGLAND QUARTERLY. 38
      (September 1965): 386-391 .

1450. Foster, Lawrence. "Free Love and Feminism: John Humphrey Noyes
      and the Oneida Community." JOURNAL OF THE EARLY REPUBLIC.
      1, 2 (Summer 1981) 165-83.

1451. FREE CHURCH CIRCULAR. Oneida Reserve, NY: Vols 3-4. January
      28, 1850-June 28, 1851.

1452. Gadsby, Edward N., Jr. "Oneida Limited: The Implementation of a
       Social Creed." Bachelor's thesis, Amherst College, 1957.

1453. Griffin, Clifford S. "Making Noyes." REVIEWS IN AMERICAN
       HISTORY. 5 (December 1977): 518-523.

1454. Haight, Norman Walter. "Faith and Freedom in Christian Utopia:
       An Analysis of the Thought of John Humphrey Noyes and the
       Oneida Community," PhD diss. Syracuse University, 1972.

1455. Hedden, Worth Tuttle. "Communism in New York, 1848-1879." THE
       AMERICAN SCHOLAR. 14 (Summer 1945): 283-292.

1456. ------. WIVES OF HIGH PASTURE. Garden City, NY: Doubleday, Doran
       & Co., 1944. (Fiction.)

1457. Hoehn, Richard A. "The Kingdom Goes Joint Stock: Learning From
       Oneida 100 Years Later." CHRISTIAN CENTURY. 98 (January
       28, 1981): 77-80.

1458. Holbrook, Stewart Hall. LOST MEN OF AMERICAN HISTORY. New York:
       Macmillan, 1946. pp. 241-266.

1459. Johnson, James E. "Charles G. Finney and Oberlin
       Perfectionism." JOURNAL OF PRESBYTERIAN HISTORY. 46
       (March 1968): 42-57; (June 1968): 128-138.

1460. Kaufmann, Moritz. SOCIALISM AND COMMUNISM IN THEIR PRACTICAL
       APPLICATION. London: Society for Promoting Christian
       Knowledge; New York: E. & J.B. Young & Co., 1883.
       Reprint. New York: AMS Press, 1976.

1461. KENWOOD KRONICLE. Kenwood, NY. 1894-1896. (Mimeographed.)

1462. KENWOOD KRONICLE. (2nd Series). Kenwood, NY. April 18,
       1898-May 18, 1899.

1463. Kephart, William M. "Experimental Family Organization: An
       Historico-Cultural Report on the Oneida Community."
       MARRIAGE AND FAMILY LIVING. 25 (August 1963): 261-271.

1464. Kern, Louis J. "Ideology and Reality: Sexuality and Women's
       Status in the Oneida Community." RADICAL HISTORY REVIEW.
       20 (Spring/Summer 1979): 181-205.

1465. Kinsley, Jesse Catharine. A LASTING SPRING: JESSE CATHARINE
       KINSLEY, DAUGHTER OF THE ONEIDA COMMUNITY. Ed. Jane
       Kinsley Rich, with the assistance of Nelson M. Blake.
       Syracuse, NY: Syracuse University Press, 1983.

1466. Lockwood, Maren. "The Experimental Utopia in America."
       DAEDALUS. 94 (Spring 1965): 401-418.

1467. Lowenthal, Esther. "Labor Policy of the Oneida Community, Limited." JOURNAL OF LABOR ECONOMY. 35 (1927): 114-126.

1468. McGee, Anita Newcomb. "An Experiment in Human Stirpiculture." THE AMERICAN ANTHROPOLOGIST. 4 (October 1891): 320-324.

1469. Mandelker, Ira L. RELIGION, SOCIETY, AND UTOPIA IN NINETEENTH-CENTURY AMERICA. Amherst: University of Massachusetts Press, 1984.

1470. Miller, George N. AFTER SEX STRUCK, OR ZUGASSENT'S DISCOVERY. Boston: Arena Publishing Co., 1895.

1471. Newcombe, Patricia Ann. "John Humphrey Noyes: Bible Communism." M.A. thesis, University of Chicago, 1958.

1472. Newhouse, Sewell. THE TRAPPER'S GUIDE: A MANUAL OF INSTRUCTIONS FOR CAPTURING ALL KINDS OF FUR-BEARING ANIMALS, AND CURING THEIR SKINS: WITH OBSERVATIONS OF TRAPPING AND HUNTING EXCURSIONS. 8th ed. Ed. John Humphrey Noyes. Community, NY: Oneida Community, Ltd., 1887.

1473. Noyes, Corinna Ackley. THE DAYS OF MY YOUTH. Kenwood, NY: By the author, 1960.

1474. Noyes, George Wallingford, ed. JOHN HUMPHREY NOYES: THE PUTNEY COMMUNITY. Oneida, NY: By the author, 1931. Reprint. Syracuse University Press.

1475. ------. THE ONEIDA COMMUNITY; ITS RELATION TO ORTHODOXY: BEING AN OUTLINE OF THE RELIGIOUS AND THEOLOGICAL APPLICATIONS OF THE MOST ADVANCED EXPERIMENT (IN APPLIED ETHICS) EVER MADE IN ANY AGE OR COUNTRY. n.p.: Fielding Star Print, [191?].

1476. ------. THE RELIGIOUS EXPERIENCE OF JOHN HUMPHREY NOYES, FOUNDER OF THE ONEIDA COMMUNITY. New York: Macmillan, 1923.

1477. Noyes, Hilda Herrick, and George Wallingford Noyes. "The Oneida Community Experiment in Stirpiculture." SCIENTIFIC PAPERS OF THE SECOND INTERNATIONAL CONGRESS OF EUGENICS, 1921. EUGENICS, GENETICS AND THE FAMILY. Vol. 1. Baltimore: Williams & Wilkins Co., 1923. pp. 374-386.

1478. Noyes, John Humphrey. THE BEREAN: A MANUAL FOR THE HELP OF THOSE WHO SEEK THE FAITH OF THE PRIMITIVE CHURCH. Putney, VT: Office of the spiritual magazine, 1847. Microfilm. Ann Arbor: University Microfilms, 1961. Reprint. New York: Ayer Company, 1969.

1479. ------. CONFESSIONS OF JOHN H. NOYES, PART I: CONFESSION OF RELIGIOUS EXPERIENCE: INCLUDING A HISTORY OF MODERN PERFECTIONISM. Oneida Reserve, NY: Leonard & Co.,

Printers, 1849. Microfilm. Ann Arbor: University
Microfilms, 1947.

1480. ------. DIXON AND HIS COPYISTS: A CRITICISM OF THE ACCOUNTS OF
        THE ONEIDA COMMUNITY IN "NEW AMERICA," "SPIRITUAL WIVES"
        AND KINDRED PUBLICATIONS. Wallingford,CT: Oneida
        Community, 1871. Microfilm. Ann Arbor: University
        Microfilms, 1961. Reprint. New York: AMS Press, 1972.

1481. ------. THE DOCTRINE OF SALVATION FROM SIN, EXPLAINED AND
        DEFENDED. Putney, VT: By the author, 1843.

1482. ------. ESSAY ON SCIENTIFIC PROPAGATION. Oneida, NY: Oneida
        Community 1875. Microfilm. Ann Arbor: University
        Microfilms, 1962. Reprint. New York: AMS Press, 1972.

1483. ------. HISTORY OF AMERICAN SOCIALISMS. Philadelphia: J.B.
        Lippincott, 1870. Reprint under title: STRANGE CULTS AND
        UTOPIAS OF 19TH CENTURY AMERICA. New York: Dover
        Publications, 1966.

1484. ------. HOME TALKS BY JOHN HUMPHREY NOYES. Vol. 1, eds. Alfred
        Barton and George Miller. Oneida, NY: Oneida Community,
        1875. Microfilm. Ann Arbor: University Microfilms, 1970.
        Reprint. New York: AMS Press, 1972.

1485. ------. MALE CONTINENCE; OR SELF-CONTROL IN SEXUAL INTERCOURSE.
        Oneida: Office of the Circular, 1866. Reprint. New York:
        AMS Press, 1970.

1486. ------. PAUL'S PRIZE. Oneida, NY, 1875.

1487. ------. SALVATION FROM SIN: THE END OF CHRISTIAN FAITH.
        Wallingford, CT: Oneida Community, 1866, 1876. Reprint.
        New York: AMS Press, 1972.

1488. ------. SLAVERY AND MARRIAGE. A DIALOGUE. N.p.: By the author?
        1850.

1489. ------. A TREATISE ON THE SECOND COMING OF CHRIST. Putney,VT,
        1840.

1490. ------. THE TWO-FOLD NATURE OF THE SECOND BIRTH. Putney, VT:
        Office of The Witness, 1841.

1491. ------. "The Way of Holiness" (A series of papers originally
        published in THE PERFECTIONIST. Putney, VT: J. H. Noyes &
        Co., 1838. Reprint. Westport, CT: Hyperion Press, 1976.

1492. Noyes, Pierrepont Burt. A GOODLY HERITAGE. New York: Rinehart,
        & Co., 1958.

1493. ------. MY FATHER'S HOUSE: AN ONEIDA BOYHOOD. New York: Farrar &
        Rinhart, Inc., 1937.

1494. ------. THE PALLID GIANT: A TALE OF YESTERDAY AND TOMORROW. New
       York: Fleming H. Revell Co., 1927.

1495. Noyes, Theodore R. REPORT ON THE HEALTH OF CHILDREN IN THE
       ONEIDA COMMUNITY. Oneida, NY: Oneida Community, 1878.

1496. Olin, Spencer C., Jr. "Bible Communism and the Origins of
       Orange County." CALIFORNIA HISTORY. 58 (Fall 1979):
       220-233.

1497. ------. "The Oneida Community and the Instability of Charismatic
       Authority." JOURNAL OF AMERICAN HISTORY. 67 (September
       1980): 285-300.

1498. Oneida Association. FIRST ANNUAL REPORT OF THE ONEIDA
       ASSOCIATION: EXHIBITING ITS HISTORY, PRINCIPLES, AND
       TRANSACTIONS TO JANUARY 1, 1849. Oneida Reserve, NY:
       Leonard & Co., Printers, 1849. Reprint. New York: AMS
       Press, 1978.

1499. ------. SECOND ANNUAL REPORT OF THE ONEIDA: EXHIBITING ITS
       PROGRESS TO FEBRUARY 20, 1850. Oneida Reserve, NY:
       Leonard & Co., Printers, 1850. Reprint. New York: AMS
       Press, 1978.

1500. ------. THIRD ANNUAL REPORT OF THE ONEIDA ASSOCIATION: EXHIBITING
       ITS PROGRESS TO FEBRUARY 20, 1851. Oneida Reserve, NY:
       Leonard & Co., Printers, 1851. Reprint. New York: AMS
       Press, 1978.

1501. ------. BIBLE COMMUNISM: A COMPILATION FROM THE ANNUAL REPORTS
       AND OTHER PUBLICATIONS OF THE ONEIDA ASSOCIATION AND ITS
       BRANCHES; PRESENTING, IN CONNECTION WITH THEIR HISTORY, A
       SUMMARY VIEW OF THEIR RELIGIOUS AND SOCIAL THEORIES.
       Brooklyn, NY: Office of the Circular, 1853. Reprint.
       Philadelphia: Porcupine Press, 1973.

1502. ------. MUTUAL CRITICISM. Oneida, NY: Office of the American
       Socialist, 1876.

1503. Oneida Community. THE AMERICAN SOCIALIST. DEVOTED TO THE
       ENLARGEMENT AND PERFECTION OF HOME. Oneida, NY: v. 1-4;
       March 30, 1876-December 28, 1879.

1504. ------. BIBLE ARGUMENT, DEFINING THE RELATIONS OF THE SEXES IN
       THE KINGDOM OF HEAVEN. Oneida Reserve? Leonard & Co.:
       1849?

1505. ------. CONSTITUTION OF THE ASSOCIATION OF PERFECTIONISTS.
       Putney, VT: 1845.

1506. ------. DAILY JOURNAL OF ONEIDA COMMUNITY. Oneida, NY: Vols. 1-3,
       1866-1868. Reprint. Philadelphia: Porcupine Press, 1973.

1507. ------. HAND-BOOK OF THE ONEIDA COMMUNITY; WITH A SKETCH OF ITS
           FOUNDER, AND AN OUTLINE OF ITS CONSTITUTION AND DOCTRINES.
           Wallingford, CT: Office of the Circular, 1867. Reprint.
           New York: AMS Press, 1972.

1508. ------. HAND-BOOK OF THE ONEIDA COMMUNITY 1875. Oneida, NY:
           Office of Oneida Circular (Wallingford, CT: Wallingford
           Printing Co.) 1875?

1509. ------. HAND-BOOK OF THE ONEIDA COMMUNITY; CONTAINING A BRIEF
           SKETCH OF ITS PRESENT CONDITION, INTERNAL ECONOMY AND
           LEADING PRINCIPLES. No 2.   Oneida, NY: Oneida Community,
           1871. Microfilm. Washington, D.C., Library of Congress.
           Photoduplication Services, 1974.

1510. ------. MUTUAL CRITICISM. Oneida, NY: Office of the American
           Socialist, 1876. Reprint. Syracuse University Press,
           1975.

1511. ------. ONEIDA CIRCULAR. A WEEKLY JOURNAL OF HOME, SCIENCE AND
           GENERAL INTELLIGENCE. Oneida & Wallingford Communities.
           v. 1-12, Nov. 6, 1851-February 22, 1864; new series. v.
           1-13, Mar. 21, 1864-Mar. 9, 1876. Brooklyn, NY [etc.]:
           1851-1876.

1512. ------. THE ONEIDA COMMUNITY: A FAMILIAR EXPOSITION OF ITS IDEAS
           AND PRACTICAL LIFE, IN A CONVERSATION WITH A VISITOR.
           Wallingford, CT: 1865.

1513. ------. THE ONEIDA COMMUNITY: ITS BUSINESS IDEALS. N.p.: 1910?

1514. Oneida Community, Limited. BY-LAWS OF THE ONEIDA COMMUNITY,
           LTD. TOGETHER WITH AN ACT TO PROVIDE FOR THE ORGANIZATION
           AND REGULATION OF CERTAIN BUSINESS CORPORATIONS PASSED BY
           THE LEGISLATURE OF NEW YORK, JUNE 21, 1875. Oneida
           Community, NY: 1881.

1515. ------. ONEIDA COMMUNITY, LIMITED: 1848-1901. N.p., n.d..

1516. Parker, Robert Allerton. A YANKEE SAINT: JOHN HUMPHREY NOYES
           AND THE ONEIDA COMMUNITY. New York: C.P. Putnam's Sons,
           1935. Reprint. Philadelphia: Porcupine Press, 1972.
           Reprint. Hamden,CT: Archon Books, 1973.

1517. PERFECTIONIST. New Haven, CT. Vols 1-2, 1834-1836.

1518. THE PERFECTIONIST AND THEOCRATIC WATCHMAN. Putney, VT: v. 1-5;
           August 20, 1837-February 14, 1846.

1519. Raynsford, James Willard, Jr. "Pierrepont B. Noyes: American
           Rhineland Commissioner." Bachelor's thesis, Williams
           College, 1942.

1520. Reed, Isaac G., Jr. "The Oneida Community of Free Lovers."
      FRANK LESLIE'S ILLUSTRATED WEEKLY NEWSPAPER. 30 (April 2,
      1870): 54-55; (April 9, 1870): 38-39.

1521. Robertson, Constance Noyes. ONEIDA COMMUNITY; AN AUTOBIOGRAPHY,
      1851-1876. Syracuse: Syracuse University Press, c1970,
      1981.

1522. ------. ONEIDA COMMUNITY: THE BREAKUP, 1876-1881. Syracuse:
      Syracuse University Press, 1972.

1523. ------. ONEIDA COMMUNITY PROFILES. Syracuse: Syracuse University
      Press, 1977.

1524. Robie, W.F. THE ART OF LOVE. Ithaca, NY: Rational Life
      Publishing Co., Inc., 1925.

1525. Robinson, C.E. [C.R. Edson], pseud. "Communism, Oneida
      Community." MANUFACTURER AND BUILDER. 25 (1893):
      282-283; 26 (1894): 94-95.

1526. Sandeen, Ernest R. "John Humphrey Noyes as the New Adam."
      CHURCH HISTORY. 40 (March 1971): 82-90.

1527. Seymour, Henry J. THE ONEIDA COMMUNITY: A DIALOGUE. N.p., n.d.
      (before 1881?)

1528. Sibley, M.Q. "Oneida's Challenge to American Culture." In
      STUDIES IN AMERICAN CULTURE; DOMINANT IDEAS AND IMAGES.
      Ed. by Joseph J. Kwiat and Mary C. Turpie. Minneapolis:
      University of Minnesota Press, 1960. pp. 41-61.

1529. Smith, Goldwin. "The Oneida Comunity and American Socialism."
      Appendix to ESSAYS ON QUESTIONS OF THE DAY: POLITICAL AND
      SOCIAL. Goldwin Smith, ed. New York: Macmillan, 1893.

1530. SPIRITUAL MAGAZINE. Putney, VT, and Oneida Reserve, NY. Vols.
      1-2, 15 March 1846-June 17, 1850.

1531. THE SPIRITUAL MORALIST. Putney, VT: Vol. 1, no. 1-2; June
      13-25, 1852.

1532. Summer, Keene. "Higher You Climb the More Lonely You Become; an
      Interview with P.B. Noyes." AMERICAN MAGAZINE. 106
      (December 1928): 26-27; 129-130.

1533. Thomas, Robert David. "John Humphrey Noyes and the Oneida
      Community: a 19th-Century American Father and His Family."
      PSYCHOHISTORY REVIEW. 6 (Fall-Winter 1977-1978): 68-87.

1534. ------. THE MAN WHO WOULD BE PERFECT: JOHN HUMPHREY NOYES AND THE
      UTOPIAN IMPULSE. Philadelphia: University of Pennsylvania
      Press, 1977.

1535. Van de Warker, E. "A Gynecological Study of the Oneida
       Community." AMERICAN JOURNAL OF OBSTETRICS AND DISEASES
       OF WOMEN. 17 (1884): 785-810.

1536. Veysey, Laurence, ed. THE PERFECTIONISTS: RADICAL SOCIAL
       THOUGHT IN THE NORTH, 1815-1860. New York: Wiley, 1973.

1537. Warfield, Benjamin B. "John Humphrey Noyes and His `Bible
       Communists'." BIBLIOTHECA SACRA. 78 (January-October
       1921): 37-72.

1538. Wayland-Smith, Francis [Gerald Thorne]. HEAVEN ON EARTH: A
       REALISTIC TALE. New York: Lovell Brothers & Co., 1896.

1539. ------. MATERIALISM AND CHRISTIANITY. Kenwood, NY: By the
       author, 1906.

1540. ------. SHALL WE CHOOSE SOCIALISM? Kenwood, NY: By the author,
       1907.

1541. Wayland-Smith, Louis. REMINISCENCES. Kenwood, NY: By the
       author, 1955.

1542. Wilson, Edmund. TO THE FINLAND STATION. New York: Harcourt,
       Brace & Co. 1940. pp. 99-111.

1543. THE WITNESS. Ithaca, NY, and Putney, VT. Vols. 1-2.
       1837-1843.

1544. Worden, Harriet. OLD MANSION HOUSE MEMORIES, BY ONE BROUGHT UP
       IN IT. Kenwood, NY, 1950.

1545. Wyatt, Philip R. "John Humphrey Noyes and the Stirpicultural
       Experiment." JOURNAL OF THE HISTORY OF MEDICINE AND
       ALLIED SCIENCE. 31 (January 1976): 55-66.

OWENITE COMMUNITIES

Robert Owen (1771-1858), a Welshman, who sought to improve working conditions and reform society in general, established a model industry at New Lanark, Scotland. He transferred his ideas to the U.S., most notably at New Harmony, Indiana (1825-1827), Yellow Springs, Ohio (1825-1826), Kendal, Ohio (1826-1829), Blue Spring, Indiana (1826-1827), Equality, Wisconsin (1843-1846), and Nashoba, Tennessee (1826-1829).

ARCHIVAL MATERIALS

1546. Illinois Historical Survey. University of Illinois. Robert Owen Papers in Manchester. Rephotographed in series "British Records Relating to America in Microform". East Ardsley, Wakefield, Yorkshire, 1966.

1547. Lichtenberger Family. Papers, 1837-1894. New York Public Library, New York.

1548. New Harmony, Indiana. Records, 1825-1835. University of Illinois, Illinois Historical Survey Collections.

1549. New Harmony, Indiana. Working Men's Institute. Manuscript Collection, 1814-1940. Library. Working Men's Institute, New Harmony, IN.

1550. Owen, Robert Dale. Papers, 1827-1877. Indiana State Library, Indianapolis.

BIBLIOGRAPHIES

1551. Bestor, Arthur Eugene. RECORDS OF THE NEW HARMONY COMMUNITY; A DESCRIPTIVE CATALOGUE OF THE MANUSCRIPT VOLUMES RESERVED IN THE WORKING MEN'S INSTITUTE, NEW HARMONY, INDIANA, AND ELSEWHERE AND REPRODUCED PHOTOGRAPHICALLY FOR THE ILLINOIS HISTORICAL SURVEY. Urbana: Illinois Historical Society, 1950.

1552. Goto, Shigeru. ROBERT OWEN, 1771-1838: A NEW BIBLIOGRAPHICAL STUDY. 2 vols. Osaka: Osaka University of Commerce, Studies, 1931-1934.

1553. National Library of Wales. A BIBLIOGRAPHY OF ROBERT OWEN, THE SOCIALIST. 2nd ed. Aberystwyth, Wales, 1925.

1554. Reese, Rena, comp. LIST OF BOOKS AND PAMPHLETS IN A SPECIAL COLLECTION IN THE LIBRARY OF THE WORKINGMEN'S INSTITUTE. New Harmony, 1909.

ARTICLES AND BOOKS

1555. Albjerg, Victor Lincoln. RICHARD OWEN, SCOTLAND, 1810, INDIANA, 1890. The Archives of Purdue, no. 2. Lafayette, IN., 1946.

1556. Allen, Nic. DAVID DALE, ROBERT OWEN AND THE STORY OF NEW LANARK. Edinburgh: Moubrary House Press, 1986.

1557. Armytage, W.H.G. "William Maclure, 1763-1840: A British Interpretation." INDIANA MAGAZINE OF HISTORY. 47 (March 1951): 1-20.

1558. Atsushi, Shirai. "William Godwin and Robert Owen." KEIO ECONOMIC STUDIES. 7 (1970): 64-77.

1559. Banta, Richard E. "New Harmony's Golden Years." INDIANA MAGAZINE OF HISTORY. 44 (March 1948): 25-36.

1560. Barger, Melvin D. "Robert Owen: The Woolly-Minded Cotton Spinner." THE FREEMAN. 26 (February 1976): 101-109.

1561. Bestor, Arthur E. "Review of 'The Diaries of Donald MacDonald, 1824-1826.'" NEW YORK HISTORY. 24 (January 1943): 80-86.

1562. Blau, Joseph Leon, ed. SOCIAL THEORIES OF JACKSONIAN DEMOCRACY: REPRESENTATIVE WRITINGS OF THE PERIOD 1825-1850. New York: Hafner Publishing Co., 1947; Liberal Arts Press, 1954.

1563. Boewe, Charles E. PRAIRIE ALBION; AN ENGLISH SETTLEMENT IN PIONEER ILLINOIS. Carbondale: Southern Illinois University Press, 1962.

1564. Booth, Arthur John. ROBERT OWEN, THE FOUNDER OF SOCIALISM IN ENGLAND. London: Trubner, 1869.

1565. Brown, Paul. AN ENQUIRY CONCERNING THE NATURE, END AND PRACTICABILITY OF A COURSE OF PHILOSOPHICAL EDUCATION. Washington City: Printed for the author, by J. Gideon, Jr. 1822.

1566. Browne, Charles Albert. "Some Relations of the New Harmony Movement to the History of Science in America." SCIENTIFIC MONTHLY. 42 (June 1936): 483-497.

1567. Butt, John. ROBERT OWEN OF NEW LANARK; 1771-1858: A BICENTENNIAL TRIBUTE. Glasgow: The Open University in Scotland, 1980. Reprinted from Industrial Archaeology. Vol. 8, no. 2, May 1971.

1568. ------, ed. ROBERT OWEN, PRINCE OF COTTON SPINNERS: A SYMPOSIUM. Newton Abbott: David & Charles, 1971.

1569. Campbell, Alexander. "Letters from Europe--No. I." MILLENNIAL
      HARBINGER. 3rd series. 4 (May 22, 1847): 420.

1570. Carmony, Donald Francis, and Josephine M. Elliott. "New
      Harmony, Indiana: Robert Owen's Seedbed for Utopia."
      INDIANA MAGAZINE OF HISTORY. 76 (September 1980): 160-261

1571. CINCINNATI LITERARY GAZETTE. 2 (October 30, 1824) to 3
      (September 10, 1825).

1572. Claeys, Gregory. MACHINERY, MONEY AND THE MILLENNIUM: THE NEW
      MORAL ECONOMY OF OWENITE SOCIALISM, 1815-60. Princeton:
      Princeton University Press, 1987.

1573. ------. "Paternalism and Democracy in the Politics of Robert
      Owen." INTERNATIONAL REVIEW OF SOCIAL HISTORY. 27
      (1982): 161-207.

1574. Cole, David. HISTORY OF ROCKLAND COUNTY, NEW YORK, WITH
      BIOGRAPHICAL SKETCHES OF ITS PROMINENT MEN. New York:
      J.B. Beers & Co., 1884. pp. 156-157.

1575. Cole, George Douglas Howard. THE LIFE OF ROBERT OWEN. 2nd ed.
      London: Macmillan and Co., Ltd., 1930.

1576. ------. "Owen and Owenism." ENCYCLOPAEDIA OF THE SOCIAL
      SCIENCES. New York: Macmillan, 1930, reissued 1937. s.v.

1577. ------. ROBERT OWEN. Boston: Little, Brown, 1925.

1578. Cole, Margaret, Isabel (Postgate). ROBERT OWEN OF NEW LANARK.
      New York: Oxford University Press; London: Batchworth
      Press, 1953.

1579. Cottman, George S. "The New Harmony Movement." INDIANA
      MAGAZINE OF HISTORY. 1 (1905): 157-159.

1580. Courtauld, George. ADDRESS TO THOSE WHO MAY BE DISPOSED TO
      REMOVE TO THE UNITED STATES OF AMERICA, ON THE ADVANTAGES
      OF EQUITABLE ASSOCIATIONS OF CAPITAL AND LABOUR, IN THE
      FORMATION OF AGRICULTURAL ESTABLISHMENTS IN THE INTERIOR
      COUNTRY. INCLUDING REMARKS OF MR. BIRKBECK'S OPINIONS
      UPON THIS SUBJECT. Sudbury, England: Printed and sold by
      J. Burkitt, 1820.

1581. Cullen, Alexander. ADVENTURES IN SOCIALISM: NEW LANARK
      ESTABLISHMENT AND ORBISTON COMMUNITY. Glasgow: J. Smith &
      Son, 1910. Reprint. New York: AMS Press, 1970.

1582. Davidson, Marshall B. "Carl Bodmer's Unspoiled West." AMERICAN
      HERITAGE. 14 (April 1963): 43-65.

1583.   de la Hunt, Thomas James, comp. HISTORY OF THE NEW HARMONY
        WORKING MEN'S INSTITUTE, NEW HARMONY, INDIANA, FOUNDED BY
        WILLIAM MACLURE, 1838-1927. Evansville, IN: Printed and
        engraved by Burkert-Walton Co., 1927.

1584.   Denehie, Elizabeth Smith. "The Harmonist Movement in Indiana."
        INDIANA MAGAZINE OF HISTORY. 19 (June 1923): 188-200.

1585.   THE DISSEMINATOR OF USEFUL KNOWLEDGE. New Harmony, IN., January
        16, 1828-March 4, 1841.

1586.   Dolleans, Edouard. ROBERT OWEN (1771-1858). Paris: G.
        Bellais, 1905.

1587.   Dos Passos, Katharine, and Edith Shay. "New Harmony, Indiana."
        THE ATLANTIC MONTHLY. 166 (November 1940): 604-611.

1588.   THE ECONOMIST: A PERIODICAL PAPER EXPLANATORY OF THE NEW SYSTEM
        OF SOCIETY PROJECTED BY ROBERT OWEN. London, January 27,
        1821-March 9, 1822.

1589.   Elliott, Josephine Mirabella. "Madame Marie Fretageot:
        Communitarian Educator." COMMUNAL SOCIETIES. 4 (Fall
        1984): 168-182.

1590.   ------. "The Owen Family Papers." INDIANA MAGAZINE OF HISTORY.
        60 (December 1964): 330- 352.

1591.   ------, ed. ROBERT DALE OWEN'S TRAVEL JOURNAL, 1827.
        Indianapolis: Indiana Historical Society, 1977, c1978.

1592.   ------. TO HOLLAND AND TO NEW HARMONY. ROBERT DALE OWEN'S TRAVEL
        JOURNAL, 1825-1826. Indianapolis: Indiana Historical
        Society, 1969.

1593.   Estabrook, Arthur H. "The Family History of Robert Owen."
        INDIANA MAGAZINE OF HISTORY. 19 (March 1923): 63-101.

1594.   Everett, Linus S. AN EXPOSURE OF THE PRINCIPLES OF THE "FREE
        INQUIRERS." Boston: B.B. Mussey, 1831.

1595.   Flower, George. HISTORY OF THE ENGLISH SETTLEMENT IN EDWARDS
        COUNTY, ILLINOIS. Chicago: Chicago Historical Society,
        1882.

1596.   THE FREE ENQUIRER. 1825-1835.

1597.   Fretageot, Nora (Chadwick), and W.V. Mangrum. HISTORIC NEW
        HARMONY: OFFICIAL GUIDE. Evansville, IN: Keller-Crescent
        Co., 1914, 1934.

1598.   Galloway, William Albert. THE HISTORY OF GLEN HELEN. Columbus,
        OH: Printed by the F.J. Heer Co., 1932. pp. 47-53.

1599. Gould, Kenneth M. "Robert Owen: Backwater of History?"
      AMERICAN SCHOLAR. 7 (Spring 1938): 153-170.

1600. Grant, A. Cameron. "New Light on an Old View: Comb's Phrenology
      and Robert Owen." JOURNAL OF THE HISTORY OF IDEAS. 29
      (April/June 1968): 293-301.

1601. Gray, John. A LECTURE ON HUMAN HAPPINESS. Philadelphia: J.
      Coates, 1826. Microfilm. New York: New York Public
      Library, 1951.

1602. Hahn, Manfred. NEW HARMONY, ODER, DIE VERSUCHE DES
      PRAKTISCHEN BEWEISES GEGEN DIE KAPITALISTISCHE
      GESELLSCHAFT: VORMARXISTISCHER SOZIALISMUS ALS
      COMMUNITIES. Bremen: Universitat Bremen, 1983.

1603. Hamy, E.T. "Les voyages du naturaliste Ch. Alex. Leseur dans
      l'Amerique du Nord, 1815-1837." JOURNAL DE LA SOCIETE DES
      AMERICANISTES DE PARIS. 5 (1904).

1604. Harrison, John Fletcher Clews. "Owenite Communitarianism in
      Britain and America." COMMUNAL SOCIETIES. 4 (Fall 1984):
      243-248.

1605. ------. "The Owenite Socialist Movement in Britain and the United
      States." LABOR HISTORY. 9 (Fall 1968): 323-337.

1606. ------. QUEST FOR THE NEW MORAL WORLD: ROBERT OWEN AND THE
      OWENITES IN BRITAIN AND AMERICA. New York: Scribners,
      1969. Published in London by Routledge and K. Paul, under
      title: ROBERT OWEN AND THE OWENITES IN BRITAIN AND
      AMERICA; THE QUEST FOR THE NEW MORAL WORLD.

1607. ------. SOCIAL REFORM IN VICTORIAN LEEDS: THE WORK OF JAMES HOLE,
      1820-1895. Leeds: Thoresby Society, 1954.

1608. ------, comp. UTOPIANISM AND EDUCATION: ROBERT OWEN AND THE
      OWENITES. New York: Teachers College Press, Columbia
      University, 1968.

1609. Harvey, Rowland Hill. ROBERT OWEN: SOCIAL IDEALIST. Berkeley
      and Los Angeles: University of California Press, 1949.

1610. Hebert, William. A VISIT TO THE COLONY OF HARMONY IN INDIANA.
      London: Printed for G. Mann, 1825. Reprinted in Lindley,
      INDIANA AS SEEN BY EARLY TRAVELERS. pp. 339-340.

1611. Heilbroner, Robert L. THE WORLDLY PHILOSOPHERS. New York:
      Simon & Schuster, 1953. pp. 96-126.

1612. Hendrickson, Walter Brookfield. DAVID DALE OWEN, PIONEER
      GEOLOGIST OF THE MIDDLE WEST. Indianapolis: The Indiana
      Historical Bureau, 1943.

1613. ------. "An Owenite Society in Illinois." INDIANA MAGAZINE OF
      HISTORY. 45 (June 1949): 175-182.

1614. THE HERALD OF THE NEW MORAL WORLD AND MILLENNIAL HARBINGER,
      DEVOTED TO THE INTEREST OF THE INDUSTRIOUS AND PRODUCING
      CLASSES, AND THE ELEVATION OF MANKIND. Ed. by J.M.
      Horner. New York, January 6, 1841-August 1842.

1615. Hermann, Janet Sharp. THE PURSUIT OF A DREAM. New York: Oxford
      University Press, 1981.

1616. Hubbard, Elbert. ROBERT OWEN IN LITTLE JOURNEYS TO THE HOMES OF
      GREAT BUSINESS MEN. East Aurora, NY: Roycrofters, 1909.

1617. Hunt, Thomas. "The Past and Present of the Colony of
      `Equality'." THE NEW MORAL WORLD. 13 (August 2, 1845):
      472-475.

1618. Hurst, Roger A. "The New Harmony Manuscript Collections."
      INDIANA MAGAZINE OF HISTORY. 37 (March 1941): 45-49.

1619. Ismar, F.A. THE SCHOOL OF INDUSTRY, AT NEW HARMONY STATE OF
      INDIANA, AND MADAME MARIA DUCLOS FRETAGEOT; A LETTER TO
      MR. WILLIAM MACLURE. New Harmony, IN: Printed for the
      author, 1830.

1620. Jones, Arnita Ament. "From Utopia to Reform." HISTORY TODAY
      [Great Britain]. 26 (1976): 393-401.

1621. Jones, Lloyd. LIFE, TIMES AND LABOURS OF ROBERT OWEN. London:
      Labour Association, 1890. Reprint. New York: AMS Press,
      1977.

1622. Jordan, David Starr, and Amos W. Butler. "New Harmony."
      SCIENTIFIC MONTHLY. 25 (November 1927): 468-470.
      Reprint. INDIANA ACADEMY OF SCIENCE. PROCEEDINGS. 37
      (1928): 59-62.

1623. Knortz, Karl. ROBERT OWEN AND SEINE WELTVER BESSERSVERSUCHE.
      Leipzig: E. Demme, 1910.

1624. Knox, Julia LeClerc. "The Unique Little Town of New Harmony."
      INDIANA MAGAZINE OF HISTORY. 32 (March 1936): 52-58, 282.

1625. Kolmerton, Carol A. "Egalitarian Promises and Inegalitarian
      Practices: Women's Roles in the American Owenite
      Communities, 1824-1828." JOURNAL OF GENERAL EDUCATION. 33
      (Spring 1981): 31-44.

1626. Lang, Elfrieda. "The Inhabitants of New Harmony According to
      the Federal Census of 1850." INDIANA MAGAZINE OF HISTORY.
      42 (December 1946): 355-394.

1627. Leopold, Richard William. ROBERT DALE OWEN: A BIOGRAPHY. Cambridge, Harvard University Press, 1940. Reprint. New York: Octagon Books, 1969.

1628. "Life Visits New Harmony." LIFE 19 (September 17, 1945): 133-139.

1629. Lindley, Harlow, ed. INDIANA AS SEEN BY EARLY TRAVELLERS; A COLLECTION OF REPRINTS FROM BOOKS OF TRAVEL, LETTERS AND DIARIES PRIOR TO 1830. Indianapolis: Indiana Historical Commission, 1916.

1630. Lockwood, George Browning. THE NEW HARMONY COMMUNITIES. Marion, IN: The Chronicle Co., 1902. Reprinted and revised as THE NEW HARMONY MOVEMENT. New York: D. Appleton and Co., 1905. Reprint. New York: AMS Press, 1971.

1631. Lockridge, Ross Franklin. THE OLD FAUNTLEROY HOME. New Harmony, IN: Published for the New Harmony Memorial Commission by courtesy of Mrs. Edmund Burke Ball, 1939.

1632. McCabe, Joseph. ROBERT OWEN. London: Watts & Co., 1920.

1633. Macdonald, Donald. "The Diaries of Donald Mcdonald, 1824-1826." INDIANA HISTORICAL SOCIETY PUBLICATIONS. 14 (1942): 145-379.

1634. M'Knight, James. DISCOURSE EXPOSING ROBERT OWEN'S SYSTEM AS PRACTISED BY THE FRANKLIN COMMUNITY, AT HAVERSTRAW. New York, 1826.

1635. Maclure, William. EDUCATION AND REFORM AT NEW HARMONY; CORRESPONDENCE OF WILLIAM MACLURE AND MARIE DUCLOS FRETAGEOT, 1820-1833. Ed. by Arthur E. Bestor, Jr., Indianapolis: Indiana Historical Society, 1948. Reprint. Clifton, NJ: A.M. Kelley, 1973.

1636. ------. OPINIONS ON VARIOUS SUBJECTS, DEDICATED TO THE INDUSTRIOUS PRODUCERS. 3 vols. New Harmony, 1831-1838.

1637. ------. "Sketch of His Life." AMERICAN JOURNAL OF SCIENCE. 47 (April-June 1844): 1-17.

1638. Miliband, Ralph. "The Politics of Robert Owen." JOURNAL OF THE HISTORY OF IDEAS. 15 (April 1954): 233-245.

1639. MILLENNIAL GAZETTE, nos. 1-16, March 22, 1856-July 1, 1858. Reprint. New York: AMS Press, 1973.

1640. Monaghan, Jay, ed. "From England to Illinois in 1821: The Journal of William Hall." JOURNAL OF THE ILLINOIS STATE HISTORICAL SOCIETY. 39 (March, June 1946): 35, 45-47, 51-57, 211, 215, 217, 221, 235, 238-45.

1641. Moore, J. Percy. "William Maclure--Scientist and Humanitarian."
       PROCEEDINGS OF THE AMERICAN PHILOSOPHICAL SOCIETY. 91
       (1947): 234-249.

1642. Morris, James M. "Communes and Cooperatives: Cincinnati's
       Early Experiments in Social Reform." CINCINNATI
       HISTORICAL SOCIETY BULLETIN. 33 (Spring 1975): 57-80.

1643. Morrison, Frances. THE INFLUENCE OF THE PRESENT MARRIAGE SYSTEM
       UPON THE CHARACTER AND INTERESTS OF FEMALES CONTRASTED
       WITH THAT PROPOSED BY ROBERT OWEN. Manchester: A.
       Heywood, 1838.

1644. Morton, Arthur L. THE LIFE AND IDEAS OF ROBERT OWEN. New York:
       International Publishers, 1969.

1645. Morton, Samuel George. A MEMOIR OF WILLIAM MACLURE, ESQ.
       Philadelphia: The Academy of Natural Sciences of
       Philadelphia, 1844.

1646. THE NEW HARMONY GAZETTE. New Harmony. October 1, 1825-October
       22, 1828. Continued as THE NEW-HARMONY AND NASHOBA
       GAZETTE, or THE FREE ENQUIRER. 2nd series, 5 vols.; 3rd
       series, 2 vols. New York: October 29, 1828-June 28, 1835.

1647. THE NEW MORAL WORLD: AND GAZETTE OF THE RATIONAL SOCIETY.
       London, November 1, 1834-August 16, 1845. Reprint. New
       York: Greenwood Corp., 1969.

1648. Owen, Robert. AN ADDRESS DELIVERED AT THE COMMENCEMENT OF THE
       ASSOCIATION OF ALL CLASSES AT ALL NATIONS. MAY 1, 1835.
       London: Printed by C. Baker, 1835.

1649. ------. ADDRESS DELIVERED BY ROBERT OWEN, AT A PUBLIC MEETING,
       HELD AT THE FRANKLIN INSTITUTE IN THE CITY OF PHILADEL-
       PHIA, ON MONDAY MORNING, JUNE 25, 1827. TO WHICH IS
       ADDED, AN EXPOSITION OF THE PECUNIARY TRANSACTION BETWEEN
       THAT GENTLEMAN AND WILLIAM M'CLURE. TAKEN IN SHORT HAND
       BY M.T.C. GOULD. Philadelphia: M.T.C. Gould, 1827.

1650. ------. ADDRESS DELIVERED BY ROBERT OWEN, OF NEW LANARK,
       WEDNESDAY, THE 27TH OF APRIL, 1825, IN THE NEW CHURCH OF
       NEW HARMONY, INDIANA. TOGETHER WITH THE CONSTITUTION OF
       THE PRELIMINARY SOCIETY; AND THE PROPOSED RULES AND
       REGULATIONS FOR THE ESTABLISHMENT OF A PERFECT COMMUNITY.
       Cincinnati: Published by the Society, 1825.

1651. ------. ADDRESS ON SPIRITUAL MANIFESTATIONS, DELIVERED BY ROBERT
       OWEN, AT THE LITERARY INSTITUTION, JOHN STREET, FITZROY
       SQUARE, ON FRIDAY, JULY, THE 27TH, 1855. London: J.
       Clayton and Son, 1855.

1652. ------. ADDRESS ON THE HOPES AND DESTINIES OF THE HUMAN SPECIES
       ... London: J. Watson, 1836.

1653. ------. AN ADDRESS TO THE SOCIALISTS ON THE PRESENT POSITION OF
       THE RATIONAL SYSTEM OF SOCIETY; AND THE MEASURES REQUIRED
       TO DIRECT MOST SUCCESSFULLY THE OPERATIONS OF THE
       UNIVERSAL COMMUNITY SOCIETY OF RATIONAL RELIGIONISTS,
       BEING THE SUBSTANCE OF TWO LECTURES, DELIVERED IN LONDON,
       PREVIOUS TO THE MEETING OF CONGRESS, IN MAY 1841 ...
       London: Home Colonization Society, 1841.

1654. ------. THE BOOK OF THE NEW MORAL WORLD, CONTAINING THE RATIONAL
       SYSTEM OF SOCIETY, FOUNDED ON DEMONSTRABLE FACTS,
       DEVELOPING THE CONSTITUTION AND LAWS OF HUMAN NATURE AND
       OF SOCIETY. London: E.Wilson, 1836; New York: G. Vale,
       1845.

1655. ------. THE CATECHISM OF THE NEW MORAL WORLD. Manchester: A.
       Heywood, 1838?

1656. ------. THE COMING MILLENNIUM. (FIRST SERIES.) TRACT NO. 1-6;
       (SECOND SERIES.) TRACT NO. 7-12. London: 1855.

1657. ------. COMMUNISM; (PRIMITIVE CHRISTIANITY) ADVOCATED BY ROBERT
       OWEN, OF LANARK, DUBLIN, 1823.

1658. ------. THE CRISIS; OR THE CHANGE FROM ERROR AND MISERY TO TRUTH
       AND HAPPINESS ... London: B.D. Cousins, 18?

1659. ------. DEBATE ON THE EVIDENCES OF CHRISTIANITY, CONTAINING AN
       EXAMINATION OF THE "SOCIAL SYSTEM" AND OF ALL THE SYSTEMS
       OF SCEPTICISM OF ANCIENT AND MODERN TIMES, HELD IN THE
       CITY OF CINCINNATI, OHIO, FROM THE 13TH TO THE 21ST OF
       APRIL, 1829, BETWEEN ROBERT OWEN OF NEW LANARK, SCOTLAND,
       AND ALEXANDER CAMPBELL OF BETHANY, VIRGINIA, REPORTED BY
       CHARLES H. SIMS [I.E. SIMMS] STENOGRAPHER, WITH AN
       APPENDIX WRITTEN BY THE PARTIES. Bethany, Va., A.
       Campbell, 1829; London: R. Broombridge, 1839. Microfilm.
       Ann Arbor: University Microfilms, 1966.

1660. ------. A DEVELOPMENT OF THE PRINCIPLES AND PLANS ON WHICH TO
       ESTABLISH SELF-SUPPORTING HOME COLONIES; AS A MOST SECURE
       AND PROFITABLE INVESTMENT FOR CAPITAL, AND AN EFFECTUAL
       MEANS PERMANENTLY TO REMOVE THE CAUSES OF IGNORANCE,
       POVERTY, AND CRIME. London: Home Colonization Society,
       1841. Microfilm. Ann Arbor: University Microfilms, 1966.

1661. ------. A DEVELOPMENT OF THE ORIGIN AND EFFECTS OF MORAL EVIL,
       AND OF THE PRINCIPLES AND PRACTICES OF MORAL GOOD,
       EXEMPLIFIED IN THE FOLLOWING PROOFS OF THE IRRATIONALITY
       OF THE OLD IMMORAL WORLD, CONTRASTED BY AN EXPOSITION OF
       THE PRINCIPLES AND PRACTICES WHICH WILL ENSURE THE
       RATIONALITY OF THE NEW MORAL WORLD. Manchester: A.
       Heywood; London: Hetherington, 1838.

1662. ------. A DIALOGUE, IN THREE PARTS BETWEEN THE FOUNDER OF "THE
       ASSOCIATION OF ALL CLASSES OF ALL NATIONS," AND A STRANGER
       DESIROUS OF BEING ACCURATELY INFORMED RESPECTING ITS
       ORIGIN AND OBJECTS. Manchester: A Heywood, 1838.

1663. ------. A DISCOURSE ON A NEW SYSTEM OF SOCIETY; AS DELIVERED IN
       THE HALL OF REPRESENTATIVES OF THE UNITED STATES, IN
       PRESENCE OF THE PRESIDENT OF THE UNITED STATES, THE EX-
       PRESIDENT, HEADS OF DEPARTMENTS, MEMBERS OF CONGRESS, ETC.,
       ON THE 7TH OF MARCH, 1825. Washington: Printed by Gales &
       Seaton, 1825. Microfilm. Ann Arbor: University Micro-
       films, 1968.

1664. ------. INSTITUTES OF CANON LAW. London: J.T. Hayes, 1864.

1665. ------. LECTURES ON THE MARRIAGES OF THE PRIESTHOOD OF THE OLD
       IMMORAL WORLD, DELIVERED IN THE YEAR 1835, BEFORE THE
       PASSING OF THE NEW MARRIAGE ACTS. Leeds: Author, 1835.

1666. ------. THE LIFE OF ROBERT OWEN. WRITTEN BY HIMSELF. WITH
       SELECTIONS FROM HIS WRITINGS AND CORRESPONDENCE. 2 vols.
       London: E. Wilson, 1857-1858. Reprint. Clifton, NJ:
       Augustus M. Kelley, 1967.

1667. ------. MANIFESTO OF ROBERT OWEN, THE DISCOVERER AND FOUNDER OF
       THE RATIONAL SYSTEM OF SOCIETY, AND OF THE RATIONAL
       RELIGION. Manchester: A.Heywood, 1840.

1668. ------. THE MARRIAGE SYSTEM OF THE NEW MORAL WORLD; WITH A FAINT
       OUTLINE OF THE PRESENT VERY IRRATIONAL SYSTEM; AS
       DEVELOPED IN A COURSE OF TEN LECTURES. ... Leeds: J.
       Hobson, 1838.

1669. ------. THE NEW RELIGION; OR, RELIGION FOUNDED ON THE IMMUTABLE
       LAWS OF THE UNIVERSE, CONTRASTED WITH ALL RELIGIONS
       FOUNDED ON HUMAN TESTIMONY, AS DEVELOPED IN A PUBLIC
       LECTURE, DELIVERED BY MR. OWEN, OCTOBER 20, 1830. London:
       J. Brooks, 1830.

1670. ------. A NEW SOCIETY AND OTHER WRITINGS BY ROBERT OWEN. Ed.
       Ernest Rhys. New York: E.P. Dutton, 1927.

1671. ------. A NEW VIEW OF SOCIETY; OR, ESSAYS ON THE PRINCIPLE OF THE
       FORMATION OF THE HUMAN CHARACTER, AND THE APPLICATION OF
       THE PRINCIPLE TO PRACTICE. BY ONE OF HIS MAJESTY'S
       JUSTICES OF PEACE FOR THE COUNTY OF LANARK. London:
       Printed for Cadell and Davies, by R. Taylor and Co., 1813.

1672. ------. NEW VIEW OF SOCIETY. TRACTS RELATIVE TO THIS SUBJECT: V.
       12. PROPOSALS FOR RAISING A COLLEGE OF INDUSTRY OF ALL
       USEFUL TRADES AND HUSBANDRY. BY JOHN BELLERS. (REPRINTED
       FROM THE ORIGINAL, PUBLISHED IN THE YEAR 1696). REPORT TO
       THE COMMITTEE OF THE ASSOCIATION FOR THE RELIEF OF THE

MANUFACTURING AND LABORING POOR. A BRIEF SKETCH OF THE
RELIGIOUS SOCIETY OF PEOPLE CALLED SHAKERS. WITH AN
ACCOUNT OF THE PUBLIC PROCEEDINGS CONNECTED WITH THE
SUBJECT, WHICH TOOK PLACE IN LONDON IN JULY AND AUGUST
1817. London: Longman, Hurst, Rees, Orme, and Brown,
1818. Reprint. Clifton, NJ: Augustus Kelley, 1967; New
York: AMS Press, 1972.

1673. ------. ORATION, CONTAINING A DECLARATION OF MENTAL INDEPENDENCE,
DELIVERED IN THE PUBLIC HALL, AT NEW HARMONY, IND., BY
ROBERT OWEN, AT THE CELEBRATION OF THE FOURTH OF JULY,
1826. New Harmony, IN, 1826. Microfilm. University of
Illinois, Library, 1950.

1674. ------. OUTLINE OF THE RATIONAL SYSTEM OF SOCIETY, FOUNDED ON
DEMONSTRABLE FACTS, DEVELOPING THE CONSTITUTION AND LAWS
OF HUMAN NATURE; BEING THE ONLY EFFECTUAL REMEDY FOR THE
EVILS EXPERIENCED BY THE POPULATION OF THE WORLD. London:
Cousins, Printer, 183-?

1675. ------. PAMPHLETS AND ADDRESSES ON SOCIALISM. London,
1818-[1844].

1676. ------. THE PROBLEM OF THE AGE SOLVED. New York, 1847.

1677. ------. REASONS FOR EACH LAW OF THE NEW CONSTITUTION PROPOSED TO
BE INTRODUCED FIRST INTO THE STATE OF NEW YORK, AFTERWARDS
INTO EACH STATE OF THE UNION, AND THEN FROM THE UNIVERSAL
AND UNCHANGING TRUTH OF THE PRINCIPLES AND INNUMERABLE
ADVANTAGES IN PRACTICE TO ALL OTHER NATIONS. AND, ALSO, A
CONTRAST BETWEEN THE OLD AND NEW SYSTEMS OF SOCIETY.
Washington, 1846.

1678. ------. ROBERT OWEN'S ADDRESS TO THE HUMAN RACE ON HIS
EIGHTY-FOURTH BIRTHDAY, MAY 14TH, 1854. (FROM THE
REPORTER'S NOTES AND MR. OWEN'S MS.) London: E. Wilson
etc., 1854.

1679. ------. ROBERT OWEN'S GREAT PRELIMINARY MEETING ON THE FIRST DAY
OF THE YEAR, 1855, IN WHICH BY HIS PREVIOUS ADVERTISEMENTS
MR. OWEN HAD ANNOUNCED THAT THE TRUE MILLENNIAL STATE OF
HUMAN EXISTENCE SHOULD COMMENCE. WITH HIS REASONS
PREFIXED FOR CALLING THESE MEETINGS. 2nd ed. London: E.
Wilson, 1855.

1680. ------. ROBERT OWEN'S MILLENNIAL GAZETTE, EXPLANATORY OF THE
PRINCIPLES AND PRACTICES BY WHICH, IN PEACE, WITH TRUTH,
HONESTY, AND SIMPLICITY, THE NEW EXISTENCE OF MAN UPON THE
EARTH MAY BE EASILY AND SPEEDILY COMMENCED. London,
1856-1858.

1681. ------. ROBERT OWEN'S OPENING SPEECH, AND HIS REPLY TO THE REV.
ALEX. CAMPBELL, IN THE RECENT PUBLIC DISCUSSION IN
CINCINNATI, TO PROVE THAT THE PRINCIPLES OF ALL RELIGIONS

ARE ERRONEOUS, AND THAT THEIR PRACTICE IS INJURIOUS TO THE
HUMAN RACE. ALSO, MR. OWEN'S MEMORIAL TO THE REPUBLIC OF
MEXICO, AND A NARRATIVE OF THE PROCEEDINGS THEREON ... FOR
THE PURPOSE OF ESTABLISHING A NEW POLITICAL AND MORAL
SYSTEM OF GOVERNMENT, FOUNDED ON THE LAWS OF NATURE, AS
EXPLAINED IN THE ABOVE DEBATE WITH MR. CAMPBELL.
Cincinnati: Pub. for R. Owen, 1829.

1682. ------. SECOND LECTURE ON THE NEW RELIGION; OR, RELIGION FOUNDED
ON THE IMMUTABLE LAWS OF THE UNIVERSE, CONTRASTED WITH ALL
RELIGIONS FOUNDED ON HUMAN TESTIMONY, AS DEVELOPED IN A
PUBLIC LECTURE, ... DEC. 15, 1830. London: J. Brooks
[etc.], 1830.

1683. ------. THE SOCIAL BIBLE, BEING AN OUTLINE OF THE RATIONAL SYSTEM
OF SOCIETY, FOUNDED ON DEMONSTRABLE FACTS DEVELOPING THE
CONSTITUTION AND LAWS OF HUMAN NATURE, BEING THE ONLY
EFFECTUAL REMEDY FOR THE EVILS EXPERIENCED BY THE
POPULATION OF THE WORLD ... London: B.D. Cousins [182-?]

1684. ------. SOCIALISM, OR THE RATIONAL SYSTEM OF SOCIETY; THREE
LECTURES DELIVERED IN THE MECHANICS' INSTITUTE, LONDON, ON
THE 30TH MARCH, AND 3RD AND 6TH APRIL, 1840, IN REPLY TO
THE ERRORS AND MISREPRESENTATIONS MADE ON THE SUBJECT OF
SOCIALISM IN BOTH HOUSES OF PARLIAMENT, BY THE LONDON CITY
MISSION, BY A LARGE PORTION OF THE DAILY AND WEEKLY PRESS,
AND IN THE SERMONS AND LECTURES DELIVERED AND PUBLISHED BY
THE CLERGY AND MINISTERS THROUGHOUT THE KINGDOM. FIRST
LECTURE. London: Effingham Wilson, 1840.

1685. ------. SYLLABUS OF FOUR MORNING AND FOUR EVENING COURSES OF
LECTURES AT THE EGYPTIAN HALL ... ON THE RATIONAL SYSTEM
OF SOCIETY, DERIVED SOLELY FROM NATURE AND EXPERIENCE ...
VERSUS SOCIALISM, DERIVED FROM MISREPRESENTATION ... AND
VERSUS THE PRESENT SYSTEM OF SOCIETY, DERIVED FROM THE
INEXPERIENCED AND CRUDE NOTIONS OF OUR ANCESTORS ...
London: Home Colonization Society, 1841.

1686. ------. THIRD PORTION OF PART VI OF THE NEW EXISTENCE OF MAN UPON
THE EARTH. WITH AN APPENDIX CONTAINING A RECORD OF
SPIRITUAL COMMUNICATIONS FROM FEBRUARY, 1854, TO FEBRUARY,
1855. WITH TWELVE TRACTS ON THE COMING MILLENNIUM.
London: Effingham Wilson, 1855.

1687. ------. A TREATISE OF DOGMATIC THEOLOGY. 2nd ed. London: J.T.
Hayes, 1887.

1688. Owen, Robert Dale. "Frances Wright, General Lafayette and Mary
Wollstonecraft Shelley." ATLANTIC MONTHLY. 32 (October
1872): 448-459.

1689. ------. MORAL PHYSIOLOGY; OR A BRIEF AND PLAIN TREATISE ON THE
POPULATION QUESTION. 10th ed. London: Holyoake & Co.,
1859.

1690. ------. "My Experience of Community Life." ATLANTIC MONTHLY. 31 (September 1873): 1-16.

1691. ------. ROBERT DALE OWEN'S TRAVEL JOURNAL, 1827. Ed. Josephine M. Elliott. Indiana Historical Society Publications, vol. 25, no. 4. Indianapolis: Indiana Historical Society, 1978.

1692. ------. "The Social Experiment at New Harmony. A Chapter of Autobiography." ATLANTIC MONTHLY. 32 (August 1873): 224-236.

1693. ------. TO HOLLAND AND TO NEW HARMONY: ROBERT DALE OWEN'S TRAVEL JOURNAL. Ed. Josephine M. Elliott. Indiana Historical Society Publications, vol. 23, no. 4. Indianapolis: Indiana Historical Society, 1969.

1694. ------. TWENTY-SEVEN YEARS OF AUTOBIOGRAPHY: THREADING MY WAY. New York: G.W. Carleton, 1874.

1695. Owen, William. DIARY OF WILLIAM OWEN, FROM NOVEMBER 10, 1824, TO APRIL 20, 1825. Joel W. Hiatt. Indianapolis: Bobbs-Merrill, Co., 1906. Reprint: Clifton, NJ: A.M. Kelley, 1973. Microcard edition: TRAVELS IN THE OLD SOUTH, II, 49. Louisville: Lost Cause Press, 1960.

1696. OWENISM AND THE WORKING CLASS. SIX PAMPHLETS AND FOUR BROADSIDES, 1821-1834. London, various publishers, 1821-1834. Reprint, New York: Arno Press, 1972.

1697. Paulding, James Kirke. THE MERRY TALES OF THE THREE WISE MEN OF GOTHAM. New York: G. & C. Carvill, 1826. Microfilm. Ann Arbor: University Microfilms, 1962.

1698. Pears, Thomas Clinton, Jr. NEW HARMONY, AN ADVENTURE IN HAPPINESS: PAPERS OF THOMAS AND SARAH PEARS. Indianapolis: Indiana Historical Society, 1933. Reprint. Clifton, NJ: Augustus M. Kelley, Publishers, 1973.

1699. Peattie, Donald Culross. "Frontier Utopians: Say, Rafinesque and Others." In GREEN LAURELS. New York: Simon & Schuster, 1936. pp. 244-268.

1700. Podmore, Frank, ROBERT OWEN: A BIOGRAPHY. 2 vols. London; New York: D. Appleton and Co., 1907.

1701. Pollard, Signey, and John Salt, eds. ROBERT OWEN: PROPHET OF THE POOR. London: Macmillan, 1971.

1702. Pitzer, Donald E. "Education in Utopia: The New Harmony Experience." Indiana Historical Society Lectures, 1976-1977. THE HISTORY OF EDUCATION IN THE MIDDLE WEST. Indianapolis: Indiana Historical Society, 1978. pp. 75-101.

1703. ------, ed. ROBERT OWEN'S AMERICAN LEGACY: PROCEEDINGS OF THE
       ROBERT OWEN BICENTENNIAL CONFERENCE (Thrall Opera House,
       New Harmony, IN, October 15 and 16, 1971). Indianapolis:
       Indiana Historical Society, 1972.

1704. RADICAL PERIODICALS OF GREAT BRITAIN. New York: Greenwood
       Reprint Corp., 1968.

1705. Rodman, Jane. "The English Settlement in Southern Illinois,
       1815-1825." INDIANA MAGAZINE OF HISTORY. 43 (December
       1947): 329-362.

1706. Sargent, William Lucas. ROBERT OWEN AND HIS SOCIAL PHILOSOPHY.
       London, 1860. Reprint. New York: AMS Press, 1978.

1707. Sears, Louis Martin. "New Harmony and the American Spirit."
       INDIANA MAGAZINE OF HISTORY. 38 (September 1942): 225-
       230.

1708. ------. "Robert Dale Owen as a Mystic." INDIANA MAGAZINE OF
       HISTORY. 24 (March 1928): 15-25.

1709. Simons, Richard. "A Utopian Failure." INDIANA HISTORY
       BULLETIN. 18 (February 1941): 98-114.

1710. Stephen, Leslie. "Robert Owen." DICTIONARY OF NATIONAL
       BIOGRAPHY. Ed. Sidney Lee. London: Smith, Elder & Co.,
       1895. Vol. 42, pp. 444-452.

1711. Sylvester, Lorna Lutes, ed. "Miner K. Kellogg: Recollections of
       New Harmony." INDIANA MAGAZINE OF HISTORY. 64 (March
       1968): 39-64.

1712. Taylor, Barbara. EVE AND THE NEW JERUSALEM; SOCIALISM AND
       FEMINISM IN THE NINETEENTH CENTURY. New York: Pantheon,
       1983.

1713. Thrift, Ronald. TWO PATHS TO UTOPIA: AN INVESTIGATION OF ROBERT
       OWEN AND NEW LANARK AND BRIGHAM YOUNG IN SALT LAKE CITY.
       Ph.D. Diss. University of New Mexico, 1976.

1714. Timmons, Wilbert H. "Robert Owen's Texas Project."
       SOUTHWESTERN HISTORICAL QUARTERLY. 52 (January 1949):
       286-293.

1715. Trollope, Frances. DOMESTIC MANNERS OF THE AMERICANS. London:
       Printed for Whittaker, Treacher & Co., 1832.

1716. Van Cleave, Harley J. "The New Harmony Venture and Its Relation
       to Natural Science." BIOS. 22 (December 1951): 263-275.

1717. Volwiler, Albert T. "Robert Owen and the Congress of
Aix-la-Chapelle, 1818." SCOTTISH HISTORICAL REVIEW. 19
(January 1922): 96-105.

1718. Weiss, Harry Bischoff, and Grace Ziegler. THOMAS SAY: EARLY
AMERICAN NATURALIST. Springfield, IL: C.C. Thomas, 1931.

1719. "William Maclure and Education for a Good Society" with
responses from Charles Burgess and William A. Boram.
HISTORY OF EDUCATION QUARTERLY. 3 (June 1963): 58-80.

1720. Williams, Mentor L. "Paulding Satirizes Owenism." INDIANA
MAGAZINE OF HISTORY. 44 (December 1948): 355-365.

1721. Wilson, William E. "Social Experiments on the Wabash: New
Harmony, Indiana." In A VANISHING AMERICA, THE LIFE AND
TIMES OF THE SMALL TOWN. New York: H. Holt, 1964. pp.
79-93.

Kendal Community (1826-1829)

Also known as Friendly Association for Mutual Interests at
Kendal, this Owenite Community was located in Stark County, Ohio
by two individuals from New Harmony.

ARCHIVAL MATERIALS

1722. Kendal Society. Minutes, 1828-1829. Massillon Public Library,
       Massillon, OH.

ARTICLES AND BOOKS

1723. De Pillis, Mario S. "Cleng Peerson and the Communitarian
       Background of Norwegian Immigration." NORWEGIAN-AMERICAN
       STUDIES AND RECORDS. 21 (1962): 136-157.

1724. ------. "Still More Light on the Kendal Colony: A Unique Slooper
       Letter." NORWEGIAN-AMERICAN STUDIES AND RECORDS. 20
       (1959): 24-31.

1725. Fox, Wendall P. "The Kendal Community. OHIO ARCHAEOLOGICAL AND
       HISTORICAL QUARTERLY. 20 (January 1911): 176-219.

1726. Perrin, William Henry, editor. HISTORY OF STARK COUNTY, WITH AN
       OUTLINE SKETCH OF OHIO. Chicago: Baskin & Battery, 1881.

Nashoba Community (1826-1829)

Founded by Frances Wright, an Owen disciple, as a place where
slaves could earn their freedom. Located in Shelby County,
Tennessee.

ARTICLES AND BOOKS

1727. Brown, Anna B.A. "A Dream of Emancipation." NEW ENGLAND
       MAGAZINE. New Series. 30 (June 1904): 494-499.

1728. D'Arusmont, Frances (Wright). BIOGRAPHY, NOTES AND POLITICAL
       LETTERS OF FRANCES WRIGHT D'ARUSMONT. Dundee, Scotland:
       J. Myles; New York: J. Windt, 1844.

1729. ------. COURSE OF POPULAR LECTURES AS DELIVERED BY FRANCES WRIGHT
       IN NEW YORK, PHILADELPHIA AND OTHER CITIES OF THE UNITED
       STATES. New York: Office of the Free Enquirer, 1829.
       Microfilm. Ann Arbor: University Microfilms, 1965.

1730. Davis, J. Treadwell. "Nashoba: Frances Wright's Experiment in Self-Emancipation." THE SOUTHERN QUARTERLY. 11 (October 1972): 63-90.

1731. Eckhardt, Celia Morris. "Fanny Wright: Rebel & Communitarian Reformer." COMMUNAL SOCIETIES. 4 (Fall 1984): 183-193.

1732. ------. FANNY WRIGHT: REBEL IN AMERICA. Cambridge: Harvard University Press, 1984.

1733. Elliott, Helen. "Frances Wright's Experiment with Negro Emancipation." INDIANA MAGAZINE OF HISTORY. 35 (June 1939): 114-157.

1734. Emerson, O.B. "Frances Wright and Her Nashoba Experiment." TENNESSEE HISTORICAL QUARTERLY. 6 (December 1947): 289-314.

1735. Gilbert, Amos. MEMOIR OF FRANCES WRIGHT, THE PIONEER WOMAN IN THE CAUSE OF HUMAN RIGHTS. Cincinnati: Longley Bros., 1855. Microfilm. Ann Arbor: University Microfilms, 1965.

1736. Heineman, Helen L. "`Starving in that Land of Plenty?': New Backgrounds to Frances Trollope's Domestic Manners of the Americans." AMERICAN QUARTERLY. 24 (December 1972): 643-660.

1737. Owen, Robert Dale. "Frances Wright, General Lafayette and Mary W. Shelley." ATLANTIC MONTHLY. 32 (October 1873): 448-459.

1738. Parkes, Edd Winfield. "Dreamer's Vision: Frances Wright at Nashoba (1825-1830)." TENNESSEE HISTORICAL MAGAZINE, 2d Series. 2 (January 1932): 75-86.

1739. ------. NASHOBA. New York: Twayne, 1963.

1740. Payne-Gaposchkin, Cecilia Helena. "The Nashoba Plan for Removing the Evil of Slavery: Letters of Frances and Camilla Wright, 1820-1829." HARVARD LIBRARY BULLETIN. 23 (July 1975): 221-251; (October 1975): 429-461.

1741. Pease, William H., and Jane H. Pease. A New View of Nashoba." TENNESSEE HISTORICAL QUARTERLY. 19 (June 1960): 99-109.

1742. Perkins, Alice J.G., and Theresa Wolfson. FRANCIS WRIGHT, FREE ENQUIRER. THE STUDY OF A TEMPERAMENT. New York: Harper & Bros., 1939. Reprint. Philadelphia: Porcupine Press, 1972.

1743. Matthews, Paul Aaron. "Frances Wright and the Nashoba Experiment: A Transitional Period in Antislavery Attitudes." EAST TENNESSEE HISTORICAL SOCIETY PUBLICATIONS. 46 (1974): 37-52.

1744. Wright, Frances. VIEWS OF SOCIETY AND MANNERS IN AMERICA, ed.
           by Paul Baker. Cambridge : Belknap Press of the Harvard
           University Press, 1963.

1745. Waterman, William Randall. FRANCES WRIGHT. Columbia University
           Studies in History, Economics, and Public Law, 15. New
           York: Columbia University, 1924. Reprint. New York: AMS
           Press, 1973.

PILGRIMS (1817-1818)

Also known as the Mummyjums, they first settled in Woodstock, Vermont. Later took a pilgrimage under the leadership of Isaac Bullard. They ended in Arkansas.

ARTICLES AND BOOKS

1746. Flint, Timothy. RECOLLECTIONS OF THE LAST TEN YEARS PASSED IN OCCASIONAL RESIDENCES AND JOURNEYINGS IN THE VALLEY OF THE MISSISSIPPI. Boston: Cummings, Hillard & Co., 1826. Reprint. New York: Knopf, 1932. Reprint. New York: Da Capo, 1968. pp. 275-280.

1747. Ham, F. Gerald. "The Prophet and the Mummyjums: Isaac Bullard and the Vermont Pilgrims of 1817." WISCONSIN MAGAZINE OF HISTORY. 56 (Summer 1973): 290-299.

1748. Nuttall, Thomas. JOURNAL OF TRAVELS INTO THE ARKANSAS TERRITORY. In EARLY WESTERN TRAVELS, 1748-1846. Ed. Reuben Gold Thwaites. Vol. 13. Cleveland: A.H. Clark, 1904-1907. pp. 294-295.

1749. Thompson, Zadock. HISTORY OF STATE OF VERMONT, FROM ITS EARLIEST SETTLEMENT TO THE CLOSE OF THE YEAR 1832. Burlington, VT.: Edward Smith, 1833. pp. 202-204.

PLOCKHOY'S COMMONWEALTH (1663-1664)

The first communal society known to have been formed in America. A group of Dutch Mennonites, under the leadership of Pieter Corneliszoon Plockhoy settled on the Delaware River, in New Netherlands.

ARTICLES AND BOOKS

1750. Downie, John. PETER CORNELIUS PLOCKBOY [sic], PIONEER OF THE FIRST CO-OPERATIVE COMMONWEALTH, 1659. HIS LIFE AND WORK. COMMENTARY BY JOHN DOWNIE, 2d ed. Manchester, England: Co-Operative Union, n.d.

1751. Harder, Leland David. "Pioneer of Christian Civilization in America." MENNONITE LIFE 4 (January 1949): 41-45, 49.

1752. ------. "Plockhoy and His Settlement at Zwaanendael, 1663." DELAWARE HISTORY 3 (March 1949): 138-154.

1753. ------, and Marvin Andrew. PLOCKHOY FROM ZURIKZEE; THE STUDY OF A DUTCH REFORMER IN PURITAN ENGLAND AND COLONIAL AMERICA. Newton, KS.: Board of Education and Publication, General Conference Mennonite Church, 1952. Contains both of Plockhoy's writings: THE WAY TO PEACE ... and A WAY PROPOUNDED.

1754. Plockhoy, Pieter Corneliszoon. KORT ENKLAER ONTWERP. Amsterdam, 1662.

1755. ------. A WAY PROPOUNDED TO MAKE THE POOR IN THESE AND OTHER NATIONS HAPPY, BY BRINGING TOGETHER A FIT SUITABLE AND WELL QUALIFIED PEOPLE UNTO ONE HOUSEHOLD-GOVERNMENT, OR LITTLE-COMMON-WEALTH. London, 1659.

1756. ------. THE WAY TO PEACE AND SETTLEMENT OF THESE NATIONS, FULLY DISCOVERED IN TWO LETTERS, DELIVERED TO HIS LATE HIGHNESSE AND ONE TO THE PRESENT PARLIAMENT ... BY PETER CORNELIUS, VAN ZURICK ZEE. London, 1659.

1757. Smith, George L. RELIGION AND TRADE IN NEW NETHERLAND: DUTCH ORIGINS AND AMERICAN DEVELOPMENT. Ithaca: Cornell University Press, 1973. pp. 231-235.

ST. NAZIANZ COMMUNITY (1854-1874)

A Roman Catholic communal group, founded by German immigrants in Manitowoc County, Wisconsin, under the leadership of Father Ambrose Oschwald.

ARTICLES AND BOOKS

1758. Beck, Frank. "Christian Communists in America: A History of the Colony of Saint Nazianz: Wisconsin, During the Pastorate of Its Founder, Father Ambrose Oschwald, 1854-1873," MA thesis, St. Paul Seminary, 1959.

1759. Johnson, Paul Robert. "St. Nazianz, Wisconsin: Landscape Persistance in a German Communal Settlement, 1854-1983." Ph D diss. University of Oklahoma, 1984.

1760. Schlicher, J.J., trans. "History of St. Nazianz." WISCONSIN MAGAZINE OF HISTORY. 31 (September 1947): 84-91.

1761. Titus, W.A. "Historic Spots in Wisconsin: St. Nazianz, A Unique Religious Colony." WISCONSIN MAGAZINE OF HISTORY. 5 (December 1921): 160-165.

THE SHAKERS (1787-   )

Founded by Mother Ann Lee in England, she met with greater
success in America. Distinct Shaker communities were formed in
New England, New York, Ohio, Indiana, and Kentucky, of which two
colonies remain (at Sabbathday Lake, Maine and Canterbury, New
Hampshire).

BIBLIOGRAPHIES

1762. Richmond, Mary L. SHAKER LITERATURE: A BIBLIOGRAPHY. 2 vols.
       Hancock, MA.: The Shaker Community, Inc., and distributed
       by the University Press of New England, 1977. Because
       this bibliography was so thorough in works by and about
       the Shakers, there is no need to duplicate it in this
       bibliography. Instead, it will include only those
       materials published since Mrs. Richmond's work. The
       exceptions will be to mention the Andrews' volumes again
       and the Desroche study, classics for Shaker studies.

ARTICLES AND BOOKS

1763. Andrews, Edward Deming. THE COMMUNITY INDUSTRIES OF THE
       SHAKERS. Albany, NY.: University of the State of New
       York, 1933. Reprint. Charleston, MA.: Emporium
       Publications, 1972. Reprint. Philadelphia: Porcupine
       Press, 1972.

1764. ------, and Faith Andrews. FRUITS OF THE SHAKER TREE OF LIFE:
       MEMOIRS OF FIFTY YEARS OF COLLECTING AND RESEARCH.
       Stockbridge, MA.: The Berkshire Traveller Press, 1975.

1765. ------. THE GIFT TO BE SIMPLE: SONGS, DANCES AND RITUALS OF THE
       AMERICAN SHAKERS. New York: J.J. Augustin Publisher,
       1940. Reprint. New York: Dover, 1962.

1766. ------. THE PEOPLE CALLED SHAKERS: A SEARCH FOR THE PERFECT
       SOCIETY. New York: Oxford University Press, 1953. New
       enlarged edition. New York: Dover, 1963.

1767. ------. "The Shaker Children's Order." WINTERTHUR PORTFOLIO 8.
       Ed. Ian M.G. Quimby. Charlottesville: University Press of
       Virginia, 1973. pp. 201-214.

1768. ------. SHAKER FURNITURE: THE CRAFTSMANSHIP OF AMERICAN COMMUNAL
       SECT. New Haven: Yale University Press, 1937. Reprint.
       New York: Dover, 1964.

1769. ------. VISIONS OF THE HEAVENLY SPHERE: A STUDY IN RELIGIOUS
ART. Charlottesville: Published for the Henry Francis du
Pont Winterthur Museum by the University Press of
Virginia, 1969.

1770. ------. WORK AND WORSHIP: THE ECONOMIC ORDER OF THE SHAKERS.
Greenwich, CT: New York Graphic Society, 1974. Reprint as
WORK AND WORSHIP AMONG THE SHAKERS, New York: Dover
Publications, 1982.

1771. "Ann Lee's Birthday." THE AMERICAN BOOK OF DAYS. Comp. James
M. Hatch. 3rd Ed. New York: H.W. Wilson, 1978. pp.
218-221.

1772. "An Artist Among the Shakers" [John Benson Lossing]. AMERICAN
HERITAGE. 31 (April/ May 1980): 69-73.

1773. Bail, Hamilton Vaughan. "Zadock Wright: That `Devilish' Tory of
Hartland." VERMONT HISTORY. 36 (Autumn 1968): 186-203.

1774. Bainbridge, William Sims. "The Decline of the Shakers: Evidence
from the United States Census." COMMUNAL SOCIETIES. 4
(Fall 1984): 19-34.

1775. ------. "Shaker Demographics 1840-1900: An Example of the Use of
U.S. Census Enumeration Schedules." JOURNAL FOR THE
SCIENTIFIC STUDY OF RELIGION. 21 (December 1982):
352-365.

1776. Barker, R. Mildred. HOLY LAND: A HISTORY OF THE ALFRED SHAKERS.
Sabbathday Lake, ME: United Society, 1983.

1777. ------. POEM AND PRAYERS. Sabbathday Lake, ME: Shaker Press,
1983.

1778. ------. THE SABBATHDAY LAKE SHAKERS. Sabbathday Lake, ME: Shaker
Press, 1978.

1779. Bednarowski, Mary Farrell. "Outside the Mainstream: Women's
Religion and Women Religious Leaders in Nineteenth-Century
America." JOURNAL OF THE AMERICAN ACADEMY OF RELIGION. 48
(June 1980): 207-231.

1780. Brewer, Priscilla J. "The Demographic Features of the Shaker
Decline, 1787-1900." THE JOURNAL OF INTERDISCIPLINARY
HISTORY. 15 (Summer 1984): 31-52.

1781. ------. "Emerson, Lane, and the Shakers: A Case of Converging
Ideologies." NEW ENGLAND QUARTERLY. 55 (June 1982):
254-275.

1782. ------. "`Numbers are Not the Thing for Us to Glory In':
Demographic Perspectives on the Decline of the Shakers."
COMMUNAL SOCIETIES. 7 (1987): 25-35.

1783. ------. SHAKER COMMUNITIES, SHAKER LIVES. Hanover, NH.:
       University Press of New England, 1986.

1784. Brown, Sandra G. "Shaker History in the George Arents Research
       Library. COURIER (Syracuse). 8 (January 1971): 3-10.

1785. Burns, Amys. THE SHAKERS; HANDS TO WORK, HEARTS TO GOD. New
       York: Aperture, 1988.

1786. Burress, Marjorie Byrnside, ed. WHITEWATER, OHIO; VILLAGE OF
       SHAKERS, 1824-1916: ITS HISTORY AND ITS PEOPLE. n.p.,
       1979.

1787. Butler, Hal. "Shakertown, A Community of Quality." HOME &
       AWAY. 2 (July/August 1981): 22-25.

1788. Butler, Linda, and June Sprigg. INNER LIGHT: THE SHAKER LEGACY.
       New York: Alfred A. Knopf, 1985.

1789. Byrd, William S. LETTERS FROM A YOUNG SHAKER: WILLIAM S. BYRD
       AT PLEASANT HILL. Ed. Stephen J. Stein. Lexington, KY.:
       The University Press of Kentucky, 1985.

1790. Campbell, D'Ann. "Women's Life in Utopia: The Shaker Experiment
       in Sexual Equality Re-appraised--1810-1860." NEW ENGLAND
       QUARTERLY. 51 (March 1978): 23-38.

1791. Carter, Duncan A., and Laurence W. Mazzeno. "Dicken's Account of
       the Shakers and West Point: Rhetoric or Reality?" THE
       DICKENSIAN. 72 (September 1976): 130-139.

1792. Chemotti, Mary Rae. "Conformity and Digression in Communitarian
       Building: Shaker Architecture at Pleasant Hill, Kentucky."
       MA thesis, University of Kentucky, 1977.

1793. ------. "Outside Sources for Shaker Building at Pleasant Hill."
       THE KENTUCKY REVIEW. 2 (1981): 49-74.

1794. Crosthwaite, Jane F. "The Spirit Drawings of Hannah Cohoon:
       Window on the Shakers and Their Folk Art." COMMUNAL
       SOCIETIES. 7 (1987): 1-15.

1795. Dahlen, Martha. "A Faithful Harvest." HORTICULTURE. (March
       1979): 60-70.

1796. Desroche, Henri. THE AMERICAN SHAKERS. Amherst, MA:
       University of Massachusetts Press, 1971.

1797. Emlen, Robert P. "The Early Drawings of Elder Joshua Bussell."
       ANTIQUES. 103 (March 1978): 632-637.

1798. ------. "The Great Stone Dwelling of the Enfield, New Hampshire
       Shakers." OLD-TIME NEW ENGLAND. 69 (Winter-Spring 1979):
       69-85.

1799. ------. "The Hard Choices of Brother John Cummings" [Enfield, NH].
       HISTORICAL NEW HAMPSHIRE. 34 (Spring 1979): 54-65.

1800. ------. "Raised, Razed, Raised Again: The Shaker Meetinghouse at
       Enfield, New Hampshire, 1793-1902." HISTORICAL NEW
       HAMPSHIRE. 30 (Fall 1975): 133-146.

1801. ------. SHAKER VILLAGE VIEWS. Hanover, NH: University Press of
       New England, 1987.

1802. Foster, Lawrence. "Shaker Spiritualism and Salem Witchcraft:
       Social Perspectives on Trance and Possession Phenomena."
       COMMUNAL SOCIETIES. 5 (1985): 176-193.

1803. Ferguson, Richard G., Jr. "Central Themes in Shaker Thought."
       REGISTER OF THE KENTUCKY HISTORICAL SOCIETY. 74 (June
       1976): 216-229.

1804. Garrett, Clarke. SPIRIT POSSESSION AND POPULAR RELIGION: FROM
       THE CAMISARDS TO THE SHAKERS. Baltimore: Johns Hopkins
       University Press, 1987.

1805   Gillon, Edmond. SHAKER VILLAGE. Chester, PA: Schiffler, 1986.

1806. Gooden, Rosemary D. "A Preliminary Examination of the Shaker
       Attitude Toward Work." COMMUNAL SOCIETIES. 3 (Fall
       1983): 1-15.

1807. Gordon, Beverly. SHAKER TEXTILE ARTS. Hanover, NH.: Published
       by the University Press of New England with the
       Cooperation of the Merrimack Valley Textile Museum and
       Shaker Community, Inc., 1980.

1808. Halley, A. "Lotte Jacobi: Canterbury, New Hampshire 1959."
       MASSACHUSETTS REVIEW. 24 (Spring 1983): 113-124.

1809. Hill, Horbert R. "Indiana Too Had a Shakertown--
       Communitarianism and the Millennium." OUTDOOR INDIANA.
       39 (July-August 1974): 23-33.

1810. Horgan, Edward R. THE SHAKER HOLY LAND: A COMMUNITY PORTRAIT.
       Harvard, MA.: The Harvard Common Press, 1982.

1811. Hulings, Martha A. SHAKER DAYS REMEMBERED. Albany, NY.: Shaker
       Heritage Society, 1983.

1812. Humez, Jean McMahon. GIFTS OF POWER. THE WRITINGS OF REBECCA
       JACKSON, BLACK VISIONARY, SHAKER ELDRESS. Amherst:
       University of Massachusetts Press, 1981.

1813. Jacob, Mary Jane. "The Impact of Shaker Design on the Work of Charles Sheeler." MA thesis, University of Michigan, 1976.

1814. Janzen, Donald E. THE SHAKER MILLS ON SHAWNEE RUN: HISTORICAL ARCHAEOLOGY AT SHAKERTOWN AT PLEASANT HILL, MERCER COUNTY, KENTUCKY. Report of Archaeological Investigations, 1975-1978. Pleasant Hill: Pleasant Hill Press, 1981.

1815. Johnson, Brother Theodore E. IN THE EYE OF ETERNITY. Gorham, ME: United Society of Shakers and the University of South Maine, 1983.

1816. Joy, A.F. WE ARE THE SHAKERS: MOTHER ANN'S STORY. Winona, MN: Apollo Books, 1985.

1817. Joziatis, Brenda. "Renaissance at Shaker Village" (Canterbury, New Hampshire). NEW HAMPSHIRE PROFILES. (May 1979): 17-21.

1818. Kassay, John. THE BOOK OF SHAKER FURNITURE. Amherst: The University of Massachusetts Press, 1980.

1819. Keig, Susan Jackson. TRADE WITH THE WORLD'S PEOPLE: A SHAKER ALBUM. Hamilton, Ohio: Becket Paper Co., 1976.

1820. Klein, Janice. "Ann Lee and Mary Baker Eddy: The Parenting of New Religions." JOURNAL OF PSYCHOHISTORY. 6 (Winter 1979): 361-375.

1821. Kratz, C. Eugene. "The New York Shakers and Their Dwelling Places." THE CLARION, AMERICA'S FOLK ART MAGAZINE. (Fall 1979): 36-45.

1822. Kreiser, Larry. "Shaker Accounting Records at Pleasant Hill: 1830-1850." THE ACCOUNTING HISTORIANS JOURNAL. 13 (Fall 1986): 19-36.

1823. Lahutsky, Nadia. "Women and Sectarian Communities: The Case of the Shakers." Unpublished paper presented at Association of Disciples for Theological Discussions, St. Louis, Mo., October 5, 1985.

1824. McKinstry, E. Richard. THE EDWARD DEMING ANDREWS MEMORIAL SHAKER COLLECTION. New York: Garland, 1987.

1825. Marshall, Kathryn. "The Shaker Community//Image Word: Covenant of Joy." EPIPHANY. 3 (Spring 1983): 88-97.

1826. Miller, Amy Bess. HANCOCK SHAKER VILLAGE/THE CITY OF PEACE: AN EFFORT TO RESTORE A VISION, 1960-1985. Hancock, MA.: Hancock Shaker Village, 1984.

1827. Morse, Flo. THE SHAKERS AND THE WORLD'S PEOPLE. New York:
       Dodd, Mead & Co., 1980.

1828. Moser, Thomas. HOW TO BUILD SHAKER FURNITURE. With measured
       drawings by Christian Becksvoort. New York: Sterling
       Publishing Co., 1979.

1829. Muller, Charles, and Timothy D. Rieman. THE SHAKER CHAIR.
       Canal Winchester, OH.: The Canal Press, 1984.

1830. Muller, Charles R. THE SHAKER WAY. Worthington, OH.: Ohio
       Antique Review, 1979.

1831. Neal, Julia. THE KENTUCKY SHAKERS. Lexington, KY.: University
       Press of Kentucky, 1977.

1832. Nickless, Karen K., and Pamela J. Nickless. "Trustees, Deacons,
       and Deaconesses: The Temporal Role of the Shaker Sisters,
       1820-1890." COMMUNAL SOCIETIES. 7 (1987): 16-24.

1833. Patterson, Daniel W. GIFT DRAWING AND GIFT SONG: A STUDY OF TWO
       FORMS OF SHAKER INSPIRATION. Sabbathday Lake, ME.: The
       United Society of Shakers, 1983.

1834. ------. "Shaker Music." COMMUNAL SOCIETIES. 2 (Autumn 1978):
       53-64.

1835. ------. THE SHAKER SPIRITUAL. Princeton: Princeton University
       Press, 1979.

1836. Pearce, John E. "The Last of the Shakers?" THE LOUISVILLE
       COURIER-JOURNAL MAGAZINE. (October 18, 1984): 12-20.

1837. Piotrowski, Mona M. "The Enfield Shakers." In THE CHALLENGE OF
       CHANGE: THREE CENTURIES OF ENFIELD, CONNECTICUT HISTORY.
       Canaan, NH: Published for the Enfield Historical Society
       by Phoenix Publishing, 1977. pp. 30-56.

1838. Procter-Smith, Marjorie. WOMEN IN SHAKER COMMUNITY AND WORSHIP:
       A FEMINIST ANALYSIS OF THE USES OF RELIGIOUS SYMBOLISM.
       Lewiston, NY.: Edwin Mellen Press, 1985.

1839. Purcell, L. Edward. THE SHAKERS. New York: Crescent Books,
       1988.

1840. Ray, Mary Lyn. "A Reappraisal of Shaker Furniture and Society."
       WINTERTHUR PORTFOLIO 8. Ed. Ian M.G. Quimby.
       Charlottesville: University Press of Virginia, 1973.
       107-132.

1841. Rotundo, Barbara. "Crossing the Dark River: Shaker Funerals
       and Cemeteries." COMMUNAL SOCIETIES. 7 (1987): 36-46.

1842. Rubin, Cynthia Elyce. "Shaker Industries." THE CLARION. (Fall
        1979): 46-57.

1843. Sasson, Diane. THE SHAKER SPIRITUAL NARRATIVE. Knoxville: The
        University of Tennessee Press, 1983.

1844. Setta, Susan M. "The Appropriation of Biblical Hermeneutics to
        Biographical Criticism: An Application to the Life of the
        Shaker Founder, Ann Lee." HISTORICAL METHODS. 16 (Summer
        1983): 89-100.

1845. ------. "From Ann The Christ to Holy Mother Wisdom: Changing
        Goddess Imagery in the Shaker Tradition." ANIMA: AN
        EXPERIENTIAL JOURNAL. 7 (Fall Equinox 1980): 5-13.

1846. ------. "The Mother-Father God and the Female Christ in Early
        Shaker Theology." JOURNAL OF RELIGIOUS STUDIES. 12
        (1984): 56-64.

1847. THE SHAKER MESSENGER. Holland, MI. Fall 1978-   (Supersedes
        THE WORLD OF SHAKER).

1848. Shakers. IN TIME AND ETERNITY: MAINE SHAKERS IN THE INDUSTRIAL
        AGE. Sabbathday Lake, ME: United Society, 1986.

1849. "The Shakers of Ohio: An Early Nineteenth Century Account."
        CINCINNATI HISTORICAL SOCIETY BULLETIN. 29 (Summer 1971):
        127-138.

1850. Shaver, Elizabeth D. THE WATERVLIET SHAKER CEMETERY, ALBANY,
        N.Y. Albany: The Shaker Heritage Society, 1986.

1851. Sherburne, Trudy Reno. AS I REMEMBER IT: A DETAILED
        DESCRIPTION OF THE NORTH FAMILY OF THE WATERVLIET, N.Y.,
        SHAKER COMMUNITY. Holland, MI: The World of Shaker, 1987.

1852. Sprigg, June. BY SHAKER HANDS. New York: Alfred A. Knopf,
        1975.

1853. ------. "Documented Shaker Furniture in the Collection of
        Hancock Shaker Village." Catalog. Ellis Memorial
        Antiques Show, 1978. Boston: Boston Center for the Arts,
        1978. pp. 25-33.

1854. ------. "Hancock Shaker Village: 'The City of Peace'." ANTIQUES.
        120 (October 1981): 884-895.

1855. ------. "Out of this World: The Shakers as a Nineteenth-Century
        Tourist Attraction." AMERICAN HERITAGE. 31 (April/May
        1980): 65-68.

1856. ------. SHAKER DESIGN. New York: Norton, 1986.

1857. Starbuck, David R., and Margaret Supplee Smith. HISTORICAL
      SURVEY OF CANTERBURY SHAKER VILLAGE. Boston University,
      1979.

1858. Stein, Stephen J. "Community, Commitment, and Practice: Union
      and Order at Pleasant Hill in 1834." JOURNAL OF THE EARLY
      REPUBLIC. 8 (Spring 1988): 45-68.

1859. Taylor, Michael Brooks. "Developments in Early Shaker Ethical
      Thought." Ph D diss. Harvard University, 1976.

1860. ------. "`Try the Spirits': Shaker Responses to Supernaturalism."
      JOURNAL OF RELIGIOUS STUDIES. (Ohio). 7 (Fall 1979):
      30-38.

1861. Thomas, James C. "Shaker Architecture in Kentucky." FILSON
      CLUB HISTORICAL QUARTERLY. 53 (January 1979): 26-36.

1862. Van Kolken, Diana. INTRODUCING THE SHAKERS. Bowling Green, OH:
      Gabriel's Horn Publishing Co., 1985.

1863. Wertkin, Gerard C. "The Flame is Never Ceasing: Continuity in
      Shaker Life at Sabbathday Lake." THE CLARION. (Fall
      1979): 58-67.

1864. ------. THE FOUR SEASONS OF SHAKER LIFE: AN INTIMATE PORTRAIT OF
      THE COMMUNITY AT SABBATHDAY LAKE. New York: Simon &
      Schuster, 1986.

1865. Whitson, Robley Edward, ed. THE SHAKERS: TWO CENTURIES OF
      SPIRITUAL REFLECTION. New York: Paulist Press, 1983.

1866. Williams, Richard E. CALLED AND CHOSEN: THE STORY OF MOTHER
      REBECCA JACKSON AND THE PHILADELPHIA SHAKERS. Ed. Cheryl
      Dorschner. Metuchen, NJ.: The Scarecrow Press & The
      American Theological Library Association, 1981.

1867. Wisbey, Herbert A., Jr. THE SODUS SHAKER COMMUNITY. Lyons,
      NY.: Wayne County Historical Society, 1982.

1868. Yoder, Don. "The Spiritual Lineage of Shakerism." PENNSYLVANIA
      FOLKLIFE. 28 (Spring 1978): 2-14.

1869. Youngerman, Suzanne. "Shaking is No Foolish Play: An
      Anthropological Perspective on the American
      Shakers--Person, Time, Space, Dance--Ritual." PhD diss.
      Columbia University, 1983.

SKANEATELES COMMUNITY (1843-1846)

Organized by John Collins, an abolitionist, in Onandaga County,
New York, with a strong Fourierist influence.

ARTICLES AND BOOKS

1870. Collins, John Anderson. A BIRD'S EYE VIEW OF SOCIETY AS IT IS,
       AND AS IT SHOULD BE. Boston: Printed by J.P. Mendum,
       1844.

1871. THE COMMUNITIST. Mottville, NY.: 1844-March 1846.

1872. Grant, H. Roger. "The Skaneateles Community: A New York Utopia."
       NIAGARA FRONTIER. 22 (Autumn 1975): 68-72.

1873. Leslie, Edmund Norman. HISTORY OF SKANEATELES AND VICINITY,
       1781-1881. Auburn, NY.: C.P. Cornell, 1882.

1874. Post, Albert. POPULAR FREETHOUGHT IN AMERICA, 1825-1850. New
       York: Columbia University Press, 1943. pp. 181-183.

1875. Ripley, George. "The Skaneateles Community." THE HARBINGER. 1
       (September 27, 1845): 253-254.

1876. Wells, Lester G. "The Skaneateles Communal Experiment,
       1843-1846." Onandaga Historical Association, Syracuse,
       NY., 1953.

TEUTONIA (1827-1831)

Also known as the Society of United Germans, it was founded in
Columbiana County, Ohio, by Peter Kaufman.

ARCHIVAL MATERIALS

1877. Kaufmann, Peter. Papers. Ohio Historical Society. Columbus,
　　　　Ohio.

UNION HOME (1844-1846)

Formed by John Wattles with a group of spiritualists in Randolph
County, Indiana.

ARTICLES AND BOOKS

1878. Heiss, Willard C. "Hiram Mendenhall and the Union Home
　　　　Community." FRIENDS HISTORICAL ASSOCIATION. BULLETIN.
　　　　44 (Spring 1955); 43-50.

SOCIETY OF THE WOMAN IN THE WILDERNESS
(1694?-1748)

Founded by Johann Kelpius, a mystic from Germany. The sect was
formed at Coxsackie, Pennsylvania, in anticipation of the
millennium.

ARTICLES AND BOOKS

1879. Alderfer, E. Gordon. "Johannes Kelpius and the Heritage of
       Mysticism." In A METHOD OF PRAYER. New York: Harper &
       Bros., 1951. pp. 11-73.

1880. Benz, Ernst. DIE PROTESTANTISCHE THEBAIS. Wiesbaden: Franz
       Steiner, 1963. pp. 93-101.

1881. Grummer, Henry V. "Kelpius and His Followers." GERMANTOWN
       CRIER. 5 (1953): 9-10, 26-27.

1882. Hartzell, Lawrence. "Music and the Mystics of the Wissahickon."
       JOURNAL OF GERMAN-AMERICAN STUDIES. 13 (Winter 1978):
       81-86.

1883. "Johann Jakob Zimmermann (1634-1693)." ALLGEMEINE DEUTSCHE
       BIOGRAPHIE 45. Berlin: Duncker & Humblot, 1900, 1971. pp.
       270-271.

1884. Kelpius, Johannes. THE DIARIUM OF MAGISTER JOHANNES KELPIUS,
       with annotations by Julius Fredrich Sachse. Lancaster,
       PA.: Press of the New Era Printing Co., 1917. In
       Pennsylvania German Society. PROCEEDINGS AND ADDRESSES,
       November 13, 1914. 25 (1917).

1885. Klein, K.K. "Magister Johannes Kelpius Transylvanus der Heilige
       und Dichter vom Wissahickon in Pennsylvanien," in
       FESTSCHRIFT SEINER HOCHWURDEN D. DR. FRIEDRICH TEUTSCH.
       Hermannstadt, 1931. pp. 57-77.

1886. Lashlee, Ernest L. "Johannes Kelpius and His Woman in the
       Wilderness." In G. Muller and W. Zeller, eds. GLAUBE,
       GEIST, GESCHICHTE. Leiden: E.J. Brill, 1967. pp.
       327-338.

1887. Learned, Marion Dexter. LIFE OF FRANCIS DANIEL PASTORIUS: THE
       FOUNDER OF GERMANTOWN. Philadelphia: W.J. Campbell, 1908.

1888. Seidensticker, Oswald, trans. and ed. "The Hermits of the
       Wissahickon." PENNSYLVANIA MAGAZINE OF HISTORY. 11
       (1887): 427-441.

ZOAR (1817-1898)

The Society of Separatists of Zoar, a group of German pietists
under the leadership of Joseph Bimeler(Baumeler), established a
colony in Tuscarawas County, Ohio.

ARCHIVAL MATERIALS

1889. Kaufmann, Peter. Papers. Ohio Historical Society. Columbus.

1890. Nixon Family. Papers, 1816-1936. Ohio Historical Society,
      Columbus.

1891. Rotch Family. Rotch-Wales Papers, 1677-1838. Friends of the
      Historical Library of Swarthmore College, Swarthmore, PA.

1892. Society of Separatists of Zoar. Records, 1818-1911. Western
      Reserve Historical Society. Cleveland.

ARTICLES AND BOOKS

1893. Bimeler, Joseph Michael. ETWAS FURS HERZ! Zoar, 1860-1861.

1894. ------. DIE WAHRE SEPARATION. Gedruckt in Zoar. 1856-1860.

1895. Bognar, E.J. "Blast-Furnaces Operated by the Separatist Society
      of Zoar, Ohio." OHIO ARCHAEOLOGICAL AND HISTORICAL
      QUARTERLY. 39 (July 1930): 503-513.

1896. Dobbs, Catherine R. FREEDOM'S WILL: THE SOCIETY OF SEPARATISTS
      OF ZOAR, AN HISTORICAL ADVENTURE OF RELIGIOUS COMMUNISM IN
      EARLY OHIO. New York: The William-Frederick Press, 1947.

1897. Gunn, Alexander. THE HERMITAGE-ZOAR NOTE BOOK AND JOURNAL OF
      TRAVEL. New York: The DeVinne Press, 1902.

1898. Handler, Mimi. "Christmas in Zoar." EARLY AMERICAN LIFE. 19
      (December 1988): 26-35.

1899. Hillquit, Morris. "The Colony of Zoar." THE PENNY MAGAZINE. 6
      (1837): 411-412.

1900. Howe, Henry. "The Zoar Society." HISTORICAL COLLECTIONS OF
      OHIO, Vol. 3. AN ENCYCLOPEDIA OF THE STATE. Columbus:
      Henry Howe & Son, 1891. pp. 384-396.

1901. Huntington, Webster P. "Gunn of the Zoarites." THE OHIO
      MAGAZINE. 1 (1906): 499-510.

1902.   Landis, George B.   "Separatists of Zoar."   American Historical
            Association.   ANNUAL REPORT, 1898-1899.   pp. 163-220.

1903.   Meyers, David William.   "The Machine in the Garden: The Design
            and Operation of the Separatist Society of Zoar."   MBA
            thesis.   Ohio State University, 1980.

1904.   Morhart, Hilda Dischinger.   THE ZOAR STORY.   Dover, OH.: Seibert
            Printing Co., 1967.

1905.   Nixon, Edgar Burkhardt.   "The Society of Separatists of Zoar."
            Ph D diss. Ohio State University, 1933.

1906.   ------.   "The Zoar Society: Applicants for Membership."   OHIO
            STATE ARCHAEOLOGICAL AND HISTORICAL QUARTERLY   45 (October
            1936): 341-350.

1907.   Ohio Historical Society.   ZOAR, AN OHIO EXPERIMENT IN
            COMMUNALISM.   Columbus: The Society, 1960, c1952.

1908.   Randall, Emilius Oviatt.   HISTORY OF THE ZOAR SOCIETY FROM ITS
            COMMENCEMENT TO ITS CONCLUSION: A SOCIOLOGICAL STUDY IN
            COMMUNISM.   3rd ed.   Columbus: F.J. Heer, 1904.   First
            published in OHIO ARCHAEOLOGICAL AND HISTORICAL
            PUBLICATIONS.   8 (July 1899): 1-100.   Reprint.   New York:
            AMS Press, 1971.

1909.   Society of Separatists.   COLLECTION OF SELECTED SPIRITUAL SONGS,
            FOR CONGREGATIONAL SINGING AND FOR PRIVATE USE IN
            CHRISTIAN FAMILIES.   Zoar, OH., 1855.

1910.   Snyder, Tricia and Gil, and Paul A. Goudy.   ZOAR FURNITURE,
            1817-1898: A PRELIMINARY STUDY.   New Philadelphia, OH.:
            The Tuscarawas County Historical Society, 1978.

1911.   "Zoar: Separatist Village."   COLONIAL HOMES.   10
            (January-February 1984): 74-97, 136, 140, 142.

ADDENDA

1912. Blake, John B. "Mary Gove Nichols, Prophetess of Health."
      PROCEEDINGS OF THE AMERICAN PHILOSOPHICAL SOCIETY. 106
      (June 29, 1962).

1913. Cazden, Robert E. A SOCIAL HISTORY OF THE GERMAN BOOK TRADE IN
      AMERICA TO THE CIVIL WAR. Columbia, SC: Camden House,
      1984. pp. 671-709.

1914. Foster, Lawrence. "The Rise and Fall of Utopia: The Oneida
      Community Crises of 1852 and 1879." COMMUNAL SOCIETIES. 8
      (1988): 1-17.

1915. Green, Ernest J. "The Labadists of Colonial Maryland (1683-
      1722)." COMMUNAL SOCIETIES. 8 (1988): 104-121.

1916. Hall, John R. "Jonestown and Bishop Hill: Continuities and
      Disjunctures in Religious Conflict." COMMUNAL SOCIETIES.
      8 (1988): 77-89.

1917. Munoz, V. ROBERT OWEN: A CHRONOLOGY. W. Scott Johnson, transl.
      New York: Gordon Press, 1979.

1918. Myerson, Joel. THE BROOK FARM BOOK: A COLLECTION OF FIRST-HAND
      ACCOUNTS OF THE COMMUNITY. New York: Garland, 1986.

1919. Oschwald, Ambrose. DIE AUGENSALBE ODER ZEITCHARACTERISTIK FUR
      SIEBENTE GROSSE ZEITPERIODE ALS BEITRAGE ZU AMBROS
      OSCHWALDS MYSTISCHEN SCHRIFTEN. J.M. Laeuterer, ed.
      Augsburg: L. Doll, 1854.

1920. Richards, Irving T. "Mary Gove Nichols and John Neal." NEW
      ENGLAND QUARTERLY. 7 (June 1934).

1921. Spurlock, John C. FREE LOVE: MARRIAGE AND MIDDLE-CLASS
      RADICALISM IN AMERICA, 1825-1860. New York: New York
      University Press, 1988.

1922. Warren, Alvin. "Reminiscences of Berlin Heights." OUR NEW
      HUMANITY. 1 (June 1896).

1923. Wayland-Smith, Ellen. "The Status and Self-Perception of Women
      in the Oneida Community." COMMUNAL SOCIETIES 8 (1988):
      18-53.